Eighty-Five Plus

About the Authors

Sally Bould received her Ph.D. in sociology from Bryn Mawr College. Dr. Bould is an associate professor of sociology at the University of Delaware. Her research has focused on social policy issues, especially those involving family policy and poverty. Recently she has published research on the relationship between unemployment and early retirement and the importance of early Social Security retirement benefits in preventing poverty. Her articles have appeared in *Population Research and Policy Review*, *Social Problems*, *Social Science Quarterly*, *The International Journal of Sociology and Social Policy*, *The Journal of Marriage and the Family*, *The American Journal of Economics and Sociology*, and *The Journal of Applied Behavioral Science*. She is an associate editor of *The Journal of Applied Behavioral Science*.

Beverly Sanborn received her M.S.W. from the School of Social Welfare at the University of California, Los Angeles, She is director of training for Alzheimer Family Centers, Inc., in San Diego, California. She has been designing and developing programs in the human services for the past 20 years, with her most extensive experience in service delivery to the elderly. She was project director in the development of a master plan for respite care for Los Angeles County and has been a consultant on respite care for the American Association on Aging. Ms. Sanborn has presented numerous workshops and seminars in the field of social services for the elderly, particularly for victims of Alzheimer's disease and their families. She is a licensed clinical social worker and has a private practice working with caregivers of the frail elderly.

Laura Reif, R.N., received her Ph.D. in sociology from the University of California. Dr. Reif is an associate professor at the University of California, San Francisco and is director of UCSF's graduate program in gerontological nursing. She has conducted a pioneering study on how delivery of home care can be improved by consolidating services under a single umbrella organization and has authored many articles on noninstitutional approaches to long-term care. Her recent research focuses on private insurance options for financing long-term home care and on evaluating the quality of services provided by home health agencies. She is a founding editor of *Home Health Care Services Quarterly* and co-editor of the book *International Perspectives on Long-Term Care*.

Eighty-Five Plus
The Oldest Old

Sally Bould

Beverly Sanborn

Laura Reif

Wadsworth Publishing Company
Belmont, California
A Division of Wadsworth, Inc.

Sociology Editor: Serina Beauparlant
Production: Greg Hubit Bookworks
Designer: Lois Stanfield
Print Buyer: Randy Hurst
Copy Editor: Patricia Harris
Cover: Steve Osborn

Printed in the United States of America

1 2 3 4 5 6 7 8 9 10—93 92 91 90 89

Library of Congress Cataloging in Publication Data

Bould, Sally, 1941–
  Eighty-five plus : the oldest old / by Sally Bould, Beverly
Sanborn, Laura Reif.

  Bibliography: p. 199
  Includes index.
    1. Aged—United States—Social conditions.   2. Social work with
the aged—United States.   3. Aged—Longterm care—United States.
I. Sanborn, Beverly.   II. Reif, Laura.   III. Title.
HQ1064.U5B675   1989
305.2'6'0973—dc19   88-20729
ISBN 0-534-09846-0

To the residents and staff of
White Farm Lodge

Contents

Preface

*D*uring the summer of 1984 I lived with my daughter Erika (age four) in staff quarters at White Farm Lodge, Richmond upon Thames, London, England, an old-age home where the average age of the residents was 85. I was also supervising students who were doing volunteer work throughout the borough of Richmond upon Thames under the coordination of Louis Minster, then the borough's director of social services. My students and I obtained firsthand experience not only of old-age homes but also of service delivery planning in a community with a high proportion of the very old. We saw the difficulties that this community was facing in caring for the very old at home as well as the budget squeeze that was restricting access to long-term nursing home care. When I returned to the United States, a glance at the population projections for the very old led me to believe that the United States would soon surpass the British in the proportion of its population among the very old. In fact, by the year 2005, a higher proportion of our population is expected to be in the 80-and-over category than that of any other country except Sweden and Norway. Furthermore, difficulties in getting into nursing homes in the United States were already very much in evidence.

Amid intense discussions of this experience, Beverly Sanborn, my future co-author, made the following observation: "You know," she said, "people who reach 90 are different." It was a practitioner's intuition arising from years of experience in case management for elderly clients. After all, there are as many years between 60 and 90 as there are between 20 and 50. For many of our parents, for ourselves, and certainly for today's young people, there may be an extra decade of life we have not planned on. Fortunately, the National Institute on Aging had already looked at the projections for the future and had established an initiative to focus on the oldest old, those 85 and over. It appeared that there would be enough information on this critical age group for a comprehensive overview of their situation. Not only is this age group a fascinating one, its study also highlights many of the critical issues among all elderly: the frail elderly; the elderly poor; the elderly needing the help of family and friends; elderly women managing alone. Those 85 and over represent a vanguard group, offering an opportunity for understanding the many issues that need to be dealt with in the decade of the 1990s.

One critical issue is, of course, health. Examining the healthy and vigorous 85-year-old enables us to visualize separating the aging process from any disease process. It may be possible to prevent much of the disability found among the oldest old. Nevertheless, the preponderance of disease and disability among the oldest old today, and their inability to pay cash for the help they need, led us to identify a third coauthor, Laura Reif, who could bring with her firsthand experience with the ill and disabled oldest old and the health care system.

We now had a team representing the disciplines of sociology, nursing, and social work; we also had an emerging social issue that would inevitably grow larger with each year. The next question was, how would today's students relate to the concerns of individuals more than half a century older? I assigned students in my Sociology of Aging course to interview individuals in this age range. I was prepared to deal with a range of excuses as to why this assignment could not be completed; however, to my amazement, no one asked to be excused. Every student found someone to interview, most often a family member. Indeed, the demographic change had affected my very classroom; having a grand-mother in her eighties was common among my middle-class students. Moreover, the assignment was completed with enthusiasm—the students saw it as an exciting opportunity to get in touch with their families. With this personal involvement, it was easy to get students involved in the many issues of the oldest old. They read earlier drafts of various chapters of this book and provided helpful feedback.

This book was originally conceptualized around the dominant themes of independence and dependence found in the literature. We intended to develop these issues in the context of Hendricks and Hendricks's model of individual resources—physiological, personal-psychological, social-familial, and economic. But a careful examination of these individual resources, especially social-familial resources, resulted in an argument for an alternative model of interdependence. As we examined the daily lives of the oldest old who had aged successfully, we began to understand that independence was not a characteristic of their life-style; interdependence, reciprocity, and helping networks were. An interdependent life-style, furthermore, provided activity and contact with friends. These factors have long been thought to be important components of successful aging.

The model of interdependence provides a useful framework within which to analyze community resources as well as individual resources. Even for the vigorous oldest old who are in good health, an autonomous, independent life-style often is not possible, since many have given up driving as either too expensive or too dangerous or both. Given the limited transportation alternatives in many communities, oldest old persons have to rely on helping networks of friends, family, and neighbors. Other communities may need to consider the oldest old in their transportation planning.

One reaction to our discussion of the oldest old was, "Isn't it depressing?" The answer is, not really, not if you look at the possibilities of extending active life into the nineties and beyond. It's quite challenging; it requires a commitment to the prevention of disability, including the allocation of research funds for those less glamorous disabling problems of urinary incontinence and osteoarthritis. Health education for a long and active life needs to begin at an early age. And communities need to be involved in promoting interdependence by effective conserving of elders' other resources (economic, personal-psychological, and social-familial) and by helping them build an interdependent life-style.

Acknowledgments

I would like to thank May Greisman, who patiently read all of my various drafts. The manuscript is much more readable thanks to her careful attention. Candace Clark provided an important stimulus and some concrete suggestions for developing the concept of interdependence. My coauthors, Beverly Sanborn and Laura Reif, provided endless and invaluable critiques as well as a practitioner's perspective on the chapters I wrote (Chapters One through Four and Chapter Six). They also put up with my constant pressure for them to finish the chapters they were each working on. Chapters Five and Seven reflect the joint efforts of Beverly Sanborn and myself. Chapter Eight is authored solely by Laura Reif.

The book would not have been possible without the cooperation of staff members at Agency A and Agency B. Their clients provided invaluable insight into the world of the oldest old and the caregivers of the oldest old. These individuals, staff members, and clients must all be thanked anonymously.

The students in my Sociology of Aging classes also patiently read earlier drafts and enthusiastically provided interviews. Among the students who put in extra time and provided valuable comments, Ann Boeker and Vicki Hamelberg are noteworthy. I would also like to thank my friends and colleagues Wallace Dynes, Judith Gordon, Sally Stan, Howard Robboy, John Ferguson, Carmela Carlyle, Howard Bould, and Terri Pope-Maciolek for their thoughtful critiques. Thanks are also due to the following reviewers who provided helpful suggestions: Vern Bengston, University of Southern California; Stephen Cutler, University of Vermont; Chad Gordon, Rice University; Jon Hendricks, University of Kentucky; Marilyn Schmit, Cardinal Stritch College.

None of this would have been possible without the careful attention of the secretaries in the sociology department at the University of Delaware: Carol Anderson, Claire Blessing, Judy Watson, Anna Wu, and Eleanore Morrow.

Sally Bould

Chapter One

Introduction

*T*he new octogenarian feels strong as ever when he is sitting back in a comfortable chair. He ruminates, he dreams, he remembers. He doesn't want to be disturbed by others. It seems to him that old age is only a costume assumed for those others; the true, the essential self is ageless. In a moment he will rise and go for a ramble in the woods, taking a gun along, or a fishing rod, if it is spring. Then he creaks to his feet, bending forward to keep his balance, and realizes that he will do nothing of the sort. The body and its surroundings have their messages for him, or only one message: "You are old."—Malcolm Cowley, a writer born in 1898, in his book *The View from 80.*

While much current attention to the elderly emphasizes their youthfulness (Streib, 1983), there seems to be a point at which people become "old." Although there is a great deal of variation, for most people this point seems to be reached sometime between 80 and 90 years of age. Speaking from personal experience in his book *The View from 80,* Malcolm Cowley describes the reality of old age for him:

—Everything takes longer to do—bathing, shaving, getting dressed or undressed
—Travel becomes more difficult and you think twice before taking out the car

—Many of your old friends have vanished and it is harder to find new ones
—There are more and more little bottles in the medicine cabinet, with instructions for taking four times a day
—[You hesitate] on the landing before walking down a flight of stairs
—[You spend] more time looking for things misplaced than [you spend] using them after [you have] found them
—It becomes an achievement to do thoughtfully, step by step, what [you] once did instinctively (Cowley, 1980:3, 4, 54)

Of course, there is a great deal of individual variation. In response to Malcolm Cowley's earlier article, one reader wrote to him, "All this came on me after I was 85, instead of after I was 80," and another respondent, age unknown, reacted by claiming, "You're only as old as you feel. Old age is just a rumor!" (1980:x–xiv). Nevertheless, a sample of elders 81 years of age and over chose to describe themselves as "old," not simply "elderly" or "senior citizens." Those between the ages of 71 and 80 described their group as elderly but those 81 and over as "old" (Osteen and Best, 1985). Seventy-year-olds, according to Malcolm Cowley (1980:2), "have the illusion of being middle-aged even if they have been pushed back on the shelf. The 80-year-old looks at the double-dumpling figure and admits that he is old. The last act has begun, and it will be the test of the play."

In writing this book about the last stage of life—the fifth age—we have chosen those 85 and over. This choice reflects current initiatives by the National Institute of Mental Health to focus on this age group—the oldest old.[1] The oldest old, those 85 and over, have experienced the most rapid increase in life expectancy among those 65 and over since 1970. This has resulted in an unprecedented expansion of the number of people in this age group. Yet this rapid expansion of life expectancy has not brought greater possibilities for active life. Thus far, it has only increased the years during which there is a high risk of becoming disabled (Manton and Soldo, 1985). It has also led to the overriding fear of the oldest old, which is not of death but of "becoming helpless":

. . . It is the fear of being as dependent as a young child, while not being loved as a child is loved, but merely being kept alive against one's will. It is the fear of having to be dressed by a nurse, fed by a nurse, kept quiet with tranquilizers (as babies with pacifiers), and of ringing (or not being able to

---

[1]The choice of 85 and over is an arbitrary but practical one, since the Census Bureau and other government agencies, such as the National Center for Health Statistics, provide data on those 85 and over but not on those 80 and over or 90 and over. See Suzman and Riley (1985).

ring) for a nurse to change one's sheets after soiling the bed. "My only fear about death," Mrs. Scott-Maxwell says, "is that it will not come soon enough. . . . Happily I am not in such discomfort that I wish for death, I love and am loved, but please God I die before I lose my independence." (Cowley, 1980:57)

The oldest old represent a fifth age: an age when issues of retirement are 20 or more years in the past; an age when the dominant theme is most likely to be issues of self-determination versus dependence. For the individual, a key concern is remaining in charge of one's life. An individual's primary worry is becoming dependent on others for help in his or her daily life. For society, the dominant concern is limiting public dependence in terms of the costs of daily care for those who are no longer able to pay for it. Both these concerns are highlighted by the fact that nearly one out of three of the oldest old are likely to be institutionalized in a nursing home at some point (Vicente et al., 1979).[2] This book explores these issues and seeks to develop a framework in which better alternatives for the oldest old can be developed.

Can we as a society provide viable life-style alternatives for this unique subpopulation as it more than doubles from 2.39 million in 1980 to 5.16 million by the year 2000?[3] What kind of help should be available for the oldest old, and how will this help be paid for? Current research concerning the needs and resources of people in this subpopulation can provide critical information for everyone in planning for a future wherein half of the children born in the United States are expected to reach 85 years of age. This book examines the situation of the oldest old and the issues that the rapid growth of this subgroup raises for our future. People who are now 85 and over form a vanguard group, critical for understanding the impact of impending changes in our population profile.

The rapid increases in longevity experienced by those 65 and over, and especially those 85 and over, will significantly change the profile of the population of the United States and other developed countries in the

---

[2]A national study of Medicare enrollees indicated that with equivalent self-rated health, functional ability, marital status, and payment source, "an 85 year old is two and one half times more likely to enter a nursing home than is a 75 year old" (Cohen, Tell, and Wallack, 1986:790).

[3]These projections are from the U.S. Social Security Administration's (1984) calculations based on intermediate assumptions of mortality rates. Even with the highest estimated mortality rates, by the year 2000 the number would still reach 4.57 million. The most generous assumption concerning the reduction in mortality rates results in a projection of 5.74 million by the year 2000. The Social Security Administration's projections are very close to those of the U.S. Bureau of the Census (1984d). See Rosenwaike (1985b) for details.

decades ahead. While the growing number of young old (65–74 years of age) has produced its most powerful impact on work and retirement issues, the growing number of oldest old is likely to have its greatest impact on the need for society to provide programs that promote self-determination. Special attention needs to be given to research into the processes of aging and the diseases that disable the very old. Unfortunately, much of the research in aging fails to examine this unique group because it subsumes them into the 65-and-over category.

Dependence Versus Self-Determination

The most critical need in the future will be for programs and policies that reduce the risk of dependence and promote self-determination. It is essential that policies clarify the ambiguous term "dependence" (Bond, 1976), especially when it is conceptualized as the opposite of independence. The issue of dependence for the elderly as a whole is often a symbolic one, but for the oldest old the fear of dependence in their daily existence is often very real.

In discussions of dependence among the elderly, the term has taken on numerous meanings. Estes, Swan, and Gerard (1981) and Townsend (1981) have conceptualized all elderly as dependent due to their structural position in industrialized society. Their exclusion from the workplace makes them dependent on government policies and/or a former employer to provide an adequate pension and/or income from a social security program. This income is often meager, and the extra costs incurred because of health problems can quickly exhaust any savings the elderly have put aside for their old age. When economic resources become extremely limited, the elderly may become directly dependent on government provision of cash and medical help in the form of programs for the poor. Alternatively, dependence is often used synonymously with institutionalization in a nursing home; everyone living in the community is assumed to be independent. Other researchers have realized that chronic disability can result in dependence even for those living in the community.

It is a goal of this book to develop a more comprehensive definition of dependence that reflects the importance of limited economic, physical, personal, and social-familial resources. *Dependence* will be defined as *a loss of self-determination that results from requiring the help of others but being unable to negotiate the terms of the help received.* Resources are critical in negotiating needed help; they can preserve personal choice for the elder (Haber, 1986). Those who require the help of others are those who can no longer maintain their own home and/or perform the necessary activities of daily living. They may need help in home management activities such as shopping or in personal care activities such as bathing.[4] Even when help is needed, however, dependence can be avoided and self-determination preserved as long as the help can be paid for. Abundant economic resources could be used to negotiate the terms of the help received. The ability to provide something in return for help received, even within the family, is important in avoiding dependence. Community programs and resources are important in reducing the total amount of help needed from family and friends, especially for transportation and housing needs. Such programs lower the risk of becoming dependent on others.

Because the concept of dependence used in this book involves an understanding of the complex interaction of individual resources (economic, social-familial, personal, and physical) and community resources, there is no simple measure that will provide an accurate estimate of the dependent population among the oldest old. Simple measures such as the percentage who need help in their daily lives ignore the fact that the help may be paid for or provided as a community service. Indeed, the concept of dependence developed here is one that would require a careful investigation of each individual situation. Nevertheless, a few statistics indicating the possible extent of dependence among the oldest old are in order here. Overall, a reasonable guess is that nearly 45% of the oldest old are dependent in the sense that they can no longer negotiate the terms of the help that they need. The largest dependent group is composed of nursing home residents—23% in 1980 (see Table 2.1). For those living in the community, a key indicator of a high dependency risk is the inability to go outside the home without the help of another person; 19% of the oldest old need this level of assistance (Feller, 1986: Table 11). Another indicator of dependence, which no doubt includes many of those who need help getting outside, is that of living in the home of a relative other than a spouse; 20% of all persons 85 and over live in the home of a relative (Table 2.1, note d). Those who live in the home of a relative may be dependent simply because they lack adequate economic resources.

---

[4]The necessary tasks of daily living include (1) home management tasks, or instrumental activities of daily living (IADLs), such as shopping, housework and money management; and (2) personal care tasks, or personal activities of daily living (PADLs), such as dressing, using the toilet, bathing, walking, and eating. See Katz et al. (1963) and Chapter Three for more details.

A Loss of Self-Determination

A move to a nursing home represents a loss of self-determination (Haber, 1986). Persons who are institutionalized become dependent because they are under the "care and custody" of the institution and its employees. While substantial income and assets may permit a greater choice of institutions, once in the institution, the resident is no longer in control but is subject to nonnegotiable restrictions on almost every activity of his or her daily life, including eating, sleeping, and going outside. Although residents are often locked inside the building, they cannot lock others out of their rooms. There is no privacy, no control over who comes into their rooms, and no choice of who helps them to the toilet. Personal preferences are not respected by institutions; even individuals with large amounts of money have no choice over who helps them. Indeed, having lots of money does little good, since there are very limited possibilities for spending it and any purchases may be stolen. The classification of those living in nursing homes or other institutions as dependent is, moreover, consistent with the widely held view of life in a nursing home (Townsend, 1981; Haber, 1986).

The following statement from a resident of the "Murray Manor" nursing home illustrates this loss of control and consequent dependence:

> Marsha Cush: "Just think yourself to be in a place like this. How would you feel? It's very hard to take. Very hard. It can almost heart break. 'Cause you got your own home. You got everything in it. You do what you please. You buy what you want . . . what you want to eat, what you want to drink. Nobody in here . . . what they give you, you gotta eat. If you don't eat, you go hungry. Lots of times, I walk away hungry. It's clean. Sure. Everything is nice. The people around are nice with me. Those that do work, they do nice. And everything as far as that goes is nothing to complain about that. But, as I say, if I could help myself to be on my own, I wouldn't be in here five minutes." (Gubrium, 1975:87–88)

While Murray Manor is a "nice place," other nursing homes often are not. In any nursing home, the staff has arbitrary authority, and the role of the patient is to "just go along with the daily routine and do what they [are] told," as one observant aide put it:

> Well, primarily they just have to do what they're told. And stay put where they're told to stay put. They just can't go wandering all over the place. They have to stay in their rooms. If they don't stay in their rooms and start wandering around, they'll be restrained in their room. There are some very harsh discipline reactions when taken. (Manard, Woehle, and Hellman, 1977:29–30)

Independence or Interdependence

This examination of the oldest old classifies those living in institutions as dependent because of their loss of self-determination. Nevertheless, all those living in the community are not automatically classified as independent. Indeed, the stress on independence as the primary alternative to dependence obscures a third possibility: that of interdependence. In an interdependent situation, the elder looks for and/or needs care and help from others and provides care and help for them in return. Interdependence is a give-and-take with others; it involves reciprocal helping relationships. The American value system, however, stresses independence and often does not even recognize interdependence. This is true of Western culture in general; a book entitled *Dependence or Interdependency in Old Age* (Munnichs and Van den Heuvel, 1976) devotes all but a few paragraphs to discussions of dependence and independence. Cultural values have taught Americans to fear dependence (Clark, 1972) but have provided no other alternative for an elder who can no longer maintain complete independence.

The importance of independence is reflected in the "ideal" life-style. Clark (1972:272) found that her elderly subjects "had an almost frantic quality when they spoke of the necessity of preserving complete autonomy in order to preserve self esteem." Case material is often used to illustrate this achievement of autonomy by an elder living alone and being able to pay for all needed services—being completely in charge of his or her life. For example, the *New York Times* headlined an article reporting on a survey of the elderly "Still Independent Despite Limitations" (January 25, 1987). In the article, the case of Miss Ulanov, 82 years old, was highlighted:

> In many ways, Miss Ulanov is typical of the elderly who live alone. She is a widow, and she rents her apartment in Greenwich Village. She has no income other than Social Security and is increasingly anxious about making ends meet and not being able to get around as well as she used to. "I've been self-sufficient and independent all my life," Miss Ulanov said. "Now, with my failing health and rising expenses, I don't know what will happen."

This sort of reporting reflects American values that stress autonomy and rugged individualism. Independence, strictly defined, requires that the elder live alone and either not need help or be able to pay cash for any help needed. Only a small minority of the oldest old could possibly follow an independent life-style, however, since only 20% live alone *and* are able to do all of their daily tasks themselves.[5] An additional 10% live alone and need help but are not likely to have enough money to pay for it. For those elders who are able, independence is a life-style choice. Those who highly value independence prefer not to be involved in helping networks; their need for autonomy rules out the reciprocal obligations of give-and-take relationships. They prefer being beholden to no one and having no one beholden to them. The risk of the independent life-style is that if health gets poor or cash gets low, these persons have no developed helping network; they have no history of give-and-take (Clark, 1987).

In spite of the strength of the cultural ideal of independence, the reality for many of the elderly appears to be closer to interdependence than to independence. Many elders who could choose an independent life-style prefer interdependence. Although they live alone and do not need help, many of these elders are deeply embedded in family support networks of give-and-take.[6] Often this interdependent life-style involves friends and neighbors as well as family. For the oldest old who live alone and need help, an interdependent life-style can preserve self-determination. Elders can reciprocate for any help needed. Furthermore, they probably will have built up credit by helping others, so if a need suddenly becomes severe, there is likely to be someone there to help. While the preferences of the few who can sustain their autonomy must be respected, this ideal of independence is simply not a viable goal for the vast majority of oldest old. Interdependence, in contrast, permits self-determination without the rigorous requirements of rugged individualism.

In conceptualizing policy issues for the oldest old, there is an urgent need to recast the "ideal" situation as one of interdependence and to orient policies toward promoting interdependence. The trap of the false dichotomy of independence versus dependence could thus be avoided and programs that enhance reciprocity could be developed. Less fanfare needs to be given to those "hale and hearty" individuals who live alone, still drive a car or use a taxi at 90, and are "dependent on no one." More attention should be paid to those oldest old who have effectively used

---

[5]Thirty percent of those 85 and over live alone (see Chapter Two, Table 2.1). Of these, only two-thirds are able to perform all the activities of daily living themselves (Feller, 1986).

[6]See Stoller and Earl (1983) for a discussion of helping networks among those who do and do not need help. Cohler (1983) has argued that elders may prefer autonomy and independence in old age as a progression toward interiority, or a looking inward. Examples from Choler and Grunebaum (1981) suggest that elders may resent adult children who place too many demands on their time and energy; these elders were in their fifties and sixties, however.

their personal and familial resources in building networks of reciprocity and in using an appropriate model of interdependence to cope with limited physical, social, and economic resources in extreme old age. Throughout most people's lives, the reality is not total independence but interdependence within the family and the community. Approximately half of those 65 and over are living with a spouse in what is probably an interdependent life-style. Less individualistic cultures more readily acknowledge this interdependence (Tobin, 1987).

Interdependence can be simply a matter of a choice of life-style involving reciprocal helping and a convenient division of labor. For those few oldest old couples where both are in good health, it is likely that their interdependent life-style—each doing tasks to help out the other—is a result of years of living together. Studies of helping behavior among mothers and adult daughters show that reciprocal helping patterns are common (Thompson and Walker, 1984). Daughters may provide help during an illness, for instance, while mothers provide help with shopping when the daughter's schedule is hectic. While each could manage on her own, they choose to help each other during difficult times. This is an optional life-style that serves as an insurance policy in times of acute need such as, say, a debilitating case of the flu. Where there is no chronic health need, the oldest old often require temporary help during acute illnesses or injuries. The interdependent life-style has the advantage of easing concerns about possible future care needs; the structure of help is already in place. Such elders do not need to fear "what will happen with failing health." They have built up reciprocal relationships of giving and receiving help.

In the case in which the elder with limited income *must* have help, interdependence is a necessity if dependence is to be avoided. Interdependence still permits full self-determination. In such cases, help given by family, friends, and neighbors can be repaid. If a neighbor helps out by providing a ride to the store once a week, the elder can reciprocate by providing supervision for school-age children during emergencies. In the long run, help is paid for, even if the elder must rely on past helping or token reciprocity. Oldest old couples can sustain reciprocity by developing a new division of labor, each helping the other in areas in which the spouse has become limited by disability.

In order to sustain interdependence when an elder requires help continuously, it is necessary that public policies not only recognize and support interdependence but also provide community supports. If the oldest old must rely on their social support networks to get around, they are at risk of falling too far in debt to be able to reciprocate. In this manner, they may overburden their helpers and lose self-determination so that they become dependent. Furthermore, helpers, while willing to help, often cannot extend themselves limitlessly without disruptive consequences. It is important not to "overdraw one's accounts" (Clark, 1987). Elders themselves do not wish to become a burden by, for example, interfering with the helper's work schedule (Brody, Johnsen, and Fulcomer, 1984). Opportunities for giving as well as receiving are important.

Community supports in the form of housing are an important element in building interdependence. Apartment complexes for the elderly can facilitate reciprocity and interdependence; these often develop into little communities of mutual aid. This was a good arrangement for Mrs. Jones:

> At 98, Mrs. Jones needed help with shopping and during illness. Several residents of the building provided this help. Mrs. Jones, on the other hand, maintained excellent eyesight and could still sew. Consequently, she stayed busy doing mending for other residents of the apartment complex. Those who did not help her in other ways would pay her for doing their mending. But this was not a business, and those whose income was limited did not pay in cash. She was clearly building up credit in case she needed help in the future.

The community should also support the special housing needs of the oldest old in terms of the interior of the house or apartment. This age group often has difficulty in bathing safely. Taking a bath is one area in which help from a neighbor or friend is often unacceptable and may result in a sense of dependence. Even the help of an adult child of the opposite sex may be problematic because it may violate norms of personal privacy. The best option, whenever possible, is to remodel the bathroom to permit the elder to safely bathe himself or herself. If this is not possible, a trained bath aide may be the best answer. Providing these options not only would ease the burden on helpers but would be an effective preventive technique to lessen risk of falling while bathing.[7]

The Social Security system is an example of a program of interdependence created by the federal government. Social Security benefit payments and contributions create interdependence rather than dependence (Kingson, Hirshorn, and Cornman, 1986). The government collects contributions from the wages of current workers. From these funds, the government provides payments to retired workers and their families.

---

[7]Falls are a very serious problem among the elderly because they often lead to disability or death. See Chapter Three.

These retired workers have already made their contributions, and today's workers, who are now contributing, will later receive payments from the contributions of workers in the future. Elders no longer have to be independent, that is, working or living off accrued assets; nor do they risk falling into financial dependence on their children.[8] This is government-sponsored intergenerational reciprocity. These programs are socially created in that the government assumes responsibility for determining how much each generation will pay and receive. The Social Security crisis in the early 1980s illustrates the vulnerability of such programs of interdependence; today's workers are skeptical about the system. Their fear is that they will not receive equivalent payments when it comes their turn to draw benefits. But the Social Security system is not like a savings account or a life annuity. Interdependence does not mean equity in a narrow sense; we are all interdependent in terms of our own economic and political future. Current criticism of Social Security ignores these links and rather appeals to values of rugged individualism and "independence" as if each of us could accurately predict and provide for our financial future.[9]

In order to develop viable policy alternatives for the oldest old, it is important to move beyond the myth of rugged American individualism and the dichotomous choice of independence versus dependence. Indeed, the oldest old can no longer afford the myth of independence, since the vast majority are faced with the stark reality that they no longer have a spouse with whom to develop interdependence when necessary. Interdependence as the most viable option for the oldest old makes sense, not only to forestall institutionalization or an undesirable move to a relative's home but also to preserve dignity and self-determination.

Dependence

It is often assumed that only those living in institutions are dependent, yet recent studies of families providing care in the home indicate that there are those in the community who are just as unable to care for themselves as those in institutions (Brody, 1985). In these cases, depen-

---

[8]In a recent Harris Survey, only 5% of all elderly persons reported receiving regular financial assistance from their children (Harris and Associates, 1986).

[9]Senator Kemp, a Republican from New York, termed the present problem of the Social Security system as "intergenerational resentment." (*The New York Times*, January 29, 1987).

dence is largely a result of severe health limitations. At least 5% of those 85 and over living in the community cannot manage to walk, dress themselves, go to the toilet, or take a bath; many of these severely limited individuals also need help in order to eat (Feller, 1986; Manton and Soldo, 1985). These individuals must relinquish control of their lives; they are entirely dependent on some combination of family help and paid or public help. There is also the dependence of elders who are physically able to dress, bathe, and eat but who have severe cognitive (mental) problems so that they need constantly to be told when to bathe, dress, and eat. In both cases, an independent life-style is out of the question. Nor is interdependence possible, since the elder can no longer sustain any degree of give-and-take and must adapt to nonreciprocal relationships. Although physically able, the severe Alzheimer's patient is perhaps most dependent. Mrs. Smith, for example, has lost her capacity to negotiate the terms of the help she receives:

> Martha Smith, age 83, is dependent on her husband, John, age 85. She has severe Alzheimer's disease and is now in the final stages. She requires constant care. She cannot even remember to go to the bathroom, though she will usually urinate if placed on the toilet at intervals, especially if the water faucet is running. Mrs Smith is unaware of time and place; she is usually unaware that John is her husband. She still retains the ability to speak and respond when spoken to, but she cannot carry on the ordinary give-and-take of a conversation. Furthermore, she needs attention both day and night, since she is nocturnal and spends most of the night wandering and rummaging. Mr. Smith manages by sleeping during the day while his wife is cared for at the local adult day-care center. Family and friends wonder how Mr. Smith can continue and why he does not put her in a nursing home. It is the strong emotional bond built up over sixty years of marriage that keeps him at his heavy task. He does not mind either his wife's current dependence or the physical burden of care. "I know she would do the same for me," he says, for theirs had been a very close marriage.

In these situations of dependency, caregivers like John are acting out of a strong emotional attachment. The attachment may be one of love or duty or some combination of both. Except in rare cases of wealth and prestige, hired help cannot provide this level of care. A live-in caregiver is required; without such a caregiver, the elder would be institutionalized. With a caregiver, the elder is in a nonreciprocal relationship and self-determination is severely limited. This high level of dependency is inevitable without better means of preventing and/or treating the diseases of the oldest old that cause this level of disability.

This group of persons who are highly dependent is only a small minority of those in the community. [10]

Avoidable Dependence

Many more of the oldest old are dependent due not so much to their need for help as to their limited individual resources and a lack of community resources. This may be the case, for example, with the elder who must move in with relatives; an estimated 20% of the oldest old live not in their own household but in the household of an adult child or other relative (see Table 2.1, note d). The lack of affordable housing often renders the elder dependent on the adult child by requiring that the child's household make room for the elder. Household space and schedules must be altered, creating the potential for a situation in which the adult child is giving more than the elder can possibly pay for. The readjustment of the household to accommodate the elder's needs often exceeds the norms of reciprocity between parent and child in the United States (Brody, Johnsen, and Fulcomer, 1984). The elder's contribution of a Social Security check or light housework is likely to be insufficient to pay for this imposition. Family members often must completely readjust their lives to take care of the elder's needs. The elder is no longer in charge of his or her own space or schedule, and self-determination is limited. The elder's negotiating position is weak, and he or she is likely to feel burdensome. With important ethnic exceptions, the general view in the United States is that such a person is dependent and that the dependence is socially structured. This is why the vast majority of elders prefer their own homes, [11] where they are more likely to be in charge of negotiating the terms of the help they receive.

Of course, not all situations in which the elder is living in the household of other relatives create dependence. There are possibilities for interdependence. For example, in ethnic groups such as the Asian-

---

[10]Only 3% of the oldest old living in the community require help in order to eat (Feller, 1986). Of those living in the community who do need help with daily tasks, only 23% need such a high level of help that they can, for example, only feed themselves (Manton and Soldo, 1985).

[11]In a national Harris Survey, 86% of elders who lived alone in their own home said that this was their preferred living arrangement (Harris and Associates, 1986). In a small survey of those 80 and over, there was overwhelming agreement that being in charge of one's own home was a top priority (Tobis et al., 1986). Economists assume that living in one's own household is the preferred consumer alternative as long as income is sufficient (Schwartz, Danziger, and Smolensky, 1984; Bishop, 1986).

American, there are often strong norms that include housing and care of the elderly as a result of intergenerational reciprocity. Here elders probably will not feel themselves a burden because they have already built up credit to pay for their care in their youth by housing an elder themselves. It is interesting to note, however, that in Asian cultures traditional intergenerational reciprocity does not involve the parent and child directly. It is rather the daughter-in-law who cares for her husband's elderly parents. She, in turn, will be cared for in her later years by her son's wife.[12]

There is also the situation in which even a physically impaired elder can make reciprocal contributions to the household by, say, supervising school-age grandchildren or great-grandchildren. A newly widowed adult child may also welcome the opportunity for companionship. In poor households, the elder's economic contribution may be necessary for household maintenance; the Social Security or Supplemental Security Income (SSI) check may be an essential component of the regular income of the household. The elder may also contribute significantly to the household assets:

Mrs. Thomas, age 90, moved in with her daughter's family after suffering a stroke. There are only two bedrooms in the daughter's house. The daughter and her husband sleep in one room, and the two teenage granddaughters sleep in the other. Mrs. Thomas sleeps in the dining room. These limited facts suggest the situation to be one of burden for the daughter and dependence for the elderly parent, but this is not the case. Mrs. Thomas has sold her house, and the funds from the sale have enabled the family to buy a new car. Furthermore, there are additional funds from the sale of the house to pay for remodeling of the daughter's house. Thus, Mrs. Thomas has made a significant contribution to the household and will have even paid for her own space in the remodeled house. She has also brought her antiques and family memorabilia into the household. The family's tawdry old furniture has been replaced with her elegant antique furniture.

The daughter works only part time and finds new meaning in sharing her home with her mother. The two teenage granddaughters are enter-

---

[12]This is one reason why having a son is so critical in these cultures. With modernization and urbanization, however, the structure of reciprocity is breaking down, due in part to the refusal of daughters-in-law to provide care, especially in urban areas (Gibson, 1985; Tobin, 1987). Perhaps there is no "primordial commitment" and the needful child is not bound to a reciprocal giving of care when the parent becomes needful (see Brody, 1986). By caring for the child in infancy, the parent has not built up credit toward care in his or her old age. Care of a dependent aged parent is given above and beyond the bonds of parent-child reciprocity, thus putting the elder in a dependent situation.

tained by their grandmother's memorabilia and stories. Mrs. Thomas feels that she has made generous contributions to the household and that whatever care she requires is paid for.

There is no way of estimating how instances of elders living in a relative's household entail avoidable dependence and how many represent interdependence.[13] In many, if not most, of these cases, however, dependence is probably due not to serious physiological problems but to a lack of personal income and community resources that limits the elder's options. As Dowd notes, even if government policies provide incentives for families to take in their elders, "the net effect of such a non-reciprocal exchange of resources would be to increase the old person's dependency" (1980:53). It is the oldest old who are at highest risk of being made prematurely dependent by our social policies because they are least able to sustain autonomous (and probably largely fictional) independence or to develop interdependence in a marriage. It is the oldest old who are most likely to need a community that provides adequate public transportation and housing for the elderly. For the majority of oldest old who need help with activities of daily living, there is a choice between interdependence, which allows for some self-determination, and dependence, which allows for little or no self-determination. Unfortunately, many of the oldest old find themselves in dependent situations unnecessarily; their self-determination is curtailed not so much by physiological incapacity as by limited community resources in combination with their own limited economic and social support network resources.

The aim of this book is to set forth a framework by which mechanisms can be developed to enhance self-determination and prevent dependence. Preventing the dependence inherent in nursing home use is not sufficient. More emphasis needs to be placed on dependence prevention for the oldest old in the community. This will require special attention to the individual resources available to the oldest old now and in the future. Enhancing the individual resources of the oldest old will

---

[13]The situation is potentially very different when the oldest old person is living with relatives in his or her own household. In this situation, the elder probably has not had to give up being in charge and probably has not had to move. The oldest old person may even own the house and therefore provide substantial help to a widowed or divorced adult child who needs a new home or is in a difficult financial situation. It can be estimated that 7% of those 85 and over live in their own household with relatives other than a spouse. Although the Census Bureau's definition of "householder" is vague, it is likely that those elders reported as householders are in a better negotiating position than those reported as living in a relative's household.

preserve their self-determination. The responsibility for enhancing the individual resources of this vulnerable group lies with everyone—national and state governments, the local community, and the front-line practitioner, as well as family and friends of the oldest old.

Individual Resources

One way to begin to plan for maximizing interdependence and minimizing dependence in this vulnerable age group is to assess their individual resources. What individual resources are available on which to build reciprocity and interdependence? What are the indications of serious gaps in individual resources that suggest a high risk of becoming dependent? Severely limited resources in one area, such as limited economic resources, may not result in dependence as long as other resources, such as good health, are available. Oldest old persons who have severely limited resources in more than one area probably have a higher dependency risk and may require community programs to prevent a rapid deterioration of self-determination.

Table 1.1. Dimensions of Individual Resources

Type of Resource	Key Indicators of Serious Resource Limitations	Where Discussed
Physiological	Needs assistance in activities of daily living; institutionalized (IADL and PADL limitations)	Chapter 3
Social-familial	Assistance required is more than social support network is able to provide and/or the person can reciprocate. Death or disability in social-familial network	Chapters 4, 5
Personal-psychological	Needs help in coping and in developing resources. Has few interpersonal skills. Neighbors, friends, family, and practitioners indicate that person has "given up" or is "too difficult"	Chapter 4
Economic	Is unable to purchase additional help needed. Income near poverty level; assets very limited	Chapter 6

A conceptual framework that is useful in analyzing the nature and extent of an individual's resources is provided by Hendricks and Hendricks (1986:105–106). These are resources available to the individual, resources he or she can use to negotiate the terms of reciprocity in obtaining needed help. They are also resources that the oldest old are likely to run out of, thereby risking dependence (see Table 1.1). Here we identify four dimensions of individual resources by modifying the outline of Hendricks and Hendricks (1986:105–106).

- *Physiological resources* are defined as the physical and mental ability to perform the tasks necessary for daily living. A lack of physiological resources means that the help of another person is required in order to perform one or more necessary tasks, such as shopping or bathing.

- *Personal-psychological resources* relate to the individual's inner coping ability as well as the interpersonal skills that make the person appealing to others, especially in terms of sustaining helping networks.

- *Social-familial resources* are the social support networks, including family, friends, and neighbors, available to the individual. To whom can the elder turn for help when in need?

- *Economic resources* are primarily income and assets but would also include other commodities that could enable people to obtain from the marketplace the help they need.

For the oldest old, physiological health and physical ability comprise the most salient dimension of their dependency risk. When there are no health problems, the dependency risk is small. Nevertheless, more than half of the oldest old need help in performing the activities required for daily living—shopping, housework, money management, and meal preparation (instrumental activities of daily living or IADLs) and bathing, toileting, dressing, and walking (personal activities of daily living or PADLs). In comparison with people aged 75–84, those 85 and over are more than four times as likely to be residents in nursing homes where they receive help with most of these activities. Those oldest old still living in the community are more than twice as likely as those aged 75–84 to require help in at least one activity (Feller, 1986). Chapter Three discusses at length the kind of help they need as well as the diseases and disorders that are likely to cause their chronic need for help. Preventing dependence will require specific attention to the diseases and disorders that cause these health limitations.

The personal-psychological resources of the oldest old are defined broadly as their personal coping ability and interpersonal skills. Very limited research has been performed in this area, although coping ability, as well as morale and self-esteem, are often conceptualized as dependent on other types of resources. The oldest old may be at high risk of having limited coping ability because they may be overwhelmed by several severe health problems or the death of a best friend, or both. It is also possible that the coping abilities of the oldest old are a result of their lifetime experiences and therefore less susceptible to decline than other kinds of resources (Kahana, Kahana, and Young, 1987; McCrae, 1982). The development of interpersonal skills over a lifetime can provide the oldest old with survival techniques even in extreme situations; neighbors and acquaintances may be happy to help out, for example, because the elder is so engaging, so pleasant, or so appreciative.

The social-familial dimension includes the range of family and friends available for social interaction, self-affirmation, and direct aid. This dimension is commonly referred to as one's social support network (Kahn, 1979). For the oldest old especially, family and friends may be needed to provide much more than a friendly chat, a telephone call, or an invitation to dinner. Yet the oldest old are at high risk of having lost their families and friends. Their "birth cohort"—those born around the same time—will have shrunk to less than half its original size. The death of family and friends of similar age is common. Indeed, many have faced the death of a child. These losses not only reduce the elder's social support network, they limit the possibilities of long-term interdependent relationships. There probably is no longer a spouse available to provide convenient opportunities for reciprocal help in times of need. The role of social support is reviewed in Chapter Four, and the role of relatives, friends, and neighbors as caregivers is discussed in Chapter Five.

We discuss the economic dimension primarily in terms of personal income and assets. The official U.S. government poverty level will be used to denote a severe lack of economic resources. When including people living in institutions and in the community, a higher proportion of the oldest old live in poverty than do members of any other age group (Rosenwaike, 1985b:116, 214). Other than income and assets, the oldest old have few other resources with which to barter. Most no longer have access to social positions or occupations that could give them power. Some exceptions would be a political position, such as that held by Claude Pepper, the 85-year-old Democratic congressman from Florida, or a position of extraordinary prestige, such as that of the late Duchess of Windsor. Chapter Six discusses her special situation and examines the economic resources of this group as a whole.

Chronically Limited Resources

As this book demonstrates, many of the oldest old have inadequate resources with which to negotiate their fate and preserve their self-determination. Their resource limitations are, moreover, likely to be chronic—that is, long-term limitations that are unlikely to change. This situation can be contrasted with that of younger populations, whose resource limitations are more likely to be acute. Acute conditions involve a definite onset, a crisis, and a recovery; a chronic condition is not likely to change in the long term. An example of an acute physiological limitation would be a case of flu that causes the elder to require the temporary help of another person. A chronic condition like arthritis, however, can require long-term help; there is no expectation of recovery, although techniques may be available to ease the pain or other problems caused by an arthritic condition. For younger populations, the death of a spouse or confidant is an acute condition; recovery entails remarriage or the development of new confidant relationships. For the oldest old, however, such losses are likely to be chronic because the elders are less likely to be able to replace the spouse or confidant; they will never be able to replace the loss of a child. For the oldest old, a lack of economic resources is also likely to be chronic; their poverty is more likely to be a permanent condition from which there is little expectation of recovery (Warlick, 1983).

The oldest old may be at special risk because the stress factors in their life are chronic. Much previous research has focused on the stress of *acute* conditions or specific life events. In order to more fully understand the situation of the oldest old, more research needs to be directed toward the long-term effects of chronic conditions from which there is little hope of recovery (Essex and Lohr, 1986). For the oldest old, this lack of hope for recovery may be a stress in itself. Programs that enhance interdependence and self-determination could, perhaps, alleviate some of this stress by providing long-term options to give as well as receive help. Community services provided by both government and voluntary groups could reduce the stress of the chronic need for help by providing services that enhance reciprocity and self-determination.

Multiple Resource Limitations

Examining the framework of individual resources also leads to questions about how and when limited resources in one area can be counterbalanced by an abundance of resources in another area. The most obvious example is the trade-off of great wealth and position for self-determination in spite of severe physical or even mental limitations (see Chapter Six). There is also the case in which good health and the absence of physical limitations can allow people to stretch poverty-level budgets, since any help that may be needed can be paid for in kind; housekeeping expenses can be kept low by careful shopping and use of public transportation. Interpersonal skills may make up for losses in the social support network by facilitating the development of new friends and strengthening reciprocal bonds with neighbors. Similarly, those who have extensive family resources, especially children, are in a better position to rely on reciprocal bonds over a lifetime in order to sustain interdependence.[14]

Unfortunately, for the oldest old, limited resources in one area are often accompanied by limited resources in other areas as well. Widespread poverty and physical disability mean that there are many individuals 85 and over who are both poor *and* disabled. By the year 2000, there are projected to be 2.1 million women aged 85 and over who will be unmarried *and* limited in their ability to perform at least one of the activities of daily living; 1.2 million of these women will be living in the community (Manton and Soldo, 1985). Using Warlick's (1983) predictions, more than half of these women living in the community will be poor or near poor.[15] This means that an estimated 601,000 oldest old women in the community will have neither spouse nor cash to assist them in getting the help they need. Without special policy initiatives, these women will be at high risk of becoming dependent.

Dependence and Social Policy

Looking at the individual resources of the oldest old provides a beginning framework for assessing their opportunities for interdependence as well as community resources needed to enhance these opportunities. Only a

---

[14]Those with a large number of children are less likely to be institutionalized, thus avoiding this degree of dependence (Crystal, 1982).

[15]In 1980, the median income of unmarried women 85 years of age and older was $4,803 (Torrey, 1985:386). In 1980, the poverty-level income was $3,949, and the near-poor level of income (125% of poverty level) was $4,936. Warlick (1983) has predicted that without significant policy changes, the income picture of unmarried women is not likely to improve in the future.

minority of the oldest old can sustain a strictly independent life-style, yet all too many are put in positions of unnecessary dependence because of their own limited economic and social-familial resources combined with limited community resources. How can they get the help they need on the basis of reciprocity and interdependence? How can government policy reduce the risk of dependency and promote self-determination among the oldest old? Broader policy perspectives are needed to promote self-determination. Programs must be developed to conserve the limited individual resources of the oldest old and put these resources to effective use in enhancing interdependence and self-determination.

Estes has argued that dependence of the elderly is "shaped by public policies, economic conditions, and the political forces which affect them" (1983:19). There is no doubt that the oldest old risk a loss of self-determination due to broad economic and public policies that have left many of them without an effective way to get the help they need. If the community and the state are to take a more effective approach in preventing unnecessary dependence, there must be clear public responsibility for enhancing interdependent as well as independent life-styles (Kingson, Hirshorn, and Cornman, 1986). One example of a government policy to provide help in the context of interdependence and self-determination is in the area of medical services under Medicare, the national health insurance program for the elderly. Program benefits accrue to elders as a social right in old age based on their having contributed to society in some manner.[16] The old and disabled have earned the right to Medicare. Respect for the elderly suggests the importance of such programs, which are provided on the basis of reciprocity, not charity. Charity leads to dependence, while reciprocity leads to interdependence. Medicare is an example of how help can be provided as a right.

For the oldest old, however, much of the help needed is not included in the type of help provided by Medicare. If the medical diagnosis is osteoarthritis of the knees, the primary problem is difficulty in walking around. While pain medication can help, in many cases it will not restore full mobility. The problem is medical, but the help needed is, for example, assistance with shopping. This form of help does not qualify as medical "treatment" and does not require a licensed medical practitioner to perform; therefore, it is not covered by Medicare. Further-

---

[16]Those who are now working contribute directly to Medicare through the payroll tax. At age 65, contributors and their families become eligible. At age 72, persons who have not made sufficient contributions may become eligible if they meet other criteria.

more, if the elder requires institutionalization, Medicare will not pay for the cost of a long-term stay in a nursing home. For those who are able to stay at home with medical help, Medicare provides very little in-home help (Harvard Medicare Project, 1986). Medicare, our major effort on behalf of the elderly, is least likely to provide the kind of help most needed by the oldest old. Furthermore, current practices do little to promote self-determination and interdependence.

What Standards of Eligibility?

Our reluctance to provide help outside the control of the medical professions and institutions reflects our fear of encouraging dependence on the public purse. Ironically, our reluctance to provide help in the home often promotes dependence for the oldest old on a family or an institution. The solution, however, does not lie in establishing tough eilgibility standards with new sets of gatekeepers to enforce them. The concept of social rights and self-determination requires a less stringent test of need because interdependence and reciprocity, rather than strict independence, is the goal. Help should be granted to those who claim to need it or who appear to need it. Those who receive help should, moreover, be allowed to participate in planning the type of help they receive. As Townsend (1981) indicates, respect requires that program beneficiaries be involved in planning; this is the essence of incorporating self-determination into policy planning. Furthermore, beneficiaries should be provided opportunities to reciprocate, even if only in symbolic or token form. The implementation of stringent need eligibility criteria implies the continued application dichotomy of independence versus dependence. Inability to manage on one's own must be proved beyond any doubt before assistance is given. These strict need criteria put elders in the role of "the grateful and passive recipients of services administered by an enlightened public authority" (Townsend, 1981:22). Moving to strict need criteria entails the risk of discouraging or even disqualifying those who may be in real need for the sake of the principle that those who can care for themselves must do so. This process would only preserve the myth of independence and would push the oldest old more rapidly into dependence and institutionalization.

Why should the very old be the victims of our obsession with rugged individualism and our fears of abuse of the public purse? If we were to offer free Homemaker Chore services, would all those elders who hate housework immediately apply in order to get something for nothing? Yet one-fourth of those oldest old living in the community need help with household chores (Feller, 1986). Are we to require, rather, that their families help, or just let them live with the dirt and disorder, thereby risking a fall? Could there be a special test of eligibility for housework? This fear of abuse in the area of minimum-wage help provides an interesting contrast to the much more lenient approach to the abuse potential of Medicare by highly paid professionals.

Tough eligibility standards could cause problems for the oldest old similar to those experienced recently by the disabled. The issues raised by the Social Security Disability reviews are especially instructive for the substantial minority of those 85 and over who need help because of cognitive impairment. While the Supreme Court has ruled in favor of the rights of the mentally impaired to disability payments, this right often may not be exercised since "some truly eligible disabled persons, particularly those with mental impairments, never appeal a denial or termination of benefits because they do not fully understand their rights and have no one to assist them in the process" (Naiditch, 1984:31).

It is important to understand that requiring the elderly to prove need always entails the risk of discouraging them from applying for needed services. Currently, the Food Stamp Program and the Supplemental Security Income (SSI) program, which do require demonstration of need, are underutilized, especially by the very old (Harris and Associates, 1986; Hollonbeck and Ohls, 1984; Warlick, 1982). Rigid need criteria for cash assistance programs are probably inevitable, although the context can be defined as a social right, not charity. But the issue that confronts the oldest old is not so much the need for cash assistance programs as the need for services to help them to remain in the community or to help their families when they need a high level of caregiver support. The goal of these services should be to promote, whenever possible, self-determination and to avoid excessive dependence. These goals are not compatible with rigid tests of need. In the case of programs designed to assist caregivers, known as respite care programs, rigid need criteria could even be couterproductive. Discouraging respite care for caregivers entails a greater risk of caregiver burnout and consequent institutionalization of the elder. There is a need for accurate data to develop programs that offer greater possibilities of a fuller life for our oldest citizens and their caregivers. Ignoring the problems created by our shifting age profile can only lead to a crisis or the fear of a crisis, neither of which provides for a productive or compassionate planning environment.

Compassionate Ageism

In dealing with future changes, it may make a great deal of sense, as Dowd (1984) suggests, to make a clear distinction between the young old, many of whom wish to be treated on the basis of individualism and "independence," and the old old, who are more likely to need an interdependent life-style and acknowledgment of past contributions. The young old need to be freed from the stereotypes of aging and accorded full civil rights and equal treatment under the law. They especially need not only the right to work and to be productive but also freedom from age discrimination (Neugarten, 1982) and socially created dependence (Estes, 1983). In contrast, the old old, and especially the oldest old, need what T. H. Marshall (1963) has termed "social rights": the right of access to programs that promote their self-determination on the basis of being a citizen of the realm.

Yet this approach, which emphasizes the needs of the oldest old for help, can be justly assailed as "new ageism." New ageism, according to Kalish (1979:398), is promulgated by those advocates of the aged who focus on those among the elderly who "are least capable, least healthy and least alert." Obviously, this is also compassionate ageism (Binstock, 1985) aimed at developing sympathy and public support. Neugarten (1982) is concerned with any special attention given to age per se. It is the position of this book that compassionate ageism is necessary toward those 85 years and over if we are to develop programs and plans that will preserve their self-determination and promote interdependence. In order to do this, it is necessary to examine carefully the extent of need for help among that group at highest risk—those 85 and over.

To fail to recognize the unique problems and potentials of this subpopulation is, in effect, to let old stereotypes persist. One particularly pernicious one that contributes to dependence among the oldest old is the stereotype that physical and psychological problems are inevitably a result of reaching this very old age. When the 80-year-old begins to lose vision and has trouble balancing, the tendency is to dismiss the problem as simply "old age." This attitude persists, in part, because the aged person accepts this disability as an inevitable part of aging. But even if the oldest old do seek medical attention, the physician may also be influenced by stereotypes and fail to provide appropriate treatment—or not even take time to listen. Unaware of or insensitive to the uniqueness of the oldest old's physiology, doctors may prescribe medications that may have side effects such as cognitive impairment or falling. Thus, ignoring the special needs and risks of this population only keeps us from analyzing directly the sources of their current disability and preventing future disability.

Other critics of the focus on the oldest old suggest that we may be opening the door to cruel cutbacks in public funding for health and social services for those who have grown "too old." These dangers are already present and persistent, as exemplified by the former governor of Colorado, Richard Lamm, who reportedly stated that terminally ill old people have "a duty to die and get out of the way" (Slater, 1984, as cited in Binstock, 1985). Social policy initiatives may attempt to deny the oldest old public services for the care they need. Yet ignoring the impact of the increasing number of oldest old who need help will not protect them from cutbacks in service. Already, in many sections of the country, entry into a nursing home requires that elders or their families put forth the resources to cover a year or two of care. Those 85 and over, who are most at risk of having already exhausted their meager assets in daily living, may find that they have nowhere to go in their community when institutionalization becomes necessary. The only nursing home that will accept them as a publicly supported Medicaid beneficiary may be a hundred or more miles away.[17]

In subsequent chapters, we provide further evidence that the oldest old are a unique group requiring special attention at every level of service delivery and program planning. They are especially vulnerable because of their high risks of needing help, outliving family and friends, living alone, and being poor. In times of setting budget priorities, this group must not be overlooked. Indeed, using the 85-and-over age marker as an indicator of potential need would be a cost-effective approach in initial planning. Information on the number of people in this high-risk age category is cheaply and readily available.

Is it really so important to weed out those who are "abusing the system" because they do not really need transportation assistance and to bar them from using the van because they are "too lazy" or "too cheap" to take public transportation? And what if no public transportation exists? Let us rather assume that the elderly will best know their own service needs and will respond appropriately. This was the intent of Title III of the Older Americans Act of 1965. In fact, a sample of oldest old

---

[17]This situation is a result of restrictions on nursing home beds, limitations of Medicaid reimbursement, and rising costs in many parts of the country. For example, those living in San Diego County without private means cannot gain admission to nursing homes in their county of residence. Medicaid, the program for those with very limited assets and income, pays a per-day maximum that varies by state. In some areas, this maximum is not accepted by nursing homes as full payment.

transportation users showed that many contributed generously to the agency while others apologized for their inability to contribute more than a dollar or two.[18] If anything, the oldest old need to be encouraged to seek the services they need, not discouraged by a myriad of special eligibility criteria and endless bureaucratic paperwork.

This focus on the oldest old, Binstock argues "is highly susceptible to familiar mechanisms of distortion that may generate unwarranted stereotypes of persons in this older age range" (1985:420). Nevertheless, this book argues that the benefits outweigh the risks of the negative stereotypes that may result. If compassionate ageism causes healthy and vigorous 90-year-olds to be stereotyped as disabled and in need of help, they would probably be the first to acknowledge that they are among the lucky ones and more than willing to put up with the stereotype in order to ensure better assistance for their less fortunate peers. Furthermore, there appears to be a certain prestige to reaching 90, or especially 100, years of age. In contrast to the middle-aged or "young old" (those aged 65–74), who are likely to report their age as younger than it is, the oldest old are more likely to *exaggerate* their age (Zopf, 1986:8; Rosenwaike, 1985b:22). Especially among blacks, the self-reported age among those claiming to have attained 100 years of age is very unreliable. Increasing education and careful recording of birth certificates will probably reduce age exaggeration in the future.

The situation of the oldest old, then, is very different from that of the young old. While the young old will benefit from dispelling stereotypes of poor health and the need for help, the oldest old may be hurt by the popularizing of a view of the aged as healthy and fully capable of independence. Why should special programs be provided to help if help is not needed? If there are program cutbacks, moreover, it is the oldest old, who are in greatest need of help, who will suffer most. In 1983, when, for the first time, poverty rates among those 65 and over were lower than rates for those under 65, questions arose as to why all these programs for affluent elders were needed. The oldest old are only a small minority of the 65-and-over population, so their high poverty rates were obscured by the income data on the "average" elder. It is critical not to let the needs of this small minority, the oldest old, be hidden by the more adequate resources of the majority of elders, who are young old.

While this book stresses the immediate need to limit dependence and promote interdependent life-styles among the oldest old, it is also important to aim at long-term goals of dependency prevention. For

---

[18]This agency provided a van and a helpful driver to all elderly city residents. There was no charge for the service.

example, in the critical area of housing, plans need to be put into effect soon so that there will be an adequate supply of affordable housing suited to the needs of the oldest old. If this is not done now, many more of the oldest old may be forced to depend on an adult child for a space to live. Planning now could also alleviate future socially created dependence caused by immediate needs of this fast-growing population.

Terminology

In this text, the term "oldest old" will be used to refer to those who are 85 and over. This reflects a special National Institute on Aging (NIA) initiative. The term "young old," when it is used to refer to chronological age, has been consistently defined as those aged 65–74. Another term commonly found in the literature is "old old," which, in terms of chronological age, means those who are 75 and over.[19] This emphasis on the oldest old may lead to the use of the term "middle old" when referring to those aged 75–84 (Atchley, 1985). In this book, young old will be used to refer to those aged 65–74 and old old, to refer to those 75 and over; the oldest old are those 85 and over. In all other cases, exact ages will be indicated in the text.

Methodological Problems

As noted, the oldest old are a small minority of the total population aged 65 and over. In order to obtain a reliable picture of the oldest old, it is important to use data sets that have a large number of people in this age group. Furthermore, the usual samples of community populations not only miss those who are institutionalized but also miss many of those in the community with physical or mental impairments (Streib, 1983; Harris and Associates, 1986). For as complete a picture as possible, samples from the 1980 census and special studies using 1980 census data will be used to develop the demographic picture of the oldest old. In

---

[19]The terms "old old" and "young old" were developed by Neugarten in order to distinguish those who need a range of supportive health and social services from those who do not. It was her position that chronological age was not involved. Since then, however, others have adapted the terms to designate chronological age (Neugarten, 1982; Ragan and Wales, 1980).

terms of functional ability, the ability to perform the necessary activities of daily living without the help of another person, the data are from the National Health Interview Survey conducted by the National Center for Health Statistics (NCHS). Here, two independent community survey samples from 1979 to 1980 were combined, producing a more reliable picture of those 85 and over (Feller, 1986). In the sample, every effort was made to obtain information about the respondent even if the information had to be provided by a caregiver. This NCHS sample on disability is representative only of those three out of four oldest old who are living in the community.

The case materials of individuals 85 and over are drawn largely from clients of two agencies serving the aged (Agency A and Agency B).[20] As with any client group, this group includes a large proportion of those needing help. Sources of case materials not drawn from this group will be identified. Case materials, however, are meant to be illustrative, not representative.

Plan of the Book

Chapter 2 Demographic Characteristics of the Oldest Old This chapter provides a demographic overview and a discussion of projected growth among this subpopulation. The current demographic picture includes important information on marital status and living arrangements necessary for understanding the lives of the oldest old. For example, 80% of this group does not have a spouse. This subpopulation is expected to double by the year 2000, reaching a total of 5.16 million persons 85 years of age and over. The uniqueness of the oldest old will be examined in comparison with other elderly age groups.

Chapter 3 Health This chapter reviews the extent of functional disability among those 85 and over. It identifies those diseases and disorders most prevalent among persons 85 and over and discusses these diseases as

---

[20]Case materials describing elders with high need levels are drawn from families seeking the help of respite care services in Agency A as well as individuals under case management (receiving home visits from social workers) in Agency B. Examples of lower levels of need come from telephone interviews conducted with a random sample of individuals in contact with Agency B and using primarily transportation services only. All cases are from the United States, and all names have been changed.

contributors to the widespread functional disability of this group. The special risks of falls, drug intoxication, and urinary incontinence are also discussed in terms of risk factors. This chapter provides information on possibilities for restoring functional ability among the oldest old as well as preventing functional disability in future generations who reach this age.

Chapter 4 Personal Coping Resources and Social-Familial Resources
This chapter discusses the resources of the oldest old in two of the four areas, beginning with personal resources. What coping skills are effective at this age? How are interpersonal skills critical in preventing dependency? Social and familial resources are analyzed in terms of what is likely to be available to help this age group develop reciprocal helping networks and an interdependent life-style. The importance of being able to store credit against a future need is examined as a way to avoid dependence. Community programs can play a special role in preventing the overburdening of the elder's social support network, especially in the area of housing and transportation.

Chapter 5 Caregivers of the Oldest Old   This chapter examines the special role of the caregiver for the oldest old. What is the caregiver burden? The increasing need for caregivers, the increasing average age of caregivers, and the need for community respite care programs for caregivers are presented. The problem of a lack of caregivers is reviewed in terms of willingness, availability, and ability to provide care.

Chapter 6 Economic Resources of the Oldest Old   This chapter examines the economic resources of the oldest old as well as their special financial problems related to medical care and widowhood. More than one-fifth of this subpopulation falls below the poverty level. This chapter reviews current programs such as SSI, Medicare, and Medicaid.

Chapter 7 Formal Services   This chapter reviews the range of services available to the elderly, giving special attention to the need for services among the oldest old. The projected increase in this age group will require a review of available services in order to plan adequately for the changing age structure of our population. The focus of this chapter is on long-term care and the provision of a continuum of care. The chapter reviews the current system and identifies gaps. Possible bridges between the formal and informal systems are explored.

Chapter 8 Epilogue: The Future   This chapter describes recent trends in the organization and financing of services and analyzes the impact of these trends on the oldest old. An alternative model for providing assistance to the oldest old is proposed. Implicit in this discussion is the choice between our current fragmented service network and a system designed to deliver comprehensive, coordinated care, based on the needs of the population served.

Chapter Two

Demographic Characteristics of the Oldest Old

In order to plan for a future that promotes self-determination and prevents dependence among the oldest old, it is important to have an accurate picture of their situation. Demographic data collected by the Bureau of the Census can provide a statistical sketch of this unique population, which will be critical to program planning in the nineties and beyond. This chapter examines this type of descriptive data, which is available on characteristics such as sex, race, marital status, residence, ethnicity, and living arrangements as well as the critical demographic aspects of size and growth. This is the realm of applied demography, or demographics—the "branch of the discipline that is directed toward the production, dissemination, and analysis of demographic and closely related socioeconomic information for quite specific purposes of planning and reporting" (Rives and Serow, 1984:10). Planners, policymakers, and government officials concerned with the elderly are now examining this unique population. What is known now provides a basis for understanding what might need to be done in the future to avoid unnecessary dependence and to enhance the interdependence of this rapidly expanding group. In this chapter, demographic data are analyzed not only in planning for the oldest old but also in dispelling myths and giving the practitioner as well as the planner a sense of typical and atypical case situations.

Mortality Rates and Life Expectancy:
Factors in Growth

Given the critical role of death rates, or mortality rates, in the demographer's analysis of population growth, it was logical that demographers tracking changes in age-specific mortality rates would discover the impact of declining mortality as a factor in the rapid and unanticipated growth of the oldest old population (Suzman and Riley, 1985:183; Rosenwaike, 1985b:149). Age-specific mortality rates measure deaths per 1,000 population for a given age in a given year. The mortality rate for those aged 84 is critical in determining how many will survive to be 85 and thus enter the ranks of the oldest old. Of course, demographers must also take into account how many 84-year-olds there are to begin with who might live to be 85. But by and large, the rapid expansion in numbers of oldest old is due to rapid and unanticipated declines in mortality rates among those aged 75–84, not to any significant increase in the size of the preceding cohort aged 75–84 (Rosenwaike, 1985b:172).

Demographic projections are attempts to estimate the future size of a group—in this case, the oldest old. Critical to these projections are assumptions about mortality rates in the future as applied to the number of persons in the age group today. For example, how many persons aged 70–74 in 1980 are expected to be alive in the year 2000 at ages 90–94? These demographic projections are, of course, subject to unknown future events, such as a possible cure for cancer. Demographers, as well as others, are also focusing on a future in which a very large cohort, the baby boomers born during the years 1945–1962, will reach these older ages. When this large group reaches age 85 beginning in 2030, there will be rapid increases in the oldest old population, even with no changes in mortality rates.

Another important way to understand the growth in the size of the oldest old population is to examine their life expectancy, that is, the number of additional years they can now expect to live. The rapid increases in life expectancy among the oldest old are due, of course, to decreases in their mortality rate. This means that those who attend the 85th birthday party of a loved one can, in more than half the cases, also expect to attend his or her 90th birthday party as well. The life expectancy for those who reach age 85 is more than five years.

Another way to analyze the size of the oldest old population is to examine what proportion they comprise of all those 65 and over. Again, decreasing mortality rates and increasing life expectancy are making this age group a more significant proportion of the elderly population. In 1950, the oldest old were less than 5% of the population 65 and over; by

1980, the oldest old were nearly 9% , and by the year 2000, they are predicted to be more than 14% of the 65-and-over population (Rosenwaike, 1985b:7, 197).

For planning purposes, however, the most critical figure is the projected growth in absolute numbers of the oldest old (Rosenwaike, 1985b:185). The Social Security Administration has made three different projections about the future size of this population. These estimates are based on three different assumptions about mortality rates in the future. In this book attention is given to the middle estimate, or alternative II, in which assumptions about mortality rates include continuing declines, with greater declines for women than for men (U.S. Social Security Administration, 1984). Under these middle-range assumptions, the 85-and-over population would more than double, from 2,393,000 in 1980 to 5,161,000 in the year 2000. Between the year 2000 and the year 2040, this population would more than double again, from 5,161,000 to 13,084,000. Given the fact that past projections have seriously underestimated the number of oldest old (Rosenwaike, 1985b:187), these numbers are likely to be conservative estimates for planning purposes. If life expectancy at birth in the United States reaches 85 years of age in the year 2080, these numbers may seriously underestimate the size of the oldest old groups in the future. But even under the middle estimates, the future size of the oldest old group needs to be given immediate attention in terms of their high probability of needing help.

The Impact of Growth

The rapid growth of the oldest old population is of special concern because this is the population that is most likely to need both medical and nonmedical help from a range of formal and informal sources (Manton, 1986). An indication of the high level of need among this population is suggested by its unique living arrangements. In 1980, 23.2% of those 85 and over lived in institutions—primarily nursing homes and other homes for the aged.[1] This contrasts markedly with the 65-and-over

---

[1]Other homes for the aged might include such facilities as veterans' homes, in which the resident is under the care and custody of the institution. Those institutionalized also include a small number of patients in mental hospitals and hospitals for the chronically ill as well as inmates of correctional institutions. Of all the institutionalized oldest old, 95.8% are in homes for the aged, primarily nursing homes. Board and care facilities that provide private rooms, community meals, and light housekeeping services under minimum supervision would in most cases be classified not as institutions but as group quarters, similar to dormitories. Individuals residing in facilities in which each individual lives alone in a private apartment that includes a kitchen are classified as householders.

Table 2.1. Living Arrangements for Those 65 and Over and 85 and Over in 1980

With Spouse	With Other Relatives	Alone	In Households with Non-relatives	In Noninstitutional Group Quarters[a]	In Institutions[b]	Total
All persons 65 and over						
49.6%	14.8%[c]	27.7%	2.1%	0.5%	5.3%	100%
(N = 12,647,644)	(N = 3,785,452)	(N = 7,066,539)	(N = 523,464)	(N = 135,045)	(N = 1,340,242)	(N = 25,498,386
All persons 85 and over						
16.3%	27.2%[d]	29.8%	2.3%	1.2%	23.2%	100%
(N = 356,989)	(N = 596,144)	(N = 652,698)	(N = 51,172)	(N = 26,758)	(N = 508,918)	(N = 2,192,679)

Source: U.S. Bureau of the Census, 1984b: Tables 265, 266 (19% sample).

[a]Includes those not living in households and not living in institutions—for example, room and board houses, convents, Salvation Army shelters, and most board and care facilities that are not set up as apartment units.

[b]Includes those classified as inmates or patients; includes convalescent and nursing homes as well as rest homes for the aged. Residents are under the care and custody of the institution.

[c]Excludes those living with a spouse in their own or spouse's households.

[d]Excludes those living with a spouse in their own or spouse's households. Includes 157,635 individuals who are householders living with relatives other than a spouse (7% of all persons 85 and over); the remaining 438,509 individuals are living in the household of a relative (20% of all persons 85 and over).

population as a whole, in which only 5.3% lived in an institution in 1980 (see Table 2.1). Concern about this high proportion of the 85-and-over population that is institutionalized also centers on their increasing use of institutions. Less than 10% of those 85 and over were living in institutions in 1950, but by 1980, that proportion had more than doubled (Rosenwaike, 1985b:104). Considering the fact that the number of persons 85 and over almost quadrupled between 1950 and 1980, these numbers demand attention from a broad range of practitioners and planners. Foremost in the minds of many is the public cost of institutionalization for the elderly, which is paid for primarily through the Medicaid program.

While much of the concern about the growth of the oldest old has focused on the institutional population, more attention needs to be paid to the vast majority who do not live in institutions. How can their risk of dependence be lessened? Can institutionalization be prevented or at least postponed? Estimates were that 16 to 35 percent of the elderly in institutions could, with considerable services and family help, still live in the community (Barberis, in Rosenwaike, 1985b:111). Furthermore, institutionalization is generally the least preferred of all living arrangements. Living arrangements of the oldest old are especially important in planning for a future in which the oldest old can preserve their self-determination and interdependence.

Living Arrangements

An examination of the living arrangements of the oldest old (see Table 2.1) clearly demonstrates their uniqueness. They do not follow the pattern found among those 65 and over. As mentioned earlier, their risk of living in an institution is more than four times as great. Consequently, proportionately fewer are living in the community. Institutionalization is certainly an indicator of limited physiological resources and probably, for the oldest old, of limited familial resources as well. While almost half of those 65 and over are living in households with their spouses, only 16% of those 85 and over live in their own households with their spouses. For the oldest old, living in a family household without a spouse is almost twice as common a phenomenon as for the elderly as a whole. Similar proportions of those 65 and over and 85 and over live alone, but those 85 and older who are living alone are far more likely to need the help of another person (Feller, 1986).

In examining the living arrangements of the oldest old in Table 2.1, it is apparent that no one pattern predominates. In fact, their living arrangements are quite diverse. This evidence refutes the prevalent stereotypes that most of this age group live in a nursing home or that most of this age group live alone without families. In fact, more live in families (43%) with or without a spouse than live in institutions (23%) or alone (30%). For the oldest old, however, living with one's spouse becomes a rare arrangement, especially for women. For those 85 and over, only 39.9% of the men and 5.9% of the women are living with a spouse. This can be contrasted with the 65-to-69 age group, in which nearly 80% of the men are living with their spouses, as are more than half (52.2%) of the women (U.S. Bureau of the Census, 1984b).

While the oldest old present a diverse pattern of living arrangements, they do face a high risk of not living in their own or their spouse's households. This presents a serious problem, considering the value placed on being able to stay in one's own home (Schwartz, Danziger, and Smolensky, 1984). Furthermore, remaining in one's own household preserves possibilities for independence or interdependence and protects against dependence. Those living in their own households include persons living alone, those living with a spouse (in their or their spouse's household), or those living in their own household with other relatives or nonrelatives. Only about three out of every six (54%) persons 85 and over live in their own households. This contrasts sharply with all persons aged 65 and over, of whom five out of six (84%) are able to remain in their own households (U.S. Bureau of the Census, 1984b). Many of the oldest old have to give up their home for the home of a relative or for some form of board and care facility, where the risk of dependence is high. Others will face dependence in a nursing home.[2]

In the Community

For a more careful examination of the living arrangements of the oldest old, Table 2.2 excludes all persons in institutions and examines only those living in the community. Seventy-seven percent of the population 85 and over lived outside of institutions in 1980. Of these, a clear majority (56.6%) were living with a spouse or a relative, and a large minority (38.8%) were living alone. Only a small number were living in other arrangements, including boarding houses, monasteries, flophouses, Salvation Army shelters, board and care facilities, or households with nonrelatives.

Table 2.2. Living Arrangements for Those 85 and Over Living in the Community in 1980

With Spouse	In Own Household with Relatives[a]	In Household of Relative	Alone	With Non-relatives or in Group Quarters[b]	Total
21.2%	9.4%	26.0%	38.8%	4.6%	100%
(N = 356,989)	(N = 157,635)	(N = 438,509)	(N = 652,698)	(N = 77,930)	(N = 1,683,761)

Source: U.S. Bureau of the Census, 1984b: Tables 265, 266 (19% sample).

[a]Excludes those living with a spouse.

[b]Includes those living in households with nonrelatives and those in noninstitutional group quarters.

---

[2]Lipman and Longino (1986) classify all elderly persons who live in another's household as "residentially dependent," but in this book, only those in institutions are automatically classified as dependent.

Living in a Family Household   Contrary to the popular conception that the very old live alone, the majority of those 85 and over in the community live with families. Unlike their younger counterparts, they are less likely to be living with a spouse and more likely to be living with other family members (see Table 2.1). In the case in which the person is living in the household of relatives, the most typical arrangement is of living with an adult child in the child's household.[3] Adult children and their spouses provide the household and often assume a substantial responsibility for the care of the oldest old parent or parent-in-law. In fact, the National Health Interview Survey of 1979–1980 found that one-half of those aged 85 or over living with relatives other than a spouse were in need of help from another person in order to carry out necessary tasks of daily living.[4] Furthermore, relatives other than adult children often provide the home. One out of every five oldest persons living in a family household is living in the household of a relative who is neither a child nor a spouse (see Table 2.3).[5] Clearly, extended family networks still operate. Special attention needs to be paid to the relationship between the oldest old person and his or her relative. It is important to avoid excessive dependence for the oldest old person who must move into a child's (or other relative's) home and also to avoid an excessive sense of burden for the relative providing the home.

Those still living in their own households but with relatives other than spouses present an intriguing group for both the researcher and the practitioner. Such cases provide an opportunity to understand the kind of reciprocity that can be developed when the oldest old is the householder. Because the oldest old person has been able to maintain the status of householder, he or she is likely to be in a much better positon to develop reciprocity and interdependence. Only a small minority (16.5%) of family households are of this type, however (see Table 2.3).

While families other than spouses do play a critical role in providing help or even a home and 24-hour care, it is important to understand that

---

[3]The oldest old living in a child's household include those living in the household of a child's spouse as well.

[4]In this survey, necessary tasks of daily living include not only home management tasks or the instrumental activities of daily living (IADLs) of shopping, housework, meal preparation, and money management, but also personal care tasks or the personal activities of daily living (PADLs) of eating, getting in and out of a bed or chair, using the toilet, dressing, bathing, walking, and going outside. See Feller (1986) for a full description of the sample and measures.

[5]There is no uniform criterion set by the Census Bureau to define a householder. The determination of householder is up to the household member who fills out the form. Nevertheless, it appears that designation of the oldest old member as householder is likely to signify something very different from, say, designation as parent of the householder.

Table 2.3. Living Arrangements for Those 85 and Over Living in Family Households in 1980

With Spouse	With Other Relative in Own Household[a]	Child[b]	In Household of Relative	
			Other Relative	Total
37.5%	16.5%	26.3%	19.7%	100%
(N = 356,989)	(N = 157,635)	(N = 250,376)	(N = 188,133)	(N = 953,133)

Source: U.S. Bureau of the Census, 1984b: Table 265.
[a]Excludes those living with a spouse.
[b]Includes those living in the household of a son- or daughter-in-law.

not all of the oldest old will have a relative ready and able to provide such help if it is needed. Adult children can be especially critical for this group, who are likely to have outlived both spouses and siblings. Furthermore, there is a negative relationship between the number of children and the risk of institutionalization. The more adult children the elderly parent has, the less likely it is that he or she will be institutionalized (Crystal, 1982:45). In the year 1990, ever-married women (women who have ever been married) aged 86–90 will have, on the average, only 2.5 children, assuming that none of their children has died.[6] The parents of the baby boomers will be better off, however, because they are likely to have had at least one more child, and fewer of their children will have died.

A minority of the oldest old living in the community (21.2%) are still living with a spouse. There is a high degree of need among this group. Almost one-third (32%) of those 85 and over who are married and living with a spouse need the help of another person to carry out all the necessary tasks of daily living (Feller, 1986). For married persons 85 and over, however, the ability of the spouse to provide all of the care required may be insufficient. Nearly one in seven men is not living with a spouse for reasons other than marital discord or legal separation, and similarly, one in five married women is not living with a spouse (Rosenwaike, 1985b:81). These figures no doubt reflect the lack of ability of spouses in this age range to care for each other given the high likelihood of disability and the potentially high physical burden of care. Many of

---

[6]Metropolitan Life has estimated that a mother has a one-in-four chance of outliving her son (Metropolitan Life Insurance Company, cited in Bengtson and Treas, 1980).

these spouses are in nursing homes. Adult children, moreover, may be able to cope only with the care of one parent, not both:

> Mr. Washington, at 86, lives in a board and care facility. He manages all right with some functional disabilities. His wife, however, now lives with their daughter, two hours' drive away. He himself was no longer able to care for her and did not wish to burden his daughter with the dual care required for both. This was not a happy solution for him but was one to which he appeared to be resigned.

The critical role of families, both spouses and other relatives, is in providing help for the oldest old, as illustrated by these data. It is simply a myth that families don't care. It is also probably a myth that families can provide all the necessary help themselves. A better understanding of the potential and limitations of each family will be required in the future. In many cases, the most effective community approach for this group would be some combination of respite services for families together with direct services to the elderly. Careful attention needs to be paid to preserving interdependence and reciprocity and avoiding both feelings of dependence and feelings of burden.

Living Alone A substantial minority (38.8%) of the oldest old who live in the community live alone.[7] This figure is somewhat higher than the percentage of those 65 and over living alone in the community (29.3%). It is important, however, not to infer that those who live alone suffer severely from isolation or loneliness (Tobin, 1987; Rubinstein, 1986). It is the role of the researcher or practitioner, not the demographer, to ascertain the degree of social activity and family involvement of those who are living alone. Furthermore, it is important to recognize that living alone is probably the preferred living arrangement for the unmarried oldest old. In a survey of all those over 65 living alone, 86% said they prefer living alone (Harris and Associates, 1986). It is important that these preferences be taken into account in program planning.

Living alone does mean, however, that there is no one in the

---

[7]This percentage of oldest old living alone in the community matches quite closely the percentage found in the National Health Interview Survey of 1979–1980 (38.5%). A recent Harris Survey found that 52% of the oldest old live alone (Harris and Associates, 1986). This difference probably reflects the fact that the Harris poll was a telephone survey of persons who were physically and mentally able to respond over the telephone. Also, non-English speakers were excluded—approximately 4.5% of the oldest old in 1980 (Longino, 1988). Therefore, those living with relatives and needing care are probably underrepresented.

household with whom to develop reciprocity and interdependence in the activities of daily living. Giving and receiving help must be negotiated with persons outside the household. An important consideration here is that one of every three persons 85 and over who are living alone *does* need the help of another person in managing the activities of daily living (Feller, 1986:84). While that means that two out of three normally can manage, short-term acute illness among the 85-and-over age group can be very debilitating. Getting the flu can easily mean that the person will require help for three or four weeks. Program planning for those oldest old who live alone needs to take into account their special needs.

The Special Case of Women   One demographic fact that is obvious to everyone is that women live longer than men today. A woman's life expectancy at birth in 1984 was 78.2 years, compared with a man's 71.2 years. This means that the vast majority of the oldest old will be women. In 1980, there were only 44 men for every 100 women 85 and over (Rosenwaike, 1985b:37). The sex ratio for the oldest old has become more and more unbalanced in the last half century. In 1930 there were three men for every four women 85 and over; in 1980, there were approximately three men for every seven women (Rosenwaike, 1985a:193).[8]

Women's increasing longevity in industrialized countries has raised questions concerning the role of biology in longevity. Some researchers have even implied that a woman's life span is greater than a man's. The life span is "the length of life that is biologically possible for a given species" (Atchley, 1985:367). There is, however, no evidence that women are biologically blessed with a greater number of possible years of life than men. There is even a hint that men who reach age 100 may have some advantages in longevity compared with women, although data on persons 100 years of age or more are not reliable (Rosenwaike, 1985b:37). The world's oldest known person was a man who died at age 120. On the celebration of his or her 85th birthday, a man has a fifty-fifty chance of celebrating his 90th, whereas a woman has a more than fifty-fifty chance of celebrating her 91st (Rosenwaike, 1985b). It may be true that female sex hormones provide greater protection against coronary heart disease (Waldron, 1976), but this results in greater longevity for women at ages younger than 85; it does not provide them with a greater life span.

---

[8]It is also important to realize that the proportion of men in the 85-and-over population today is enhanced by the fact that many of this generation were immigrants and that these immigrants were disproportionately men.

Women's greater longevity, as well as their greater susceptibility to widowhood, means that they predominate among those in living arrangements that entail a high dependency risk. Of those oldest old living inside institutions in 1980, 78.8% were women; of those living outside institutions, women accounted for more than three-quarters (77.9%) of those living alone or living with relatives other than a spouse. Table 2.4 shows that the three living arrangements—in institutions, alone, or with other relatives—account for 90.4% of all women 85 and over. Those living in institutions are by definition dependent because they are in the care and custody of the institution. Oldest old women who live outside institutions, either alone or in households with other family members, are also of special concern because of their high risk of having limited economic resources and of needing the help of another person. Unmarried women of advanced age have a very high risk of poverty (Warlick, 1983). Furthermore, of those living in the community, 43.8% of the oldest old women need the help of another person in order to perform all activities of daily living; among oldest old men, only 31.0% need such help (Feller, 1986). After age 80, men are twice as likely as women to be defined as physically able (Harris et al., 1987).

The choice between these two predominant community living arrangements for older women has been explored in detail by Soldo, Sharma, and Campbell (1984). Controlling for age, they found, as predicted, that the need for assistance was an important factor; those who lived with relatives were more likely to need assistance with self-care or getting around than those who lived alone. Nevertheless, income was also important in predicting living arrangements; poor women were more likely to be living with relatives. This study, as well as the 1986 study by Bishop, suggests that when older unmarried women have sufficient economic and physiological resources, they live alone; a lack in either leads to a high probability of living with relatives. The effect is additive; unmarried women who are both poor and in need of help are more likely to be living with relatives than women who are poor but in good health or better off economically but in poor health. Bishop (1986:72) suggests that women with higher incomes and a disability purchase services so that they can continue to live alone. Thus, the high probability of living with relatives for unmarried women aged 85 and over is due to their high risk of poverty and their high risk of needing assistance. Furthermore, the task of providing help for these oldest old unmarried women is most likely to fall on women—their daughters and daughters-in-law—who may themselves be past 65 and, if widowed, possessing very limited economic resources.

Table 2.4. Living Arrangements for Women 85 and Over in 1980

With Spouse	With Other Relativesª	Alone	In Households with Non-relatives	In Noninstitutional Group Quartersᵇ	In Institutionsᶜ	Total
5.9%	30.8%	33.3%	2.3%	1.4%	26.3%	100%
(N = 90,126)	(N = 469,619)	(N = 508,009)	(N = 34,893)	(N = 20,774)	(N = 401,280)	(N = 1,524,701)

Source: U.S. Bureau of the Census, 1984b:Tables 265, 266.
ªExcludes those living with a spouse in their own or spouse's household.
ᵇIncludes those not living in households and not living in institutions.
ᶜIncludes those classified as inmates or patients; includes convalescent and nursing homes as well as rest homes for the aged.

Other Demographic Characteristics

While census information on size and potential growth, sex ratio, and living arrangements of the oldest old are probably the most critical demographic planning information for the oldest old, a number of other factors may be important at all levels of planning. For the practitioner, these may also be important in understanding the typical client, as contrasted with the atypical client, in terms of case management. Information on education, race, ethnicity, migration, and geographic distribution and income (see Chapter Six) are also available from the census.

Education

For both the program planner and the practitioner, it is important to understand the typical level of education among the oldest old. Persons who were 85 and over in 1980 attended school during the last decade of the nineteenth century and the first decade of the twentieth century. Many were immigrants, and many others were sons and daughters of immigrants. Only a minority of men (37.1%) and women (44.9%) completed at least one year of high school; nearly one-third did not complete the eighth grade. Among blacks, the typical 85-year-old in 1980 had completed fewer than seven years of elementary school, with one-quarter completing only four or fewer years.

This very low level of education is important in understanding the oldest old's difficulty in performing certain tasks, such as managing money. Also, those with low educational levels are not likely to be sophisticated users of social services and often need extra help in making it through the bureaucratic maze. These low educational levels may also result in the oldest old being more confused by any changes in their environment. Measures of cognitive impairment are likely to be higher among those with lower levels of education (Kane and Kane, 1981). Practitioners need to be especially sensitive to mental status changes in order to ascertain whether the change is the result of a disease process. It may be the result of some factor in the environment which is bewildering to a person with only a few years of education. It is important not to assume that the oldest old cannot cope with change. Lack of familiarity with bureaucratic processes combined with lack of education may be the key to the problem. This could be especially true of the oldest old rural black residents who have had very limited experience with the world of white bureaucracy and the modern hospital (Valentine, 1971). Elders with low levels of education and limited English-speaking ability also will probably need special attention in adapting to hospitals or nursing homes.

In future years, cohorts born later will certainly have higher levels of education and more experience with the bureaucratic process and the organization of institutional care. In the year 2000, the typical person aged 85–94 will have had at least some high school education, and only one-fifth will have finished less than the eigth grade. Even then, however, it will be necessary for the practitioner to take into account the educational level as well as the newness of the experience for the oldest old. New experiences, especially for those with little education and limited experience, can be confusing or frightening at any age (Lieberman and Tobin, 1983).

Minority Populations

The racial and ethnic diversity of American society is reflected in its oldest old population. Some minority groups, however, form a smaller proportion of the oldest old than they do at younger ages. Only 8% of the oldest old were nonwhite in 1980 (Rosenwaike, 1985b). The nonwhite category is overwhelmingly black (90%) but also includes persons of Asian and American Indian origin. Blacks and American Indians have a very different age structure than white populations, due to higher birth rates and higher mortality rates. Those who reach age 85 in these populations are a very select group of survivors.[9]

The black population 85 and over is the largest single minority group among the oldest old ($N = 155,137$). Furthermore, it is markedly different from the white population in terms of living arrangements. While approximately the same proportion of blacks and whites live with a spouse or live alone, blacks are much more likely than whites to be living with relatives other than a spouse and much less likely to be institutionalized. Indeed, in 1980, the rate of institutionalizaton among white oldest old (24%) was almost double the rate for black oldest old (13%).

The black family is more likely to include the oldest old, as well as children who are not biological offspring of any adult family member (i.e., nieces or nephews). Black families clearly take on substantial burdens of care. In the case of oldest old blacks 40.2% are living with relatives other than a spouse (U.S. Bureau of the Census, 1984b:Tables 265 and 266). The fact that black elderly parents tend to have had more children also increases the probability that one of the children will be able to provide care (Crystal, 1982). In addition, oldest old blacks are most likely to be living in the South, where there may be a more traditional approach to family caregiving. It could also be that discrimination and/or poverty systematically limits black families' access to institutional care (Watson, 1983). Black families especially are least able to afford any extra costs incurred by caring for an elderly relative; these families have a high probability of being poor. Furthermore, a black elderly person (over 65) living in a relative's household is more than three times as likely to be living in a poor family, in comparison with a white elderly person living in a relative's household (U.S. Bureau of the Census, 1985:41). Nevertheless, at the same level of income and disability, nonwhites are more likely to live with others than are whites (Bishop, 1986). The disabled black elderly are more likely to live with their children than are the disabled white elderly (Macken, 1986).

The black oldest old may be in a better position to negotiate the terms of their care within the family setting. Among oldest old persons living with relatives other than a spouse, blacks are more likely to be

---

[9]The hypothesis that oldest old blacks are a hardier group and thus expected to live longer than oldest old whites (the "mortality crossover") has been questioned by Rosenwaike (1985b). Evidence for greater longevity among oldest old blacks may simply be the result of age misstatement. Medicare data, however, do support a possible crossover effect in those 85 and over (Zopf, 1986).

living in their own households (32.3%) than are whites (25.7%).[10] This is probably because their economic contribution of a house and/or a regular Social Security check makes their home an attractive place for adult children or other relatives to stay. Even when the elder is living in a relative's household, there may be a strong incentive to keep the elder at home so as not to lose the contribution of the Social Security check to the household income.

Oldest old persons of Hispanic origin ($N = 36,204$) are much fewer in number than oldest old blacks or even oldest old persons born in Italy ($N = 62,100$). Nevertheless, this group deserves special attention because its numbers are most likely to grow very rapidly and it is most likely to retain bilingual or even Spanish-speaking-only characteristics. The special needs of this group reflect both limited ability in English and low levels of education. For Hispanics, as for blacks, there are further problems created by the high likelihood of poverty, especially for Mexican-American and Puerto Rican families.[11] This high overall poverty level, together with a strong preference for family care rather than institutional care, means that the burden of care for these families is likely to be high. Fortunately, there are sufficient numbers of young bilingual speakers, as well as enough concentrations of elderly Hispanic populations, that programs could be tailored specifically to meet the needs of the Hispanic elderly, including the oldest old and their families. There may already be a high level of need for special programming in New Mexico, where 29% of the oldest old are of Hispanic origin and a majority of them do not speak English (Longino, 1988).

The population 85 years of age and over in 1980 also includes a large concentration of persons who were born outside the United States and came during the peak immigration years 1900–1910. While the total number of persons of foreign birth is much greater than that of nonwhites and Hispanics combined, they are ethnically and linguistically quite diverse. Italy (62,100 persons), Poland (34,850 persons), and Russia (34,250 persons) predominate as countries of origin for the foreign-born

---

[10]Among all oldest old blacks, the chances of heading one's own household without a spouse (12.9%) are nearly twice the chances for oldest old whites (6.7%) (U.S. Bureau of the Census, 1984b:Tables 265, 266).

[11]In census data, the self-reported racial designation of Hispanics may be either black or white, and ethnicity may include any one of several different ethnic groups. Cubans tend to have higher educational levels and higher incomes than do Mexican-Americans or Puerto Ricans. Nevertheless, poverty among elderly Hispanics living in the households of relatives other than a spouse is higher (7.9%) than among elderly whites living in similar households (6.3%) (U.S. Bureau of the Census, 1985:41).

oldest old (Rosenwaike, 1985b:44). In 1980, nearly one-quarter of all whites aged 85 and over had been born in a foreign country. Furthermore, more than 300,000 of them were born in a country where the dominant language was not English. Concentrations of non-English-speaking oldest old are found in the Northeast: Connecticut (8.5%), Massachusetts (7.4%), New Jersey (8.5%), New York (9.0%), and Rhode Island (9.9%) (Longino, 1988).

The fact that this population learned English as a second language and probably had very little education can create special problems in terms of their ability to cope with new and confusing situations. This is especially true in the aftermath of a stroke or in any of a range of conditions that can result in cognitive impairment:

> Mr. Zimmerman had had a stroke. When the doctor first assessed him in the hospital, he asked him to count from one to ten. The answers Mr. Zimmerman gave were described to his family as "gibberish." The family was also informed that he had lost much of his cognitive function. They were warned that Mr. Zimmerman probably would not recognize family members. On further recovery, it came to light that Mr. Zimmerman's "gibberish" was in fact Yiddish. Under the stress of the stroke, he had, quite understandably, complied with the doctor's request by counting from one to ten in his first language, the language he had learned as a small boy.[12]

It is important to realize that even if their command of English is perfect, those whose childhood language was other than English are likely to switch to that language under physical and psychological stress. In areas with large immigrant populations, it is important to assess an elder's linguistic experience before presuming cognitive impairment.

Geographic Distribution

More than half (54.4%) of the oldest old are concentrated in ten states: California (9.7%), New York (8.6%), Pennsylvania (5.8%), Florida (5.2%), Illinois (5.1%), Texas (5.0%), Ohio (4.8%), Michigan (3.6%), Massachusetts (3.3%), and New Jersey (3.2%)(Rosenwaike, 1985b:60). States with large numbers of oldest old are at risk of incurring large expenditures for Medicaid, the program in which state funding is matched by federal funds in order to provide nursing home payments for poor persons. States pay from 23 to 50% of Medicaid costs for their residents (Muse and Sawyer, 1982). In times of federal cutbacks and state fiscal

---

[12]This case is from the unpublished research of Judith Gordon.

crises, this is a vulnerable budget item (Newcomer and Harrington, 1983; Lammers and Klingman, 1984).

For nine of the ten states mentioned above, however, the growth in the oldest old population from 1970 to 1980 was close to the national average of 59.5%. For Florida, as well as Arizona and Nevada, the growth of the oldest old population was approximately twice the national average. These states that have experienced this dramatic increase—a more than doubling of the oldest old—are faced with the greatest problems in program planning. One state, Alaska, has experienced little growth—only 5%—of its oldest old population. The rapid growth of a state's oldest old population between 1970 and 1980 reflects, to a great degree, the persons in the state who were aged 75–84 before 1970 and who will have reached their 85th birthday by 1980.

The popular image of the young old, those aged 65–69, is of a population in flux—moving into a condo, into a retirement community, or to the Sunbelt—but it is the oldest old, not the young old, who are most likely to have changed their residence in the past five years (Rosenwaike, 1985b). Furthermore, the residence changes of the oldest old are likely to be prompted by widowhood, disability, and institutionalization (Rosenwaike, 1985b). Often the move is into the children's home or to a location closer to their children because of an anticipated deterioration of health or a loss of key elements of their social support networks:

Mrs. Watson, at 86, was a vivacious, chatty, outgoing widow who had no functional disabilities and could easily maintain an independent life-style. Unlike many in her age group, she had kept up with weekly volunteer work and had also maintained a busy round of social activities. She led a very active life with a high level of involvement in her community. But her busy life in southern California was soon to come to an end. In less than two months, she was planning a move to the Pacific Northwest. Her son-in-law had been transferred more than 1,000 miles away, and she was going to move also—not to live with her daughter's family but to be nearby "just in case." She seemed cheerful enough about starting over, but the tremor in her voice suggested that this cheerfulness was the result of habit, not anticipation. In her new location it would not be easy for her to develop the range of activities she now enjoyed.

There can be no doubt that many, if not most, of these moves are difficult for both the elder and his or her family. Practitioners and program planners need to pay special attention to easing the transition to a new residence (Lieberman and Tobin, 1983).

Urban Versus Rural Areas

Planning for the service needs of the oldest old is clearly facilitated by the concentration of this group in urban areas. More than three-quarters of all oldest old live in urban areas, and more than half live in central cities or their suburbs. Black oldest old are even more concentrated (51%) in the central city itself than are whites (31%) (Rosenwaike, 1985b). This urban concentration allows for efficient targeting of those in need, use of respite facilities such as adult day-care centers, and development of specialized transportation networks.

While 23% of the oldest old live in rural areas, rural residence poses particularly difficult problems for cost-effective program development. This can become critical not only for access to programs helping the functionally disabled but also for access to basic medical care itself. The doctor visits that may require expensive taxi service in the city are simply not within the realm of possibility for rural residents, for whom taxi service is unavailable at any price and the nearest doctor may be more than 30 miles away. The problem is further exacerbated by the fact that rural oldest old are poorer than urban oldest old. Among blacks, one-half of the oldest old living in rural areas are poor. Rural areas present a critical challenge in terms of developing informal social support networks composed of nearby residents to provide essential services (Wentowski, 1981; Lozier and Althouse, 1975).

Demographics for Practitioners

While demographers and planners focus on numbers, practitioners focus on individuals: behind the demographer's numbers are individual people. Demographic data can be especially helpful for practitioners in avoiding stereotyped thinking and in sensitizing themselves to the unique experiences of many in this cohort, such as low educational levels or foreign birth. Demographic data also can enhance the development of efficient and effective approaches for the typical case and the understanding of a special situation in the atypical case.

For the oldest old, a typical case could involve a long-time widow with some limitations of activity who is living alone or with her daughter. Various services could be coordinated to help widows who are alone as well as those who are living with daughters. At this age, widowhood is typical (Blau, 1973). The care of an elderly mother is even described by

Brody (1985) as one of "normative stress," a natural course of events. Mothers and daughters or childless widows have often had much opportunity to develop patterns of reciprocity and interdependence. There is probably much potential for programs to facilitate reciprocal woman-to-woman helping networks (see Chapter Four, footnote 8).

The oldest old widower, however, is a very atypical case; his problems do not fit with the usual sequence of life events. He probably expected his wife to outlive him, but she, not he, died first. In his age group he finds mostly women, and even among the minority of men 85 and over, more men living in the community are married (49%) than widowed (44%). He may, with good reason, feel that he was one of the unlucky ones. Why me? Why couldn't I be like the average man who has a wife to take care of him until he dies? If he does need assistance, he may resent having to rely on a formal provider rather than a wife. Furthermore, an oldest old widower is more likely to be a recent widower and have to adjust to widowerhood at a later stage in life, when his own health is less robust. At age 85, remarriage is unlikely, and the recent widower in not likely to have a circle of widower friends with whom he can develop helping networks or even begin new activities. Support groups, common enough for widows, are rare for widowers, although AARP (The American Association of Retired Persons) is providing special programs for widowers. If support groups are sex-integrated, he would be likely to have to adjust to being a token man, a situation that probably is not an easy one:

> Mr. Schwartz was a very angry person. His wife had just died at age 85; he was 89. He had cared for her the last three years. It had been very difficult, and only now did he realize that she had probably had Alzheimer's disease. When he was hospitalized for an acute illness, his wife was placed in a nursing home, where she died five months later. Mr Schwartz was still free of disability, but he was unable to adjust to his new life as a widower. His case worker had recommended a support group, but there was none appropriate to his needs.

This atypical case fit neither the usual sequence of life events nor the package of services available. While agencies could do a better job of programming for unmarried men (Rubinstein, 1986:247), in many geographic areas it would not be appropriate to develop special programs designed for oldest old widowers because their numbers are so small. These widowers, however, merit special attention because of the very high risk of suicide for white men aged 85 and over (Manton, Blazer, and Woodbury, 1987:222).

Demographics as a Planning Tool

As the previous discussion indicates, demographics is an effective planning tool. It is often the most efficient planning tool as well because demographic data are generally easily accessible and relatively inexpensive. Unfortunately, until recently demographic data were usually available only for the 65-and-over age group, or at best, the 75-and-over age group. This is beginning to change as demographers and planners recognize the special needs of the fifth age, which requires an age breakdown for those 85 and over. With demographic data, programs can be developed to meet a wide range of needs and to achieve a wide range of goals. Programs can be targeted for oldest old persons being cared for by families or for individuals living alone. The special needs of minority racial and ethnic groups can be taken into account. Moreover, demographers can project their estimates into the future and provide a vital service to planners, who must always pay attention to projected needs ten to 15 years hence. How many of the oldest old are likely to be of Hispanic origin in the year 2000, and how many of them will be foreign born and need services provided in Spanish? If we are to restrict the development of more nursing home beds, what alternatives will be available for the oldest old in terms of in-home care or alternate living arrangements? These are critical questions for the future.

Demographers can provide data to define the dimensions of the oldest old population. Planners and policymakers must act promptly if a crisis of care for the oldest old is to be minimized. The danger is that without effective planning and policy development, practitioners will be left to manage crisis after crisis as the level of need escalates far beyond the capacity of the system to handle it effectively. Furthermore, programs developed in an atmosphere of crisis are likely to repeat the mistakes of the past. Now is the time to plan for programs that will promote self-determination and prevent dependence among this population at high risk.

Chapter Three

Health

Introduction

The health of the oldest old is the central concern underlying all other issues. Physiological resources are the most critical type of resource in preventing dependency. For the oldest old, good health is not so much a feeling of wellness or even the absence of disease; it means having sufficient physiological resources to carry on their daily lives without the help of another person. Looming foremost is the fear that limited physiological resources will result in dependence and even institutionalization. Institutionalization exacerbates dependence because it entails a loss of self-determination and involves either a rapid depletion in assets or public spending through Medicaid or both. Failing health has personal and psychic costs for the oldest old and their families. With no immediate prospect for a reduction in illness or disability, there is no comfort or hope in the knowledge that people are now living to advanced ages (Manton, 1986).

Needing the Help of Another Person

The critical measure of the oldest old's physiological resources is: Do they have the physical and mental capacity to manage their daily lives on their own, or do they require help from another person? A lack of adequate physiological resources results in functional disability. *Functional disability is the degree to which a chronic health problem, either physical or mental, produces a behavioral change in a person's capacity to perform the necessary tasks for daily living so that the help of another person is required.* Functional disability does not relate to any specific disease or diagnosis, and in fact, for the oldest old it is probably due to a combination of chronic health factors. Furthermore, a disease process in the oldest old will more likely manifest itself in functional disability rather than in discrete symptoms typical of the disease in a younger population (Besdine, 1985). Measures of functional disability provide a better sense of the physiological resources of the oldest old than does any listing of diseases or symptoms.

Functional disabilities affect a person's ability to attend to personal care needs, or personal activities of daily living (PADLs), and home management needs, or instrumental activities of daily living (IADLs). Personal activities of daily living, often called simply ADLs, include bathing, eating, dressing, toileting, transferring oneself in and out of bed or a chair, and walking or getting around inside the home. Persons who need help with these activities will need another person on a daily basis (except for help with taking a bath). While disabilities in the area of home management are considered to be less severe in nature, they are often critical in determining whether an individual can live alone. These IADLs include, minimally, shopping, housework, money management, and meal preparation. Other activities that may be restricted by IADL disabilities are doing laundry, getting around outside, and taking medications.[1] In this book, "activities of daily living" refers to both PADLs and IADLs, and elders are considered functionally disabled if they require the help of another person in at least one of these necessary activities.

There is another measure of disability[2] that focuses on whether a

---

[1]Spector and Katz (1985) found that the IADL scale describes 97.9% of the population in a hierarchal manner. See also Lawton and Brody (1969) and Katz et al. (1963).

[2]The most common definition of disability refers to limitations in a person's ability to perform the "major activity" with specific reference to work. This measure is not appropriate for the oldest old, since the critical issue is not their ability to work but their ability to perform the necessary activities of daily living (PADLs and IADLs). Recent changes in the National Health Interview Survey questionnaire recognize this important distinction between work-related disability and functional disability or functional limitation in performing the activities of daily living (Rosenwaike, 1985b:126).

person is *limited* in performing any of the activities of daily living (PADLs and IADLs) due to a chronic health problem. These persons, for example, may require the use of a cane for walking. They are *functionally limited* but not *functionally disabled* because they are able to manage without help. Such individuals do not risk dependence unless their limitation worsens to the point that they require others to help. Among the young old, there are many who are limited in performing at least one of the activities of daily living but who do not require the help of another person. In fact, almost one-quarter of the young old who are functionally limited can manage by themselves without help. But managing the necessary tasks of daily living on one's own with a health limitation becomes less and less possible in the older age groups. Among the oldest old, only 10% of those with a health limitation can manage the activities of daily living without the help of another person (Feller, 1986). In this book, a *functional limitation* is the need for a device *or* a person; a functional disability is the need for a person. For the oldest old, however, this distinction is less important because nearly all those who are functionally limited are also functionally disabled.

Persons aged 85 and over comprise a unique group in that due to a chronic health problem, more than half of them (54%) need the help of another person in order to manage their daily lives (Table 3.1). For those aged 75–84, only one out of every five requires the help of others. For the young old, only a tiny minority (8.4%) needs this kind of help because of a chronic health problem. Therefore, concern over not being able to manage one's own life is very real for those reaching age 85. This measure of physiological resources is the most appropriate because it provides a simple and straightforward insight into the impact of diseases and disorders on the daily lives of the oldest old.[3]

In an Institution

Elders living in institutions generally have severe health problems that limit their ability to perform daily activities. We will assume that those

---

[3]This measure, however, is not the best indicator of the impact of health problems on the caregivers of the oldest old. See Chapter Five.

Table 3.1. Elderly Persons Needing the Help of Another Person in at Least One Activity of Daily Living

Age	Living in the Community[a]		Institutionalized[b]	Total[c]
65–74	Percentage needing help	6.7%	100%	8.4%
	Number needing help	1,012	286	1,298
	(Total population)	(15,078)	(286)	(15,364)
75–84	Percentage needing help	15.7%	100%	21.8%
	Number needing help	1,093	542	1,635
	(Total population)	(6,964)	(542)	(7,506)
85 and over	Percentage needing help	39.3%	100%	54.1%
	Number needing help	620	509	1,129
	(Total population)	(1,576)	(509)	(2,085)

Note: Activities include shopping, performing household chores, preparing meals, managing money, walking, going outside, bathing, dressing, using the toilet, getting in or out of a bed or chair, and eating.
[a]National Health Interview Survey of the civilian noninstitutionalized population living in households in 1979–1980. See Feller (1986).
[b]U.S. Bureau of the Census (1984b). Excludes inmates of correctional institutions.
[c]Total population, excluding residents of group quarters and inmates of correctional institutions.

residing in an institution (other than a correctional institution[4]) do require the help of another person (Johnson and Grant, 1985:40). Although it is estimated that a small percentage of nursing home residents do not need to be institutionalized, it is reasonable to assume that all of them would need the help of another person in most home management tasks and some personal care tasks. Two common problems of nursing home residents who are 85 and over involve severe cognitive impairment (52.9%) and the need for assistance in using the toilet (68.2%); nearly all oldest old residents (94.1%) require help in taking a bath (National Center for Health Statistics, 1987b).

Most studies of the institutional population are conducted at only one point in time. The National Center for Health Statistics' nursing home survey, which was taken in 1985, shows that close to half (45.2%)

---

[4]Inmates of correctional institutions are excluded from this analysis. For those 85 and over, only 404 persons were inmates of correctional institutions. The vast majority of institutionalized oldest old (487,746) resided in nursing homes or other institutions for the aged. An additional 7,022 were patients in mental hospitals, and 13,746 were inmates of other institutions, such as hospitals for the chronically ill.

of the institutionalized population is 85 and over. But it is members of this special population who are most likely to remain in the institution for six months or more (Liu and Manton, 1983). Furthermore, those 85 and over have almost three times the risk of being placed permanently in a nursing home compared with those aged 65–74 (Vicente, Wiley, and Carrington, 1979:363). This fact is not surprising, since the oldest old have the highest risk of developing Alzheimer's disease, a common disease among those who are institutionalized for six months or more. For the young old, the nursing home is often a short-stay facility for, say, recovery from a hip fracture, and payment is primarily through Medicare (Liu and Manton, 1983). For the oldest old, a hip fracture is likely to result in permanent disability and continued institutionalization. Furthermore, there is no public social insurance available to cover their long-term stays, and very few are covered by any form of private insurance.

Persons living in institutions are classified as dependent; that is, they can no longer sustain the norm of reciprocity. They have lost control over their lives and their environments (Goffman, 1961) and are dependent on the care of others. This dependence may be only temporary for the young old, but the oldest old often face permanent dependence. Even if an individual can pay for the care received out of his or her own income and assets, this payment does not prevent dependence because the institution is not under the control of the payor. The reverse is true; the patient is at the mercy of the institution, no matter who pays the bill.[5] In these settings, the concepts of independence and interdependence no longer apply.

Institutionalization is the major form of help provided by the government for those who are functionally disabled. While the rationale is medical, the major form of help is with activities of daily living (Vladeck, 1980; Diamond and Berman, 1981). Given the high cost of providing help within institutions, it makes sense to explore further the possibilities for providing help with activities of daily living outside the institution. How extensive is the need for help in the community? If policy changes are made now, could we better preserve the independence and interdependence of the oldest old? Could the extreme dependence of institutionalization be postponed or prevented? For this purpose, the

---

[5]While there is certainly a variation in the quality of care provided by nursing homes, patients have little control over their lives even in the best or most expensive facilities. Some nursing homes are trying to give patients more say in simple matters such as when to have breakfast. These small efforts to give patients some control over their lives are important, but they still occur within the context of dependence.

Table 3.2. Elderly Persons Needing Help in Activities of Daily Living (PADLs and IADLs) Requiring Physical Mobility

Age	Shopping	Going Outside	Walking
75–84	11.6%	8.3%	8.9%
85 and over	31.2%	24.9%	23.5%

Source: National Health Interview Survey of 1979–1980. See Feller (1986), Tables 2, 14.

emphasis in this book is on those oldest old still living in the community. How can their personal, social-familial, economic, and physiological resources be developed? This chapter closely examines the physiological resources of the oldest old still living in the community.

In the Community

Functional disabilities limiting physical mobility are the disabilities that most often cause the oldest old to need help in activities of daily living (see Table 3.2). In the Health Interview Survey of 1979–1980, more oldest old persons reported needing help with shopping (31.2%) than with any other necessary activity. This is not surprising because shopping requires the ability to go outside the home; one in four (24.9%) reported that they needed help just to go outside. Similarly, nearly one in four (23.5%) required help in order to walk. This substantial minority who need help in terms of physical mobility distinguishes the 85 and over from those in the next lower age group, those aged 75–84; the oldest old are almost three times as likely to need these kinds of help.

Tasks that require physical agility also become much more difficult for the oldest old to handle. One-fourth (25.4%) of the oldest old need help to perform household chores, and nearly 16% need help in order to take a bath. Again, these levels of need are nearly three times as great as the levels found among those aged 75–84 (see Table 3.3). These are

Table 3.3. Elderly Persons Needing Help in Activities of Daily Living (PADLs and IADLs) Requiring Physical Agility

Age	Performing Household Chores	Bathing
75–84	9.9%	5.2%
85 and over	25.4%	15.7%

Source: National Health Interview Survey of 1979–1980. See Feller (1986), Tables 2, 14.

Table 3.4. Elderly Persons Needing Help in Specified Tasks of Daily Living

Age	Managing Money	Using the Toilet
75–84	5.0%	3.1%
85 and over	15.4%	9.5%

Source: National Health Interview Survey of 1979–1980. See Feller (1986), Tables 2, 14.

activities, however, that can be performed on less than a daily basis. Nevertheless, they are also activities that entail the risk of falling, so caution is necessary in judging the ability of the 85-year-old.

Other critical activities that present serious problems are using the toilet and managing money. Needing help in these areas generally precludes independence except in cases where abundant economic resources permit purchasing the service. Family support networks, however, can provide money management in an interdependent context. In both cases, the level of need for the oldest old is more than three times that of ages 75–84 (see Table 3.4).

Disability and Disease

The rapid increase in functional disability experienced by those aged 85 and over is the result of chronic health conditions. *Chronic conditions* generally develop slowly, involve a number of body functions, and are usually not reversible; there is often, however, the possibility of medical management and rehabilitation. *Acute conditions,* in contrast, involve a definite onset, a crisis, and recovery or death. Acute conditions, such as the flu, can certainly be disabling, but the disability disappears with recovery. Although an exact link between a chronic disease and the resulting functional disability is often tenuous, Besdine (1985) has made some important observations about this link.

First, diseases, both chronic and acute, often go untreated much longer in the very old because they do not report their symptoms to health providers. Elderly persons living in the community may be concealing as many as half of their symptoms (Besdine, 1985). Therefore, treatable conditions often are not diagnosed until it is too late to prevent disability.

Second, many common diseases of the elderly may have as their only indicators such nonspecific symptoms such as falling, urinary incontinence, dizziness, acute confusion, refusal to eat or drink, weight loss, and failure to thrive (Besdine, 1985:Table 22-5). The presence of one or more of these symptoms often indicates the presence or worsening of disease, but they remain unreported because they are so nonspecific. Such symptoms are considered "normal" for the oldest old, so they may be ignored as simply the result of normal aging. Specifically, however, they may be symptoms of drug intoxication, pneumonia, cancer, heart attack, or lung obstruction (pulmonary embolism) (Besdine, 1985:Table 22-6). These disorders may therefore have functional disability as their primary symptom.

Third, the link between a chronic condition and functional disability is compounded by the fact that the oldest old are likely to have more than one chronic condition. One study of oldest old persons being discharged from the hospital found that half of them had at least five diagnoses (Guhleman, 1987). Therefore, a number of chronic conditions can jointly produce functional disability. In contrast, the young old are more likely to have just one chronic condition that they are able to manage by themselves. For example, if the only chronic condition is mild arthritis, it is possible to manage by oneself with the use of a cane. Besdine provides an example more typical of the oldest old:

> An example is the old woman with unreported urinary tract infection producing frequent urgent urination which exceeds the mobility limit of her degenerative osteoarthritis and makes her incontinent. Uncorrected poor vision and urine on the floor cause a fall with a fracture of her osteoporotic hip and . . . heart failure. (1985:265–266)

Here the likely result is institutionalization; the patient will need long-term care in a nursing home. But her institutionalization could have been postponed or possibly avoided if adequate attention had been paid to her urinary and vision problems as well as her high risk of falling. Attention to preserving her physiological resources could have preserved her possibilities for self-determination.

In the following section, some of the most common chronic conditions of the very old are reviewed. These are the diseases of which a disabled 85-year-old is likely to have two or more. These diseases are examined in clusters according to presenting problems and possible risk factors. In each case, the disease is reviewed with specific attention to its possible impact on the physiological resources of the oldest old.

The Most Common Chronic Disabling Conditions of the Oldest Old

Bone and Joint Problems

The preceding review of functional disability suggests a preponderance of problems with mobility: shopping, getting outside, and even walking inside are activities for which the help of another person is often required. Some can manage alone but require the use of a cane or other device. Overall, at least half of all those 85 and over (including those in institutions) report limitations in walking around inside. Two disease processes are probably the key contributors to these mobility problems. Degenerative joint disease (osteoarthritis) and osteoporosis are leading factors affecting the mobility of the individual who has reached 85 years of age. One study showed that one-fifth of elderly persons with bone and joint problems needed the help of another person for housework and getting out of the house (Thompson et al., 1974, cited in Kelsey et al., 1979). Even without severe mobility limitations, the pain from these bone and joint diseases can seriously restrict activity. Each step may simply be too painful.

Osteoarthritis or Degenerative Joint Disease　When 85-year-olds complain of arthritis or rheumatism, chances are they are referring to osteoarthritis, or degenerative joint disease. This disease involves destruction of the tissues that allow the joint to move properly; pain results when the joint is moved. Osteoarthritis may affect only specific joints and surrounding tissue; this form of arthritis should not be confused with *rheumatoid arthritis*, which is a disease of the whole body causing inflammation of many joints. The pain of osteoarthritis no doubt contributes to the number of medications consumed. Without medication, movement may be too painful. Osteoarthritis, because it often affects weight-bearing joints and the spine, may also be a key factor in falls. The person who finds movement painful may not maintain good balance.

According to Dr. E. L. Schneider, deputy director of the NIA, research on this disease could be a key factor in improving the quality of life for our oldest old (1985). Problems with osteoarthritis are almost

Table 3.5. Medical Conditions Reported as a Cause of Disability by Elderly Persons with a Limitation in at Least One Activity of Daily Living (PADL or IADL)

Condition[a]	Percentage Reporting the Condition as a Cause of Their Limitation		
	Aged 85 and Over	Aged 75–84	Aged 65–74
Arthritis	34.9	38.0	36.9
Senility	34.6	13.5	3.3
Arteriosclerosis	33.7	37.7	33.8
Cerebrovascular disease (stroke)	27.0	31.3	30.7
Hip and other fracture	18.3	21.9	29.4
Hypertension	8.5	9.6	13.9
Diabetes	3.3	7.5	10.2
Ischemic heart disease	3.3	4.9	6.0
Cancer	1.9	4.4	6.4
Emphysema and bronchitis	1.6	4.6	8.7

Source: 1982 National Long Term Care Survey, as reported in Manton (1986).
Note: A limitation does not necessarily require the help of another person, but for the oldest old it does in nine out of ten cases.
[a]Respondents could list as many as four medical conditions as a cause.

universal by the 80th birthday (Kelsey et al., 1979). The ordinary wear and tear of life seems to result in osteoarthritis. Little is known about risk factors except that obesity is considered to worsen the wear-and-tear problems. Also, joints that are misaligned as a result of inherited factors or accidents are at higher risk. Medical treatment now can offer pain relief and reduction in swelling, but the medication can have side effects. Practitioners need to pay special attention to evaluating the risk of falling for those whose movements are painful even with medication. Among the oldest old who reported at least one limitation in activities of daily living, 34.9% indicated that arthritis was one cause of their limitation (see Table 3.5).[6]

Osteoporosis The second major bone disorder is osteoporosis, a thinning of the bone that makes it brittle. This is almost as universal as

---

[6]These data come from the 1982 National Long Term Care Survey. This was a community survey in which persons 65 and over were asked if they were limited in any way in performing the activities of daily living due to chronic health problems. Those with limitations could indicate as many as four causes for their functional limitation (Manton, 1986).

osteoarthritis except that men and blacks tend to be spared somewhat. Among women over 75, nearly 90% have some degree of osteoporosis. Osteoporosis, like osteoarthritis, can cause pain and thereby restrict mobility. Its most disabling problem, however, is the likelihood of fracture of these brittle, thin bones. Fractures can occur with only minimal stress and often require a lengthy healing process; healing may not take place at all for at least one-fourth of the hip fractures (Sheehy, 1982:32). For women, fractures of the hip, pelvis, wrist, and upper arm all increase dramatically with age (Melton and Riggs, 1983:69); vertebral fractures are also common (Roberto, 1987). Even where healing has occurred, the pain of movement may remain.

The risk factors for osteoporosis are important in estimating the risk of painful movement as well as of bone fracture. At highest risk of developing osteoporosis are women with fair skin, slender build, small muscle mass, early menopause, and a family history of osteoporosis. Life-style risk factors include smoking, low calcium intake, inactivity, and excessive consumption of substances such as alcohol and caffeine (Heaney, 1983:140). Presence of these risk factors requires special attention to the prevention of falls and careful consideration in prescribing medication that could impair balance. Among the oldest old who reported at least one limitation in any activity of daily living, 18.3% indicated that a bone fracture was one cause of their limitation (see Table 3.5).

Cardiovascular Diseases

Cardiovascular diseases are an important cause of both death and disability for the oldest old. Deaths due to heart disease gradually increase with each age group and account for almost half of all deaths of those 85 and over. Stroke as a cause of death also increases with each age group; for those aged 85 and over, approximately 14% of deaths are due to stroke (Zopf, 1986:232). Similarly, for those with any functional limitations, one-third reported arteriosclerosis as one cause and one-fourth reported stroke as one cause (see Table 3.5); since as many as four chronic conditions could be reported, it is likely that some of the oldest old suffer from the combined disabling effects of arteriosclerosis and stroke.

Among the cardiovascular diseases, heart disease is the leading cause of death but not of disability for the oldest old; only 3.3% of those with any functional limitations reported heart disease as a cause (see

Table 3.5). In contrast, arteriosclerosis, or "hardening of the arteries," is less important than the flu as a cause of death for the oldest old, but it is a very important cause of disability; 33.7% of the oldest old with any functional limitations reported arteriosclerosis as a cause. Stroke, or cerebrovascular disease, is an important cause of both death and disability (see Zopf, 1986, and Table 3.5). Prolonging active life will require special attention to the disabling cardiovascular diseases of stroke and arteriosclerosis.

Arteriosclerosis is a chronic condition affecting the arteries such that blood cannot effectively circulate throughout the body. This condition is often referred to as "hardening of the arteries," but a common form of arteriosclerosis is atherosclerosis, which is a narrowing of the arteries, especially by cholesterol deposits. The primary disabling effect is the inability of the body to operate with a minimum necessary efficiency, thus making normal daily activities beyond the individual's capacity to perform. Symptoms may be shortness of breath, pain, swelling in the legs, or simply general lack of energy. For example, the person simply may not have the energy to go shopping. In severe cases, the person cannot get out of a bed or chair without help. In fact, of oldest old persons with severe (five or six) PADL limitations, more than half reported arteriosclerosis as a cause (Manton, 1986). Furthermore, nearly half of the nursing home population reported arteriosclerosis as a chronic condition (National Center for Health Statistics, 1979).

A stroke is a condition in which part of the brain has been damaged by bleeding or by a clot or other obstruction. Because the ordinary blood supply cannot reach part of the brain, some of the brain tissue is destroyed. The result is often a severe limitation of either physical or mental abilities or some combination of both. More than 40% of the oldest old with severe PADL limitations indicated stroke (cerebrovascular disease) as a cause (Manton, 1986). The risk of having a stroke doubles with each decade of life beginning at ages 45–55 (Kerson and Kerson, 1985:222). Although efforts to prevent strokes can be critical for future generations of oldest old, much can be done to improve the individual's functioning. Most people can be trained to overcome disabilities associated with a stroke if physical therapy, speech therapy, and other rehabilitative services are begun promptly. Rehabilitation, however, requires costly short-term commitments for in-patient and out-patient treatment. Stroke victims probably have one of the highest risks of institutionalization, so rehabilitation could be cost saving as well as successful in enhancing functioning.

An underlying factor in the increased risk of stroke and heart disease among the oldest old is high blood pressure, or hypertension. The oldest old are subject to a special form of hypertension—systolic hypertension.[7] This form of hypertension is found among 25% to 35% of those over 75 (Kannel, Dauber, and McGee, 1980). It is attributed, in part, to arteriosclerosis. Systolic hypertension is a specific risk factor in stroke.

Systolic hypertension is important, moreover, because it is less clearly understood than other forms of hypertension in terms of treatment with known antihypertensive drugs. Indeed, there is a current treatment dilemma for the oldest old in terms of drug therapy for hypertension. There are two reasons to evaluate their medication more carefully. First, these antihypertensive medications may have serious side effects of mood alteration and cognitive and motor impairment among the elderly (Straus, 1985:166). Second, it is important to understand that the effectiveness of antihypertensive medication has yet to be fully demonstrated for the type of hypertension most common among the elderly.[8] In addition, the widespread prevalence of mild hypertension among the elderly indicates a need for treatment through life-style and dietary changes rather than through drug therapy (Manton and Soldo, 1985).

Vision Problems

Problems with vision are reported almost as frequently as stroke as a cause of a functional limitation (Manton, 1988). Half of the oldest old report having trouble with their vision even with glasses. Twenty-one percent report "a lot of trouble," and 12% report blindness in one or both eyes.[9] These visual problems have their primary disabling effect in terms of mobility. In one study, 20% of elderly public housing residents reported that vision problems prevented them from going outside (Gillman, Simmel, and Simon, 1986). Furthermore, for 85-year-olds, disability due to vision problems is likely to be compounded by other, more prevalent diseases that restrict mobility, such as osteoarthritis.

---

[7]Systolic hypertension is defined as a systolic blood pressure (during heartbeat) greater than 160 mm Hg accompanied by a diastolic pressure (between heartbeats) less than 90 mm Hg. See Minaker and Rowe (1985:339–340).

[8]The National Institutes of Health are now engaged in extensive testing to determine the value of treatment for systolic hypertension (Minaker and Rowe, 1985; Rowe, 1983).

[9]Data are from the National Center for Health Statistics (1986). Exploratory studies of prevalence in the community conducted by Horowitz and Cassels (1985) found that extreme vision problems affect 30% of the oldest old. Estimates are that 49% of the nursing home population cannot see to read a newspaper (Kovar, as cited in Johnson and Grant, 1985).

Serious vision problems are due to disease and are not a normal effect of growing old. The three most common disease processes that can lead to partial or complete loss of sight are (1) macular degeneration— damage to the retina; (2) cataracts—a clouding of the lens; and (3) glaucoma—damage to the optic nerve. Blindness due to glaucoma can be prevented by early detection and treatment. Cataracts can be removed by surgery, even in the 85-and-over population. Rapid progress is also being made in laser treatment of macular degeneration. Macular degeneration affects an estimated 50% of those over age 70 (Sheehy, 1982); more than one-third of the oldest old report having cataracts (National Center for Health Statistics, 1986). Problems with vision represent a very fruitful area for reducing functional disability among the oldest old in the near future. The National Society to Prevent Blindness has estimated that 50% of all geriatric blindness is preventable (American Academy of Ophthalmology, 1984).

Prevention of visual disability, however, will require more than medical progress; outreach and education programs will be needed. All too often, vision loss for the elderly is fatalistically approached as inevitable with advancing age (Faye, 1984). Even some medical practitioners may too easily assume that nothing can be done and lose the opportunity for early intervention as well as the possibility of enhancing vision with special devices (low-vision aids) and rehabilitation. The limitations of current efforts are indicated by the high incidence of vision problems and the lack of preventive and rehabilitative services among low-income elders and minority elders.

The prevention and rehabilitation of vision problems could have a significant impact on the ability of the oldest old to function independently. Preventing vision problems is important not only in preserving mobility but also in preventing falls. The years after 85 do not need to be years of disability due to poor vision. Indeed, progress in this area would not only reduce disability but enhance the quality of life for the oldest old.

Cognitive Impairment

The previous discussions referred to clusters of disease processes and estimates of the likelihood of functional disability as a result of a specific disease. Cognitive impairment, however, is itself a measure of functional disability and not of any specific set of related disease processes. Cognitive impairment is the chronic loss of mental and intellectual function, often referred to as "dementia" or "senility of old age." Someone who has cognitive impairment therefore requires the assistance of another person. The presence of even mild cognitive impairment means that another person's help is required, if only in managing money. Among the oldest old, 34.6% reported "senility" as one cause of their functional limitation (Table 3.5).

Cognitive impairment is less prevalent than hypertension or osteoporosis, but the rates increase more rapidly with age. Only 3% of persons aged 65–74 report "senility" as a cause of their functional limitation. The risk of any degree of cognitive impairment probably triples between ages 65 and 85, and the risk of severe cognitive impairment is probably 15 times as likely in those over 85. Severe cognitive impairment, moreover, is the "most common precipitating cause of institutionalization" and "is found in over 50% of the nursing home population" (Rowe, 1985a:831). Community surveys of cognitive impairment vary greatly in their results, probably due in part to different levels of institutionalization. Surveys taken in New Haven and Baltimore found that about 35% of those 85 and over living in the community were cognitively impaired. More than 40% of those 85 and older with any cognitive impairment were severely cognitively impaired (George et al., 1988). This population reflects a widespread need for caregiver support.

Cognitive impairment is *not* the result of the normal aging process; it is due to a specific disease or disorder. The most prevalent cause of cognitive impairment is Alzheimer's disease, which probably accounts for at least 70% of those who have cognitive impairment (Rowe, 1985a; Gurland et al., 1983). This disease, for which there is no effective treatment, leads to a progressive loss of mental functioning. It is more likely to occur with advancing age; estimates suggest that 20% of those over 80 have Alzheimer's disease. It is the widespread prevalence of this disease at extreme ages that probably led to the popular use of the term "senility" to refer to age-related cognitive disorders.

While Alzheimer's disease is the major cause of cognitive impairment, there are many other possible causes. Because there is no conclusive diagnostic test, diagnosing Alzheimer's disease requires ruling out all other possible causes. The second most common cause of cognitive impairment is stroke, either a major stroke or a series of small strokes in the brain (multi-infarct dementia). As discussed earlier, stroke victims can be treated to prevent further strokes; there is also a wide range of possible rehabilitation techniques.

Accurate diagnosis of the cause of cognitive impairment is essential because in 15% of the patients, the cause is treatable. Careful attention to diagnosis and treatment can result in restoration of normal functioning. Among the causes of reversible cognitive impairment are drug intoxication, congestive heart failure, hypothyroidism, renal failure, depression, anemia, vitamin B_{12} deficiency, and azotemia (Rowe, 1985a).

In assessing cognitive impairment, it is important not to simply assume that it is inevitable or normal, since the loss of mental functioning can be the symptom of heart failure or kidney disease, which need immediate attention. The problem is compounded by the fact that the oldest old most often have multiple diseases and take multiple medications; they are at risk of becoming confused as the result of both their reduced kidney functioning and their medication.

The identification of mild cognitive impairment is also hampered by underreporting of symptoms by those elders who are anxious about it and therefore not likely to report it.[10] If it is determined that the cause is not reversible, a diagnosis is still necessary to alert the health practitioner to the possibilities of rehabilitation and the need for caregiver support. Special attention should also be given to the increased risk of falling among those with cognitive impairment.

Other Common Chronic Disorders of the Oldest Old

Depression and Mental Illness

While cognitive impairment is a mental symptom with a presumed physiological cause, a major, or clinical, depression is a serious mental illness. In some cases, however, an older person who is suffering a major depression may have symptoms similar to cognitive impairment. This is another reason why accurate diagnosis is so important for the oldest old when there is any noticeable change in mental functioning. There is too often an assumption that depression, like cognitive impairment, is simply a normal aspect of aging.

There is a pervasive belief that the elderly are beset with serious mental health problems in general and depression in particular. Yet recent epidemiological studies of persons living in the community, undertaken by the National Institute of Mental Health, show that those 65 and over are least likely to suffer from a major depression as compared with younger adult age groups. Major depression affected less than 1% of

---

[10]Special attention also needs to be given those with highly developed social skills who may be masking symptoms due to fear of being labeled senile or being institutionalized (Rowe, 1985a:831).

those over 65 living in the community. This rate is less than half of major depression rates (2 to 4%) among those 25 to 44 years old. Those 65 and over were also least likely to suffer from any other serious mental health problem, including alcoholism.[11] Furthermore, the likelihood of developing major depression and other serious mental health problems was no greater for those 85 and over than for those aged 65–74 (George et al., 1988).

Even for depressive symptoms, evidence now suggests that the elderly are no more at risk than are younger adults (Turner and Noh, 1988). It appears to be a myth that growing older entails a higher risk of depression. Nevertheless, depression is a problem among the elderly, as it is with younger adults. Appropriate services should be made available for those who need them. Gurland and co-workers (1983) have used the term "pervasive depression" to describe all types of depression that need specific therapeutic intervention. A community survey of the elderly in New York City indicated that 13% of those over 65 suffered from a form of depression that should be treated (Gurland et al., 1983:55).

Pervasive depression, however, often needs neither drugs nor long-term psychotherapy. The symptoms are frequently the result of problems in daily living that have become unmanageable. They may be related to situations that can be changed, such as inappropriate living arrangements with a hostile relative, or to situations such as widowhood, which require the development of new coping skills (see Chapter Four). Furthermore, symptoms of depression that appear without any clear cause in the person's life could be a side effect of a drug. The treatment would be a change of medication.

Mental health problems of oldest old women may be very different from those of their male counterparts. An indicator of this difference is the high suicide rate for men—60 suicides per year for every 100,000 men aged 85 and over. For white men, the suicide rate more than doubles when the group aged 40–44 is compared with those aged 75–79 (Atchley, 1980; Goleman, 1985). In direct contrast, the suicide rate for women decreases by more than half when those aged 40–44 are compared with those aged 85 and over; there are only five suicides per year for every 100,000 women aged 85 and over.[12] Similarly, in the New York City

---

[11]Alcohol abuse among those over 65 was similarly low, 1.6% or less, and was at least twice as likely to occur among those aged 45–64 as among those 65 and over. In all four cities, alcohol abuse was negatively correlated with age (George et al., 1988).

[12]Cultural and ethnic factors clearly influence suicide rates. Among those 85 and over, black men have much lower rates (16 per 100,000) than white men, and rates for black women are less than one per 100,000 (Manton, Blazer, and Woodbury, 1987:222). Suicide rates for older women are higher in Germany; see Atchley (1980).

study, pervasive depression among men 80 years of age and over was four times as prevalent as for those aged 65 (Gurland et al., 1983). For elderly women, however, there was little change. These high rates of suicide and depression among extremely aged men indicate a special need to develop appropriate intervention techniques. Timing may be critical, since widowerhood is likely to be a key factor for these men.

Drug Intoxication

Unfortunately, one result of the popular belief that serious depression is common among the elderly is the widespread use of antidepressive drugs to treat symptoms of depression. In fact, antidepressive drugs can themselves produce the symptoms they are prescribed to alleviate, as illustrated in the following scenario: a person develops symptoms of depression or a reactive depression following the death of a friend; these symptoms are treated as if they represented a major depression. Antidepressant drugs are administered. The patient then develops confusion, lethargy, drowsiness, and difficulty in concentrating. This serious deterioration of mental status is a side effect of the prescribed medication.[13] These side-effect risks, combined with the very low prevalence of major depression, indicate the need for caution in prescribing antidepressive drugs. Where the depression is serious enough to warrant treatment, alternative forms of therapy should be explored. In 1973, antidepressants and tranquilizers ranked 11th and 12th, respectively, in causing adverse drug reactions in the elderly (Moore and Jones, 1985:74–76). More than one-third of all hospitalizations for drug reactions in 1986 were among those 60 years of age and older (The New York Times, March 27, 1988).

Drug intoxication in general is of critical importance because its complexity and impact are widespread among the oldest old; persons over 80 years old have a one-in-four risk of experiencing drug intoxication (Minaker and Rowe, 1985:341). The very old are at greater risk of suffering drug intoxication because of increased sensitivity to drugs as well as changes in levels of absorption, metabolism, and excretion (Hussar, 1985:138). They are also at greater risk because they are more

---

[13]Furthermore, "it is not uncommon for the situation to become even worse when a physician sees agitation, confusion, or depression in a patient for whom he or she has prescribed a psychotropic medication, fails to realize that the symptom is a drug side effect, and prescribes more of the offending agent or yet another potentially discomforting medication." See Fann and Richman (1985:318).

likely to be taking more than one drug and are, therefore, susceptible to drug-drug interactions. For example, an elderly hypertensive woman being treated with antihypertensive drugs may become fatigued and display mood alteration and depression (Straus, 1985:166). If her depression is treated with an antidepressant, she is at risk of experiencing a drug-drug interaction.

Not only is there a greater likelihood among the oldest old of two or more prescription drugs being taken concurrently, it is also likely that taking prescription drugs for both depression and hypertension creates a catch-22 pharmacological problem: the antihypertensive drug may exacerbate the depression, and the antidepressant drug may exacerbate the hypertension. Careful monitoring is therefore necessary, and any changes in mood, cognitive ability, fatigability, balance, and motor capacity should be carefully investigated. Without thorough assessment and close medical supervision, the health problems of the oldest old can be exacerbated by overdiagnosis and unnecessary or dangerous drug treatments.

Falls

The disease processes discussed above are the chronic health problems most likely to produce functional disability in the oldest old. More than one-fourth of those 85 and over are probably seriously affected in their daily functioning by eye diseases, bone and joint diseases and fractures, cardiovascular diseases, and diseases causing cognitive impairment. These health and disability problems are further compounded by the fact that they are likely to suffer from two or more of these highly prevalent disease processes as well as one of a number of less prevalent age-related diseases, such as kidney disease and Parkinson's disease. Some or all of their health problems require medication, which can result in additional problems due to drug intoxication. The cumulative effect of these highly prevalent diseases and drugs on physical mobility and cognitive functioning pose a special risk of falling for all elderly persons (Gibson et al., 1987) and especially for the oldest old.

Falls are a serious risk among the oldest old because balance problems are more common and the consequences of falling are more severe. Problems with balance are a critical factor in the increased risk of falls. Some balance problems may occur without any chronic disease. A low gait speed and a high degree of sway are indicators of risk. Balance problems are also created by mobility problems, due most likely to the prevalent chronic diseases discussed above, notably osteoarthritis, stroke, and circulatory disease. Poor vision and cognitive impairment also contribute to the risk of falling by impairing perception and judgment. Drug intoxication can also lead to increased risk of falling due to its effects on mobility, vision, balance, and judgment.

Falls, even without serious physical injury, are related to high mortality rates if the person had to lie on the ground for more than one hour. British studies indicate that half of those who experienced a "long lie" of more than one hour without physical injury were dead within six months (Wild, Nayak, and Isaacs, 1981). A long lie is especially dangerous among the very old, who have trouble regulating body temperature (Sheehy, 1982:32) and are at risk of developing hypothermia, a dangerous lowering of the body's temperature.

Serious disability due to falls is usually the result of fractures, which can occur even in minor falls. A British study found that in women over 75, 40% of falls resulted in a fracture. By the age of 90, one out of every four white women is likely to have experienced a fracture (Exton-Smith, 1977:49). The most common type of fracture is the hip fracture, which occurs at an estimated rate of 3.3% per year among white women aged 85 and over (Melton and Riggs, 1983:54). Falls appear to be most prevalent between the ages of 75 and 88 (Vellas, cited in Gibson et al., 1987); prevention of falls would no doubt extend the years of active life for the oldest old.

Osteoporosis, as explained above, makes the bones more brittle and susceptible to breaking; it also makes the healing process a lengthy one. In fact, it is estimated that at least 25% of hip fractures do not heal and that for another 25%, healing is inadequate (Sheehy, 1982:32). These healing problems, as well as the risks entailed by a long period of relative immobility, result in failure to walk again in at least half the cases. Those who do manage to walk again, however, are at a higher risk of subsequent falls.

For all elderly persons, prevention of falls requires specific attention to the physical environment. In addition, the following risk factors must be given special consideration: impaired mobility; low gait speed and high degree of sway; cognitive impairment; dizziness; poor vision; and multiple medications. Preventive measures can include an investigation of balance impairment as well as an evaluation of possible side effects of any medications being taken. For those whose problems involve primarily gait disorders and a high degree of sway, much is now being accomplished in balance assessment programs (Andres, 1987). After a fall, specific rehabilitative measures can prevent subsequent falls (Gibson et al., 1987). In additon, risk factors for osteoporosis need to be carefully assessed, since the presence of this disease can severely limit recovery from a fracture.

Urinary Incontinence

Urinary incontinence, like falling, has increasingly serious consequences as an individual approaches extreme old age. Also, urinary incontinence increases the risk of institutionalization. Put simply, urinary incontinence may be defined as the inability to voluntarily control urination. The condition may be mild and confined to wetting the bed at night, or it may be a 24-hour-a-day problem requiring a substantial modification of life-style and/or help from a caregiver. Inability to control urination is socially unacceptable and often leads to embarrassment for the elder and stress for the caregiver. Incontinence is also likely to be underreported because of the patients' embarrassment.

Recent research in the area of urinary incontinence holds the promise of effective treatment for a substantial percentage of cases of chronic incontinence, which may be controlled by medication and/or exercises. Especially in women, stress incontinence, which is caused by weakness of the bladder outlet, can often be reduced by pelvic floor exercises together with medical management (Rowe, 1985a:833). In fact, pelvic floor exercises may be an effective preventive technique. Any changes for the worse should prompt an immediate visit to the doctor, since some forms of incontinence are the result of an acute infection or of medication the individual may be taking to manage another chronic condition (Rowe, 1985a:832).

Incontinence is common among all persons aged 65 and over; approximately one-fourth of persons over 65, irrespective of age, report problems with incontinence (Macken, 1985:Table 4). Nevertheless, serious problems with the bowel and bladder occur in less than 3% of those 65–75 years of age. This increases to nearly 10% for those 85 and over living in the community (Feller, 1986:Table 31). It is the 85-year-old who is most likely to need the help of another person in managing bowel or bladder problems.

Chronic Diseases That Are Less Disabling for the Oldest Old

In a number of chronic diseases in which the risk increases with age, the disease is either less prevalent or less virulent among the oldest old.

Practitioners working with the elderly will certainly be familiar with the disabling effects of cancer, diabetes, and emphysema, yet these are not likely to be the problems for the oldest old. For cancer, often viewed as the typical disease of aging, death rates fall significantly between the ages of 65 and 85; this pattern was the same in 1968 and in 1980. Furthermore, cancer is not an important cause of long-term functional limitation, even among the young old. This is no doubt due to the fact that once cancer becomes disabling, death is usually not far off. Less than 2% of those 85 and over who report functional limitations in any activities of daily living indicate cancer as a cause (Table 3.5).

Similarly, death and disability from diabetes are higher among the young old than among the oldest old. Less than 4% of the oldest old with any functional limitation report diabetes as a cause. Emphysema and bronchitis are also more common causes of limitation among the young old than among the oldest old. Less than 2% of oldest old with any functional limitation indicated emphysema or bronchitis as a cause (Table 3.5). It is probably also true that few persons with emphysema or diabetes survive to be 85 and over.

Disability and the Future

The immediate future promises increased longevity for those 85 and over but no significant decrease in functional disability (Manton, 1986). Longer lives for the very old are likely to mean increased risk of dependence. This risk of functional disability and of need for help is of vital concern to the very old and their caregivers, health practitioners, and policymakers. Nevertheless, a number of steps can be taken to reduce the risk of disability among this subpopulation.

With the knowledge currently available, it is possible to reduce or eliminate the effects of drug intoxication. Careful attention to drug reactions could prevent or even reverse some cognitive impairment, depression, hypertension, and urinary incontinence. Immediate attention to the prevention of falls will also prevent problems in the near future. It is now possible to treat and therefore prevent some disabilities due to vision problems and urinary incontinence. Imminent research results may provide better answers for treatment of systolic hypertension and reduce the risk of disability due to stroke.

Overall, more attention needs to be paid to rehabilitation, which can reverse much functional disability. Rehabilitation techniques have been highly developed in the areas of vision problems and strokes (including multi-infarct dementia). The techniques are available, but all too often the oldest old are not reached. Problems remain undetected or underreported because they are viewed as part of normal aging, or the oldest old may be limited in taking advantage of these techniques because of cost cutting by hospitals and lack of access to outpatient rehabilitation. Thus, opportunities for reducing functional disability are lost.

Because functional disability among the oldest old is most often due to a combination of diseases and disorders, more research is needed to assess combinations of risk factors as well as the effects of life-style factors. So far, only three life-style factors have been directly implicated by research on disability among the elderly. These are smoking, a slowdown of activity, and excessive body weight.

Branch (1985) examined health practices among the elderly in a community population and found that smoking in men and a slowing down of physical activity in women doubled their risk of developing a disability within the next five years. Specific attention should be given to the slowing down of activity among men as well, since it was a significant predictor of death and disability. Indeed, any change in life-style or in cognitive behavior or motor ability in the oldest old should be carefully investigated because it may be the first symptom of a treatable medical problem or drug intoxication. As indicated earlier, in the oldest old, changes in functional ability may be the only noticeable symptoms of a disease process.

In a national study of physical ability among those aged 80 and over, Harris and co-workers found that those who weighed the most were less likely to be able to walk a distance, negotiate stairs, lift, stoop, and kneel. As expected, this study found that those with cardiovascular disease, arthritis, and vision problems were less likely to report being physically able. Unfortunately, a key variable related to physical ability was gender. Men were "at least twice as likely to meet the definition of physical ability" as women (Harris et al., 1987:385). Problems with hearing were not related to physical ability, although deafness was reported as a cause of a functional limitation in the activities of daily living for 13.4% of oldest old men and 9.5% of oldest old women (Manton, 1988).[14]

---

[14]Loss of hearing is a problem for many of the oldest old. Nearly half (48.4%) report some hearing impairment, and almost one-fifth (19.1%) report "a lot of trouble." More men than women have problems with hearing (National Center for Health Statistics, 1986).

A key question for the more distant future is the inevitability of functional disability among the oldest old. What are the possibilities of preserving active life until death? These questions are the long-range concern of everyone, but especially of policymakers, who are looking at the year 2040, when there will be approximately 13 million persons aged 85 and over; the projected life expectancy of women would be 83 years of age. What can be done now so that today's 30-year-olds will be functionally able in the year 2040?

It is remarkable that in every broad area of disease and disorder discussed above, there has been rapid progress in understanding the possibilities of prevention. Indeed, prevention over the long run promises to reduce the level of functional disability among the oldest old. Regular medical attention and life-style changes promise a fuller active life for this group.

Although life-style and behavioral changes are often difficult to implement, optimism is arising due to the success of campaigns to reduce smoking. Clearly, old habits *can* change. Changes in the traditional American diet, in exercise, and in smoking habits are viewed as important factors in the reduction of cardiovascular diseases and especially in the reduction of hypertension, circulatory problems, and stroke. Osteoporosis is now believed to be preventable with exercise and adequate dietary calcium and vitamin D, plus appropriate hormonal treatment when prescribed. New tests may indicate those at highest risk so that medical intervention can begin before bone loss occurs. This should reduce the incidence of hip and other fractures as well as some of the general "aches and pains" of the oldest old. Rapid progress in the treatment of problems of the retinal arteries and early detection and treatment of glaucoma and cataracts should reduce extreme vision problems among the oldest old.

In terms of the disease processes that are the most likely causes of disability in the oldest old, only two have thus far proved intractable. These are osteoarthritis and Alzheimer's disease. The absence of effective preventive measures and treatment methods for these two problems appear to present the biggest stumbling block for decreasing disability among those 85 and over. These diseases of the oldest old require extensive research if there is to be hope of controlling their disabling effects by the year 2040. Further research is also needed in the treatment of systolic hypertension, urinary incontinence, and the prevention of arteriosclerosis, especially in vulnerable areas such as the eye and the brain.

Aging in the Absence of Disease

It is important to develop a better understanding of the aging process among those who are free of diseases and disorders. An examination of research on normal aging presents serious problems, however, in terms of locating an adequate sample of those 85 and over without any evidence of a disease process. Particularly critical is finding persons 85 and over who are free of any cardiovascular disease. Even among the relatively low-disability group whose average age is 86, Manton and Soldo (1985) found that 27% had hypertension and 42% had "hardening of arteries." Recent research (Rowe and Kahn, 1987) suggests that it is important to go one step further and distinguish between individuals who are aging successfully and those who are merely free of disease at the time of the study.

In spite of the problems of researching normal aging as separate from any disease process, Dr. E. L. Schneider, deputy director of the National Institute on Aging (1983, 1985) has put forth an optimistic view of the future of aging in the absence of disease. Normal aging does not result in functional disability. Dependence, the need for excessive help from another person, is caused by a disease or a disorder, not aging. The normal aging process only requires that the individual adapt to diminished short-term memory, decreased ability of the lens of the eye to adjust itself, reduced skin elasticity, and diminished aerobic capacity. These changes require minor accommodations: the need to wear glasses, especially for close work; the need to make lists or talk to oneself; the desire to avoid photographs or mirrors; and the inability to run back and get whatever it was you forgot.

The most serious problem is probably the fear created by the loss of short-term memory, the fear that memory loss will progress until senility. But senility is a disease process, not a normal result of aging. The oldest old need to be reassured that forgetting what their daughter told them to do in her recent phone call is normal and can easily be compensated for. Only if they have no memory of her calling at all is it a sign of serious and possible progressive memory loss.

The most important physical loss is the loss of more than 50% of lung capacity between the ages of 30 and 90 (Rowe, 1985b:251). This becomes an important medical problem in terms of the serious risk of death from respiratory diseases. The risk of death from pneumonia and influenza is highest among those 85 and over. Other changes that may be usual, such as a decrease in the functioning of the immune system and a tendency to lose balance or to faint, are not in themselves disabling

(Besdine, 1987). They indicate only a need for more careful attention to preventing falls, colds, and flu.

This perspective of the normal aging process as one that is free from chronic disease and functional disability needs to be kept clearly in mind, especially for practitioners working with the functionally disabled who have multiple diseases. It should be assumed that any behavioral or cognitive change is not the result of normal aging but the result of a disease or disorder that needs medical attention. Additionally, practitioners working with the oldest old who need help may find that their task is a difficult one because it raises some very real questions concerning their own aging process. If health practitioners view disability and disease as inevitable with advancing age, they will begin to fear their own aging. It is important to remember that disability is the result of a disease process. Much research indicates that the future could be one of a long and healthy life free of functional disability for the oldest old.

Even when the oldest old person does need help in the activities of daily living, limited physiological resources can be compensated for by abundant economic, social-familial, and personal resources. These other resources can enable the person to sustain an independent or interdependent life-style. Limited physiological resources need not result in dependence. Preventing dependence among those oldest old who need help, however, requires effective development of these other resources. The following chapter examines the role of personal and social-familial resources in developing reciprocity and interdependence and preserving self-determination.

Chapter Four

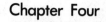

Personal Coping Resources and Social-Familial Resources

Introduction

Although physiological resources are always seen as the key to preventing dependence, personal resources and social-familial resources are more often thought of as the keys to successful aging. With effective personal resources and good family support, the oldest old can preserve a high quality of life in spite of needing a lot of help. Even an elder who is dependent can enjoy life as does Mrs. Adams:

> Mrs. Adams, at 89, lives with her daughter in her daughter's house. She is quite frail and has mild cognitive impairment. She needs help in meal preparation, housework, shopping, and bathing. Her daughter spends considerable time and effort helping her mother with these daily tasks in addition to her own work in the business she and her husband run. Yet Mrs. Adam's dependence is not a problem for her or for her daughter. Mrs. Adams is vivacious, friendly, and humorous. She was a very pretty woman and still takes a great deal of pride in her appearance. She has had her color chart done and her colors are "summer," so every day Mrs. Adams dresses in beautiful pastels. Her daughter is happy to give her aid and assistance and even pays special attention not only to the food but to the table setting and

other aspects of the atmosphere. Her mother has "such a lovely way about accepting help." The daughter is proud of her mother's whole demeanor but especially of her ability to celebrate life. Mrs. Adams's ability to accept aging and its limitations helps her daughter and her daughter's friends—who admire Mrs. Adams—to see that the process can be one of grace and dignity even with limited economic and physiological resources.

Mrs. Adams's daughter is a marvelous family resource, but Mrs. Adams also has considerable personal coping skills that allow her to accept her dependence and enjoy life. These resources make it unlikely that she will need to be institutionalized. "Supercopers" like Mrs. Adams are often indicated as examples of how to age successfully and how families can maintain a high quality of life for all members in spite of the dependent status of the elder. There has been, however, limited research on how personal coping resources or social-familial resources can prevent or limit dependence. In the area of family resources, the presence of a spouse or a large number of children does prevent or postpone in-stitutionalization. But we need a better understanding of how these social-familial resources might be used to avoid or limit dependence in the community. Can personal coping resources mitigate some of the effects of limited physiological resources and help sustain an in-terdependent life-style? Even for those with no functional disabilities, high levels of personal coping resources and social-familial resources may serve as "money saved for a rainy day." These resources could allow the oldest old to weather future health problems without becoming de-pendent. Much more research needs to be done on the role of these resources in preventing dependence. This chapter reviews the current research and suggests ways in which these resources may be utilized effectively by the oldest old.

Personal Coping Resources

For this book, we have chosen to focus on coping resources as the key psychological variable. Although the concept of coping resources has yet to be fully defined in the psychological literature, this focus seems particularly appropriate for the oldest old, who are likely to have a lot to cope with—declining health, death of friends and relatives, a necessary move to more suitable housing. Other psychological factors, such as self-esteem and mental health, are related to effective coping strategies (Lohr and Essex, 1986). Clearly, individuals with effective coping resources are likely to have higher self-esteem and better mental health than those with limited coping resources. However, it is not necessarily true that persons with high self-esteem and good mental health have effective coping resources when faced with the death of a spouse or deteriorating health. For some, such events could cause depression or a lowered sense of self-esteem. Thus, for the oldest old, effective coping resources may be necessary to preserve self-esteem and good mental health in the face of such problems. Furthermore, coping resources are likely to enable the person to sustain an interdependent life-style in spite of deteriorating health or the death of a close relative. Without effective coping resources, an older person could easily be overwhelmed by such events and end up dependent in a child's home or an institution.

The circumstances of the oldest old, furthermore, may call for the development of new personal coping skills. Someone who has not made a new friend in 40 years may need to develop new friendships with neighbors who could help out. Long-time friends or siblings of the same age simply may not be available to provide the kind of help required. The 90-year-old widow, even if she still has a best friend or sibling, is not likely to be able to depend on this relationship for help with a ride. This means that other than adult children, the oldest old will likely have to rely on younger and more recent friends and on neighbors for help. An elder who had been coping extremely well in the context of a strictly independent life-style may find that he lacks the interpersonal skills necessary to develop an interdependent life-style. In this situation his need for help may threaten his self-esteem and make him depressed. His inability to cope would increase his dependency risk; an exasperated child may prematurely insist that he come live with her, thereby making him dependent.

Consideration of the need to change coping strategies is important in planning programs to help the oldest old adapt to physical limitations and disabilities. Studies of coping among young and middle-aged adults show, for example, that a sense of being in control or of self-mastery is an important personal coping resource (Johnson and Sarason, 1978; Pearlin and Schooler, 1978). Research on the elderly, however, suggests that when faced with the stress of the loss of a friend or family member or another such life event, those with a strong belief in their ability to control their lives may simply become frustrated and cope less well than those with a less strong belief in their ability to be completely in control of their lives (Simons and West, 1984–1985). Preliminary results from the Yale Project on Stress and Coping in the Elderly suggest that type A personalities do not cope well with many of the chronic stresses of the very old. If they cannot change a situation, they are likely to "give up" (Powell, Roth, and Gelburg, 1987).

The research of Essex and Lohr (1986) supports the conclusion that for those mid-life (age 50) and older women faced with health problems, a positive "optimistic attitude" coping strategy is the most effective coping resource in reducing the possibility of depression. Such positive coping means reminding oneself that "your health is much better than the health of many women your age" and that there are "good things about your health that you have to be thankful for" (Essex and Lohr, 1986). This cognitive coping strategy was found to be more effective than a take-charge approach emphasizing action to improve health or prevent further health problems. For the old old (those 75 and over), a direct-action coping style was *not* related to life satisfaction, while positive cognitive coping was (Lohr and Essex, 1986). An optimistic-attitude coping strategy, moreover, was particularly effective in helping those with chronic physical pain and discomfort to keep their level of depression low. Since the oldest old are likely to face much physical discomfort, such a positive attitude may be an especially important coping resource. It can also be an important coping resource in dealing with the death of a close relative:

> Mrs. Brown has extraordinary personal resources in utilizing a positive cognitive coping strategy. At 90, she is frail, has some pain and poor eyesight, moves slowly, uses a cane, and needs help with household chores. Clearly, her physiological resources suggest that she is at risk of becoming dependent. Indeed, when her sister died a year ago, everyone in the family expected her to become dependent. After all, she had lived with her sister and shared all the household tasks with her for ten years. But the loss of her sister did not render Mrs. Brown dependent, nor did it make her depressed. Instead of despairing, she preferred to remember all the good times in her sister's long life of 93 years. Not only did her celebration-of-life attitude prevail but she forcefully convinced her concerned relatives that she was not going to become dependent. Indeed, she had built up an interdependent life-style not only with her sister but with others as well. She has two close friends and two nieces with whom she has built up helping networks. Although she receives more help than she gives, a balance is achieved by her hospitality. Entirely on her own, she provides heavenly meals and amusing company. Guests are not allowed to do anything. Even though she is concerned about "not getting around as good as she used to," her supercoping capacity and interpersonal skills will protect her from becoming dependent. If her health becomes worse, she does have moderate economic resources with which to continue to repay any help needed, even if the food is carry-out and the cleaning up is done by paid help. Although she is childless, she is not likely to end up in a nursing home. Her personal

resources, together with her economic and social-familial resources, will probably enable her to sustain an interdependent life-style until her death. As for her funeral, she wants it to be a celebration of her long life and not a sad occasion.[1]

Mrs. Brown's positive cognitive coping strategy allowed her to remain in charge of her life without requiring that she be able to control all the life events. For the oldest old, a sense of self-determination may come from adherence to the old prayer: "God grant me the ability to change the things I can change, the grace to accept the things I cannot change, and the wisdom to know the difference." Although there is evidence that coping patterns formed earlier in adult life continue into old age (McCrae, 1982), it may be more appropriate to change coping strategies. For the oldest old, there are many things that cannot be changed. The most effective coping strategy for dealing with poverty and unemployment during one's fifties would be to change things. But chronic poverty during one's eighties is beyond one's ability to change. Direct action and a take-charge approach may simply frustrate the person when there can be no concrete results. Although strategies like "complaining" and "sticking to oneself" may be effective coping strategies in adjusting to life in a nursing home (Kahana, Kahana, and Young, 1986), these methods may be very ineffective in sustaining helping networks in the community.

Coping strategies have been studied with respect to their impact on life satisfaction or depression, but for the oldest old it is important to examine these strategies in terms of dependency risk. A positive cognitive coping strategy, together with interpersonal skills, may be effective in building an interdependent life-style. Friends and neighbors will be more willing to help when delivering a meal does not result in having to listen to all of the day's aches and pains. Outside of the nursing home, "sticking to oneself" works only as long as one can do everything oneself. With deteriorating health, this coping strategy can rapidly break down. Also, this strategy does not develop or preserve interpersonal skills. Mrs. Carter illustrates the high dependency risk of this coping strategy:

> Mrs. Carter, age 90, lives in a nursing home although she has no serious health problems. She has given up both physically and mentally and usually sits all day in a wheelchair, not even bothering to watch TV. "I can't walk, but I don't hurt," she says as she proceeds to get up and walk to the bathroom.

---

[1]Mrs. Brown was interviewed by a student supervised by Sally Bould.

Mrs. Carter had lived an autonomous, independent life managing her deceased husband's business. With increasing age and the death of her siblings, she moved into a retirement apartment complex where special efforts were made to provide help with transportation and maintenance. Furthermore, this complex provided friendly neighbors and many activities. But she did not get involved, preferring to stick to herself. She was suspicious of these neighbors and acquaintances and feared that they did not like her. She herself was not a welcoming person, and in response to a knock on her door she would yell, "Who is it?" in an ominous tone of voice.

The crisis came when at age 82 she fell while standing on a chair attempting to change a light bulb; for such a task she could have easily sought help from a more robust neighbor or the maintenance man. Yet she never developed the ability to ask for help or to provide help in return. She broke her hip and was hospitalized. With rehabilitation, she would have been able to return to her apartment with home help. Her children were more than willing to help and to pay for any extra help needed, and as before, the apartment complex provided opportunities to give and receive help from neighbors. The problem was that her coping skills were limited to those appropriate for an autonomous, independent life-style. She would not have been able to accept such help; she could not allow a "stranger" in her apartment. Furthermore, a paid helper would never have done things "right" and probably would have been fired within days or even hours.

Therefore, an interdependent life-style was not possible for Mrs. Carter, not because she lacked economic or physiological resources or even potential social-familial resources but because she lacked the necessary personal resources. Her two children, although willing to help, were unwilling to subject their families to the stress of housing this unfriendly and often hostile parent. The nursing home and total dependence was the only option.[2]

Interpersonal Skills

Although it is obvious that Mrs. Brown has an optimistic coping attitude and Mrs. Carter has a pessimistic attitude, it is also clear that Mrs. Brown has a wide range of interpersonal skills and Mrs. Carter's are very limited. Good interpersonal skills are probably most critical for the oldest old because of their high risk of needing others' help. The ability to maintain

---

[2]Mrs. Carter was interviewed by a student supervised by Sally Bould.

a social support network of family, friends, and neighbors can be essential in preserving self-determination and avoiding dependence among the oldest old.

The oldest old, moreover, need not only the skills of maintaining social support networks but also the skills of developing new friendships, since death and disability are likely to have depleted relationships of long standing. Similarly, a move to more suitable housing may require establishing support networks with new neighbors. Interpersonal skills in developing support networks can preserve self-determination by assuring that help will be available in times of need. These skills, furthermore, prevent dependence by allowing the oldest old to remain in charge of their own households. Yet an individual like Mrs. Carter, who has lived an independent, autonomous life, may never have developed these interpersonal skills. Even with sufficient economic resources to pay for help, such individuals may alienate paid helpers as well, since using paid help requires a minimum of interpersonal skills.

It is also true that certain personality types may not be able to negotiate the delicate give-and-take required for interpersonal reciprocity. For example, a dominant and demanding personality may quickly overload and alienate a potential social support network. Even when a community provides a built-in social support network, as in rural Appalachia, that network can quickly break down under the pressure of excessive demands. Lozier and Althouse describe Mr. Meadows's failure to sustain community social support, as well as family social support, because of his lack of interpersonal skills:

> Wallace Meadows had an active and creditable career, but he never achieved a command of the porch in his old age. His own two sons migrated, and rejected his assistance to bring them home and fix them in jobs, because his demands on them were overly taxing. As a daughter-in-law said of a period when she and her husband lived across the road from Wallace, "there was no front door on our house," claiming the presumed privilege of the patriarch to demand service on his own terms and his own schedule, Wallace placed a burden on his family that was generally considered to be excessive.
>
> Like numerous other old people whose children are not residing in Laurel Creek, Wallace attempted to use the porch as a place from which to present his claims and to participate in the community beyond his direct kin. Such a strategy is by no means doomed to failure. However, Wallace expected too much of others, and his claims seemed more to be demands than requests. If he would ask for a ride in to the main forks, he might want to stop repeatedly, or to take the driver out of his way, making the act of

service relatively costly; and in exchange he could give little. With such a pattern of behavior emerging, passers-by increasingly gave evasive indications of their plans, and discouraged him from coming along. . . .

. . . In the future, failing health and decreased mobility might provide him with a justification for retiring to the porch, but to the extent that he continues to behave as a "contentious old son of a bitch," his ultimate retirement to the porch is likely to be socially supported at a much lower level than he would want. Stated otherwise, he is using up his "social credit," and will find himself in a relatively insecure position later on. (1975:12–13)

Here the practitioner may assist the elder in developing the interpersonal skills necessary to sustain helping networks. Furthermore, such interpersonal skills are necessary even when the elder can pay cash for the help needed. If Mr. Wallace had had the money to hire paid helpers, these helpers too might refuse to work for such an "impossible" person.

Social-Familial Resources

For all adult age groups, family and friends are important resources; they provide a network of social support. A social support network can also include acquaintances, neighbors, co-workers, and former co-workers. Robert Kahn (1979:85) has identified three distinct kinds of social support that these networks provide. First, they provide love, admiration, liking, and respect—a sense that someone likes us for what we are. Second, they provide affirmation of our perceptions or positions—people who share our view of the world and with whom we can feel comfortable discussing issues like politics or religion. The third kind of social support is direct aid or physical help given by network members. Although all three kinds of support are important for the oldest old, direct aid or concrete help may be essential in maintaining their own households. In cases of severe functional disability, the help provided by the person's social support network can prevent institutionalization.

Social support networks should be distinguished from *formal support services* because the former are informal in nature. For example, a friend providing help with taxes would constitute social support in the form of direct aid. Someone who uses a volunteer at the local senior center for help with taxes is making use of a system of formal aid, and this aid would not be considered social support. Similarly, assistance provided or funded by the government would be considered formal but not social support (see Chapter Seven).

The critical problem faced by the oldest old is the high likelihood of shrinkage of the size of the social support network. This problem is especially acute among age peers, both friends and family. The shrinkage is partly due to role loss, such as the loss of co-workers or fellow volunteers when the individual retires from work or volunteer activity. Shrinkage is also likely due to role loss because of death. Especially at risk of loss are the spouse role, sibling role, and role of best friend of similar age. For the woman at age 85, more than one-half of her age-mates (other women) who were alive 20 years ago are now dead; for the man at age 85, more than three-fourths of his age-mates (other men) who were alive 20 years ago are now dead (Rosenwaike, 1985b:145). This may be one reason for a decline in activities with friends for oldest old men (Field and Minkler, 1987). One's level of daily interaction may also be reduced because of role loss—for example, loss of spouse. Both daily interaction and roles can be affected by physical disability. Cumming and Henry (1961) originally examined role loss and daily interaction among the elderly by age. For the old old, defined as 75 and over, 15% had high levels of daily interaction and 8% had a large number of roles. These figures contrast markedly with those for people aged 70–74, among whom 34% had high levels of daily interaction and 22% had a large number of roles. More recent research found that among a large sample of urban widows, the old old had fewer friendship and family roles than did the young old (65–74) (Heinemann, 1985). This decline in contacts with family and friends, however, appears to be concentrated among the oldest old rather than persons aged 75–84 (Field and Minkler, 1987).

The loss of the total number of roles is, no doubt, an issue for the oldest old. Losses in family roles especially are not amenable to replacement. Even the oldest old widower is not likely to be able to find another wife. Cumming and Henry (1961) saw this process of role loss as a normal aspect of aging, but their approach has been heavily criticized by those who emphasize "activity" and urge role replacement for successful aging. This emphasis on activity and role replacement or substitution does make sense for the young old; it is probably less suitable, however, for the oldest old. In her study of urban widows, Heinemann (1985) found that for the young old, the larger number of family roles and friendship roles was correlated with greater life satisfaction. But for the old old, controlling for age and physical health problems, a larger number of roles was *not* related to greater life satisfaction. Similarly, over time the oldest old may see their grandchildren less but be just as satisfied as before (Field and Minkler, 1987).

Most researchers who have investigated social support networks have mainly counted roles, counted helpers, or counted friendship and family ties. Nevertheless, recent research suggests that it is not so much the number of links in the network as their quality or other characteristics that are important (Preston and Mansfield, 1984). In fact, the study of old old urban widows discussed above found lower life satisfaction to be related to a greater number of family ties. In a study of 1,332 men aged 60 and over, there was no relationship between the size of the friendship network or the child network on life satisfaction among men who were similar in terms of age and health (Mouser et al., 1985). More ties or roles do not, by themselves, contribute to a greater satisfaction with life. In fact, those with limited physiological resources are more likely to have more ties and greater daily interaction simply because they need the help (Stoller and Earl, 1983:68).

Quality may be as important as, or perhaps more important than, quantity, especially in providing admiration, love, and affirmation. Having a confidant may be more important than having a large family network. Research shows that people who have a confidant are much more likely to report that they are satisfied with their lives (Snow and Crapo, 1982; Liang, 1982; Conner, Powers, and Bultena, 1979; Larson, 1978). Furthermore, having a confidant may help the aged person to better survive other losses (Chown, 1981). The role of confidant is less affected by health limitations than are other roles, such as those of organization member or volunteer worker. Since confidants are often age-mates, however, the oldest old are at high risk of losing their confidants through death or disability.

Women are more likely to have confidants than are men (Dickens and Perlman, 1981), and confidants serve a strong positive function in women's lives. For men, however, the role of confidant appears to be less important (Keith et al., 1984). While the presence of a confidant adds significantly to life satisfaction for both men and women (Mouser et al., 1985), for men, being married is as important as having a confidant (Keith et al., 1984). Men who are married are most likely to name their wife as confidant. For the oldest old, however, the role of confidant is more likely to be filled by a best friend, since both men and women are unlikely to be living with a spouse at this age. For the oldest old living alone, a confidant may be critical to the development of effective coping strategies. For those living with other relatives, easy access to a confidant may ease any loss of self-esteem due to a dependent living arrangement. Even for those oldest old who are institutionalized, a confidant relationship could contribute significantly to the quality of life. Unlike other roles, this role is less limited by a person's physical disabilities. Furthermore, the nature of the role—involving the giving and receiving of love and affirmation—is one in which even those with severe physical disabilities can still fully engage:

> Mrs. White was 78 when she became friends with Mrs. Smith. When Mrs. Smith's husband died two years later, she and Mrs. Smith became best friends and confidants. Now Mrs. White is 84 and Mrs. Smith is 80. If one feels lonely, she calls up the other to join her for lunch or dinner. This is possible because they are neighbors, and even though Mrs. White has very poor vision, she can still walk over to Mrs. Smith's house. Fortunately, Mrs. Smith can still drive, so she can provide needed transportation for Mrs. White. But Mrs. White strives to repay; for example, if they go out to lunch together, Mrs. White pays the tip in return for the ride. They share many meals and much laughter. This relationship has become very important to Mrs. White since the death of her husband.[3]

Reciprocity and Dependence: Aid and Assistance

The friendship of Mrs. White and Mrs. Smith is obviously not limited to that of confidant. They are also engaged in an exchange of direct aid and assistance. Although Mrs. White needs more help because she is legally blind, she makes sure she gives in return. In her own words, she tries to "keep it even," although sometimes that means a small cash payment rather than direct help in return. Mrs. White is also able to sustain the bonds of reciprocity with Mrs. Smith because she does not have to rely on Mrs. Smith alone for all the help she requires. Mrs. White's daughter, who lives nearby, provides help with money management and transportation. Similarly, her relationship with her daughter is also one of reciprocity, including child care in the past and gift giving presently. Mrs. White's ability to give in return for the help she requires sustains the bonds of reciprocity and interdependence. She is not overburdening her social support network, nor is she risking dependence, since she is well protected by her ability to give in return for whatever she requires.

Needing the help of another person to shovel snow or get around the community does not put the elder in a dependent position[4] as long as

---

[3]Mrs. White was interviewed by a student supervised by Sally Bould.

[4]Mouser and co-workers (1985) included in their measure of dependence among older men the receiving or needing of help in shoveling snow and getting around the community. In this measurement, they ignored their earlier conceptualization of a lack of dependence resulting from resources that permit a "greater control over renegotiations" (1985:77). Clearly, such help can be paid for in cash or in kind.

the elder can reciprocate. For example, he or she can watch a neighbor's house or feed the pets during a family's vacation and thereby repay help. Simply needing help is a necessary, but not sufficient, condition for dependence in informal support systems; dependence means needing help and being unable to negotiate the terms of the help. Without the reciprocity of her social support network, Mrs. White could easily become dependent and a burden to her helpers. Without help, she could not live alone and would probably have to depend on her daughter for a place to live.

Even if elders cannot fully reciprocate, effective management of their social support networks may allow for an interdependent life-style and a large degree of self-determination. Mrs. Lewis needs more help than she can fully "pay for," yet she manages to sustain an interdependent life-style through token reciprocity and effective support network management:

> . . . Mrs. Lewis needs much help to live alone. She attempts to obligate a large number of people, each of whom can be called upon for small favors. Her landlady picks her up and takes her grocery shopping each week. A neighbor sends her a plate of hot food several times a week. After many telephone calls, she can usually locate one of several acquaintances to drive her to cash her SSI check and buy food stamps. . . . If she places too many demands on any of these helpers, she risks making them resentful or unresponsive. . . . She must work ceaselessly to find new helpers and get the old ones to respond to her needs. (Wentowski, 1981:607–608)

Mrs. Lewis is poor and frail and cannot pay for these services. Nevertheless, she always provides some token payment to her helpers. "She always repays these people in some fashion. . . . She gives jars of jelly, left-over portions of desserts, and garden produce, originally given to her" (Wentowski, 1981:607). She expects these small token gifts to pay off in substantial ways, although sometimes she expects too much:

> In one instance, Mrs. Lewis was angered by a neighbor's failure to reciprocate for borrowing her telephone. The neighbor did a few small chores for Mrs. Lewis but did not honor her promises to do larger tasks, such as mopping the kitchen floor. Mrs. Lewis complained bitterly because she felt the neighbor had misled her by making the promises. By her behavior, the neighbor was clearly indicating that Mrs. Lewis' expectations were unrealistic. Although dissatisfied, neither woman can afford to completely sever the relationship because each needs what the other has to offer. (Wentowski, 1981:607)

Clearly, Mrs. Lewis has built an effective social support network of reciprocal bonds that will survive her disproportionate need for help. It is a network composed of weak ties—a neighbor, store clerks, "the man who reads the gas meter, and the women who run the bingo at a nearby nursing home" (Wentowski, 1981:607). While such a network has its hazards and hassles, it may be an effective model for the oldest old who live alone. After all, the loss of one person in her network would not have a large impact, especially because Mrs. Lewis is constantly developing new ties. For the oldest old, a small network composed of strong, long-term ties might be less of a hassle to maintain; yet in such a network, a loss due to death or disability could be devastating. Mrs. Lewis does have the option of living with one of her two daughters in another state, but like many of her peers, she prefers to be in charge of her own household (Tobis et al., 1986; Jonas and Wellin, 1980).

Exchange Strategies for the Oldest Old

Since most of the oldest old will need the help of another person at some point, it is important to develop an understanding of various successful exchange strategies. Such strategies can help the oldest old achieve interdependence and avoid dependence. The two most common exchange strategies are the "immediate exchange strategy," involving weak ties, and the "deferred exchange strategy," involving strong ties (Sahlins, 1965). Mrs. Lewis uses the immediate exchange strategy; she both repays and expects to be repaid within a short time period. She has only weak ties within her social support network composed of neighbors and acquaintances. The risk of this strategy is that the oldest old may eventually need more help than they can repay in the short run. There is no way to store credits.

In contrast, a deferred exchange strategy involving strong ties covers a longer time period and allows the person to store credit because the repayment can be deferred. This form of exchange requires long-term, close relationships with family and friends. These are relationships of generalized reciprocity. If the oldest old have been able to build up sufficient credit in their lifetimes, they can avoid future dependence by drawing on that stored credit in times of future need:

> Mrs. Davis, at 84, does not worry about needing more help in the future. "I know my family will care for me like they always have," she says. She now needs help with transportation and heavy housework and also

needs to be reminded to take her medication for high blood pressure. These things are easy for her daughter and granddaughters to provide, since they have shared a household for 24 years. During that time, Mrs. Davis has taken the major responsibility for household management and child care while her daughter worked. She still does light housework, gardening, sewing, and shopping as long as transportation is provided. She feels secure and does not fear requiring more help in the future. She has accumulated and continues to accumulate "social credits."[5]

The risk of this strategy is that family and friends with whom one has banked credit may be unable to help when needed because of their own health problems. This is, of course, especially true in the case of a spouse or other age-mate. A large family can provide greater assurance that there will be someone able to repay.

A less common type of exchange strategy involves deferred exchange with strong community involvement. This can involve both strong and weak ties, but repayment is strongly supported by community norms. This form of exchange requires a close-knit, stable community; examples come from rural areas. Wentowski (1981:605) finds that old people in her study "who have resources (whether material or psychological) and have shared them, have developed a large number of strong ties with others. They are likely to have their needs looked after attentively." Similarly, Lozier and Althouse (1975) found that when elders in Appalachia had accumulated sufficient "social credit," they could retire to the porch and let others come and help them. Fred and his wife Edna had accumulated sufficient social credit to retire to the porch:

> Fred and Edna continued to display an interest in maintaining and improving their home. One day a new bathtub and commode were delivered, and they were placed in a conspicuous spot right up front on the porch. They remained there for about three weeks, during which time talk focused on his plans, and then three men from up the hollow came in and helped him to install them in the house. (Lozier and Althouse, 1975:10)

This form of exchange, however, is more difficult to establish in urban communities. Lozier and Althouse emphasized the security of the respected rural community elder in knowing that help would be available if needed. They contrasted this with the situation of an aged relative of one of the authors living in the city:

---

[5]Mrs. Davis was interviewed by a student supervised by Sally Bould.

This aging woman, isolated from kin in an urban neighborhood, presents herself as a "Christian woman," displaying great concern for the needs of older people who are more frail than she. Often she calls on younger people in the neighborhood to provide services for these needy old people. She is attempting to be a kind of patroness, developing a pattern of neighborhood support for old people. As she herself grows older and requires more support from neighbors, she would like to be able to rely on the community to recognize her past service and to return her due reward with dignity, but she seems plainly fearful that this may not happen. (Lozier and Althouse, 1975:15)

Although there is evidence that some rural communities provide a structure in which the elder can store credit for later need, it should not be assumed that needs of elders are taken care of better in rural areas than in urban areas. In one study, the largest unmet need in both rural and urban areas was help with household chores. But the unmet need was more than three times as great in nonmetropolitan areas than in metropolitan areas (Stoller and Earl, 1983). Clearly, some rural communities do not provide the services necessary for their elders. Urban elders, moreover, may have access to more resources such as higher income, nearby kin, and community social services.

A Balanced Reciprocity

The critical characteristic of any successful exchange strategy is that both parties feel that the exchange is just or equitable. Neither person should feel overburdened by the relationship; neither person should see himself or herself as the grateful recipient of charitable acts. Both must feel that they can negotiate the terms of the exchange. If the oldest old are unable to sustain a balanced reciprocity, they are put into a position of accepting "charity." To accept charity is, in effect, to be dependent. Wentowski (1981) finds that "paying one's own way is basic to self esteem" among the elders she studied. Giving gifts or a lunch invitation is often an important way to reciprocate in family relationships. In a small sample of able 80-year-olds, the ability to give gifts ranked very important in terms of quality of life (Tobis et al., 1986). Economic resources then can be used to sustain balanced reciprocity and to avoid charity. Monetary repayment as a form of avoiding dependence is important with more distant helpers (Jonas and Wellin, 1980) and even in family relationships:

Mrs. Evans reciprocates for help with transportation by giving gifts and invitations to lunch. She has also paid her grandson for his help with the yard work. Just recently he refused to accept her money; she became very angry and told him, "I'm not a charity case. I can pay people for their help."[6]

Having one's payment accepted may be even more important in relationships with acquaintances and neighbors. The dignity of paying one's own way is thereby preserved. Wentowski describes the consequences of failing to accept repayment:

Mr. Elder [a bachelor in his seventies] . . . does not own a car and is regularly given rides to local flea markets by Mr. Jones. As repayment, Mr. Elder calculates a fixed percentage of his daily profits and pays Mr. Jones at the end of each day. He allows no outstanding debts to obligate him to others. Mr. Jones was sick for a while, and I drove Mr. Elder to the flea market a few times. Not as yet understanding the significance of repayments, I refused money for the rides, arguing that I was making the trip anyway. In spite of the fact that he desperately desired the rides, Mr. Elder soon stopped accepting them. (1981:607)

Nonmonetary assets as well as income can be used for repayment. Using such assets, however, requires a deferred exchange strategy as well as a very delicate balance of reciprocity in negotiating the terms of the help needed. Mr. Tanner used his house and land to successfully negotiate long-term care from a neighbor:

Tanner was already quite sick when he returned, and he needed regular care. This was provided by a neighbor woman, Audrey Dooley. She did not take cash; rather, she presented her behavior as a Christian service. However, Audrey's three daughters and their husbands, all living nearby, provided a good deal of help to Tanner, and these younger people did receive payment, sometimes cash and sometimes gifts. One son-in-law, for example, got Tanner's car, with the assumption that this provided the old man with transportation when he needed it. . . .
. . . When he died, it was indeed learned that he had willed his house and land to Audrey Dooley. Although there was some disgruntled response, this disposition of the property was rapidly provided with the mantle of respectability; religious leaders in the community provided support for the view that Audrey's service had been substantial and proper and that she was entitled to receive the inheritance. (Lozier and Althouse, 1975:13–14)

---

[6]Mrs. Evans was interviewed by a student supervised by Sally Bould.

The deferred exchange strategy using assets may be a common way of negotiating help in retirement communities; evidence from the wills of one retirement community indicated that residents had named friends and neighbors in the community to inherit part of their estates (Rosenfeld, 1979).

The research of Roberto and Scott (1984–1985; 1986) and Kaye and Monk (1987) suggests the importance not only of a balanced reciprocity but also of giving. These studies indicated that among elderly friends, it was better to give more help than one received; the morale of those who received more help than they gave was lowest. The reason for this, no doubt, was that those receiving more than they gave felt dependent. They lacked sufficient economic and physiological resources to sustain a balanced reciprocity. They were forced to accept "charity."

A balanced reciprocity has also been found to be important in family relationships (Adams, 1968; Hill, 1970). One study found strong emotional ties between mothers and daughters who provided help for each other in a balanced exchange. Relationships in which mothers and daughters did not help each other, or those in which one helped more than the other, were not as close (Thompson and Walker, 1984). Unfortunately, these studies do not examine mother-child relationships over time. To what extent does an erstwhile high-reciprocity relationship decline when the adult child must give more and more while receiving less and less? What is clear from this and other studies (Bankoff, 1983) is that aged mothers often give all forms of social support to their adult daughters. Thompson and Walker (1984) found that in 21% of the adult mother-child pairs, the mother was giving more than she was receiving (see also Riley and Foner, 1968:551–552; Hill, 1970). Perhaps mothers give extra in an attempt to build up credit in case of future need. Evidence suggests that many aged parents still give help but that they become less and less able to reciprocate in ways they have in the past. Perhaps this is why the ability to give gifts is so important to the very old (Tobis et al., 1986); gift giving allows even functionally disabled elders to reciprocate. A sample of mothers who received help from their daughters generally did not describe this help as their daughters' obligation (Walker et al., 1987); if the help were an obligation, the relationship would no longer be one of reciprocity.

Strengthening the bonds between adult children and their oldest old parents may require developing new types of reciprocity for oldest old parents with increasing functional disability. Perhaps only token payments are possible, but adult children should understand their importance in preserving the elder's self-esteem. New demands on the adult children should signal a need for a reassessment of ways to reciprocate in the relationship. This approach may help prevent feelings of incompetence, which can lead to breakdown and/or atrophy of social skills (Kuypers and Bengtson, 1973). Also, it may help prevent abuse-prone situations arising from the anger of the elder forced to accept help and the resentment of the child obliged to provide it. In situations in which the parent and child never learned the art of give-and-take, practitioners could try to help them develop these social skills. Where possible, the oldest old need to know that they can still contribute, and their adult children may need to learn how to accept the contributions of their oldest old parents. In a study of elderly women with osteoporosis, 61% continued to give the same amount of help to their children and 8% increased the amount of help (Johnston and Roberto, 1987). Clearly, reciprocity can be sustained even within the limitations of chronic illness.

Role of the Public Sector: Sustaining Self-Determination

Although much thought has been given to sustaining independence among the elderly, for the oldest old it may also be critical to promote interdependence, that is, the ability to engage in balanced reciprocity. Since the resources of the elderly are limited, public programs need to step in to help sustain both independence and interdependence. If public sector programs can provide assistance in some areas of need, individuals can reduce their demands on the informal support network and be able to give as much as they receive, thereby strengthening ties and preserving self-esteem. If Mrs. Lewis, introduced above, had had access to adequate public transportation, she would have had to rely on her informal network only for shopping, occasional meals, and a few household chores. Her trips to the bank, the SSI office, and the doctor could have been managed independently. Her ability to reciprocate would have been enhanced because her few resources could have more adequately covered shopping, meal preparation, and floor mopping. Moreover, she would not have been at such a great risk of overburdening her network, and her informal support network probably could have taken on some additional tasks if necessary.

Formal Government Services Versus Informal Social Support Network Services

There is much concern today that government provision of services will weaken people's informal networks. Will friends and family help if they know that the government will do the job? This statement of the problem is a rather simplistic one. A comprehensive view suggests that government services should be provided to people with an eye to their total available resources and an efficient allocation of those resources. Overburdening people's informal support networks with transportation demands is probably an inefficient use of social-familial resources, at least in urban areas. Indeed, for people with weak ties, overburdening may result in network breakdown. Judicious coordination of public services and social network resources could be the most effective approach.[7] The goal would be to minimize each person's risk of *dependence* within the informal support network and to enable the oldest old to operate on the basis of *self-determination,* either *interdependently* or *independently.*

What the public sector can most effectively provide depends, of course, on the local community. In urban communities, where providing transportation makes sense, there is often a glaring deficiency in this essential service. More than half of a sample of urban widows of an average age of 75 received help in transportation from a friend (Roberto and Scott, 1984–1985). Some of these women may be at risk of overburdening their networks with transportation demands now or in the future. Most of our urban communities are organized around the private automobile as the primary source of transport, but this presents special problems for the oldest old. Some may not know how to drive, some may no longer possess the vision or coordination necessary, and others may not be able to afford to maintain a car. Their age-mates are likely to face similar problems and be in need of help also. For the oldest old, however, even good forms of public transportation at reduced fares may tax their physiological resources. Negotiating the high steps on the bus or the distance to the nearest bus stop may require more physical ability than many have. In high-density areas, specialized transportation may be the best way to meet the special needs of the oldest old. In rural and low-density areas, a more efficient use of public services would involve those that could be delivered weekly or even bimonthly. Where meals on wheels programs are not efficient, alternatives that require less frequent deliveries could be explored. For example, frozen meals could be delivered once a week and easily prepared with a microwave oven.

The goal of public programs for the elderly should be that of enabling them to efficiently use their private resources in order to sustain reciprocity in their informal social support system. Besides providing

---

[7]Litwak's (1985) model of assigning appropriate tasks to appropriate sectors is relevant here. Some tasks are more appropriately allocated to the public sector and/or to formal services.

help, public services should foster the development of the elder's social support network resources. Are there underutilized social support resources, such as neighbors, with whom reciprocal helping could be established? If a relationship with one family member is at risk of becoming overburdened, could tasks be allocated to other family members? Does the once-independent elder need help in shifting to an interdependent life-style requiring a delicate balance of give-and-take? For the practitioner, the broadest possible case management approach could be applied. This would include developing and managing strong reciprocal bonds in the informal support network. Case managers can effectively sustain helping networks when the elder's need for help increases (Gutkin et al., 1987).

Elders also need a more effective mechanism to store credit while they are able and vigorous:

> The problem of providing for old people in modern society is not simply a question of providing services. What is required for successful old age is the continuing existence of community or neighborhood systems which can recognize and store credit for the performance of an individual over a whole lifetime and which can enforce the obligation of juniors to provide reciprocity. Without such a system, the help that is provided to an elder robs him of his dignity, for there is no recognition that this is his due, and not a form of charity. (Lozier and Althouse, 1975:15)

The proposed Service Credit Demonstration Program (H.R. 907) would be a first step in developing a new mechanism whereby elderly volunteers could earn service credits. Their volunteer hours would be recorded, and the volunteer would be eligible to claim these hours of credit when he or she needed the help of another person.[8] Elders could thus avoid some of the indignities of being "planned for" and determine for themselves what kind of help they need and when it should be delivered. After all, they will have earned the right to this help.

The oldest old do not want to become burdens and be put in positions of dependence. Unfortunately, they face a high risk of experiencing just this outcome. Their resources for sustaining reciprocity dwindle, disturbing the delicate balance of interdependence. Instead of reciprocity we find dependence: *caregivers* who give much more than they receive and *care receivers* who must accept much more than they

---

[8]The proposed program would allow older volunteers to store credit. The Robert Wood Johnson Foundation has funded six demonstration programs under its Service Credit Banking for the Elderly. Technical assistance and direction for the program are being provided by Professor Edgar Cahn of the Southeast Florida Center on Aging at Florida International University. For further information, see Kahn (1985).

can repay in any form. Those who need such a high level of help but who do not have a caregiver are institutionalized. Tomorrow's community services must be directed at reducing the risks of both informal network dependence and institutionalization. We can reach this goal by paying careful attention to the entire range of resources available to the oldest old and to the ways in which public resources can complement and enhance individual resources. More attention needs to be paid to enhancing social-familial helping networks that are reciprocal. Interdependent elders may require *helpers*, but they do not need *caregivers*. They can give and receive help without becoming dependent on a caregiver.

Chapter Five

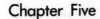

Caregivers of the Oldest Old

Beverly Sanborn and Sally Bould

Caregivers

A caregiver is a person who takes responsibility for helping a dependent elder living in the community. A dependent elder is one who can no longer maintain an independent or interdependent life-style due to inadequate physiological resources, often in combination with inadequate economic resources. The dependent elder has limited ability to negotiate the terms of the help she or he needs, so the overall responsibility for getting the necessary help shifts from the elder to the caregiver. Usually there is one *primary caregiver* who takes the overall responsibility; tasks may be delegated to secondary caregivers or to paid caregivers, but the primary caregiver is in charge. The care receiver is often asked to voice an opinion or make a choice. In some cases the care receiver may get his or her way by manipulating the caregiver, but the care receiver is ultimately dependent on the caregiver's donated help in order to manage daily tasks. A *caregiver* is different from a *helper* in that the former relationship is not one of reciprocity.

Because of the chronic limitations of the oldest old, the caregiver's responsibility is likely to extend for the remainder of the dependent elder's life. This responsibility, of course, may be shifted to an alternate caregiver or to a nursing home. Once an elder enters a nursing home, it is the institution, not any particular person, that assumes primary responsibility. Therefore, elders in nursing homes do not have caregivers as such. Their social support network of family and friends may be very important in prodding the institution to provide better care, but the responsibility for the quality of care rests with the institution.

For dependent elders living alone without a caregiver, the solution in the past was often nursing home placement. Recent attempts to keep elders at home with help have shifted the responsibility for care to the public or private agency that provides necessary services. An employee of such an agency would be a *care provider* but not a caregiver. As with the nursing home, final responsibility for care lies with the agency rather than with any single person. Caregivers are the informal system of support, in contrast to the organized, often publicly supported, formal system. Caregivers volunteer to assume the responsibility for helping; they do not function as an employee. Of course, secondary caregivers and even primary caregivers may be "paid" for their services, in cash or in other ways, by other family members or even by the state. But their caregiving activities are not formal employment. Many states have realized that making a small cash payment to family caregivers in poor families is an effective way of enabling these caregivers to function better and avoid having to resort to institutionalization of the elder.[1] The primary motivation of a caregiver, however, must be a personal commitment to providing care for the care receiver, not any cash reward (Litwak, 1985:242). It is this personal commitment that is often lacking in the formal system, where the care provider is "doing a job."

For those elders whose limited physiological and economic resources necessitate a caregiver, the presence of the caregiver can be critical in delaying or preventing institutionalization. Persons who are married and have a "built-in" spouse-caregiver are less likely than unmarried persons to be institutionalized (Cohen, Tell, and Wallack, 1986). Elders who are living alone are more likely to be institutionalized than are elders who are living with a spouse.[2] Palmore (1976) found that the presence of children decreased the risk of institutionalization. The problem of the oldest old is that they often outlive their potential caregivers.

---

[1]Thirty-three states plus the District of Columbia reported in a recent survey that they permitted "some form of financial payment of relatives for the provision of home care to clients" (Linsk, Keigher, and Osterbusch, 1986:9).

[2]Preliminary research results from a two-year follow-up of the Longitudinal Study of Aging (LSOA) indicate that disabled elders living with other relatives are more likely to be institutionalized than are elders living alone; elders living with a spouse are least likely to be institutionalized (Kovar, 1987).

Caregiver Availability

Until recently, the debate over caregiver roles focused on the *willingness* of the elderly person's family to provide care; in the public's opinion, the family was shirking its responsibilities (Shanas and Streib, 1965; Shanas, 1979). It is hoped that this debate will soon be set to rest by convincing the last skeptics that families do take care of their elderly parents (Stone, Cafferata, and Sangl, 1987). In fact, estimates are that 80% of the elderly's dependency needs are met by informal caregivers (Soldo and Myllyluoma, 1983). Caregivers of elders who need help with the personal activities of daily living (PADLs) spend "an average of four extra hours per day on caregiving activities." The majority of caregivers in this nationwide survey provided care seven days a week (Stone, Cafferata, and Sangl, 1987). New research on the oldest old needs to focus on the family's *ability* to provide this high level of care as well as on the often overlooked question of whether there will be any family member available to provide it. The rapid growth of the oldest old population, together with their specific experiences of marriage, widowhood, and child bearing, make these questions critical for community planning over the next decade. This is the population that is most likely to be in need of caregivers. Who will those potential caregivers be?

The spouse will remain the first line of defense in times of need (Cantor, 1979). Here men are at an advantage because they are more likely to have a spouse, and their spouse is also likely to be younger than they are:

> Mrs. Greene called the senior multiservice center to get a name of someone who could give her husband a bath. When she reported that he was 100 years old, the agency sent the public health nurse to make a home visit. The nurse found the apartment to be tidy and cheerful. The aroma of the evening meal on the stove wafted into the living room. Mr. Greene was still able to walk with a cane, to feed and dress himself, and to use the toilet. He simply could not manage the bath. When the nurse inquired about needs for other services, such as transportation, he became very indignant. "Young woman, I have a very young wife, and she takes good care of me. All I need is help with my bath." His young wife did appear to manage quite well. She was 85.

Even among the oldest old, almost half (48%) of the men are married. But an oldest old woman's chance of having a spouse is only 8.3%.

The second line of defense for the elderly is their children. Adult children assuming responsibility for at least some care of an aging parent is becoming the norm in our society, producing what Brody calls "normative stress" (Brody, 1985). But will there be enough offspring caregivers to go around? It is projected that by the year 2000, there will be a need for 2,484,000 adult child caregiver episodes each day (Doty, Liu, and Wiener, 1985). Even though adult children are committed to caregiving, their capacity to bear the full burden of care is likely to diminish as they themselves become aged. In 1980, about one-third of daughters at age 60 had a surviving parent, and at age 70, 3% of daughters still had a surviving parent (Watkins, Menken, and Bongaarts, 1987:349). These numbers are expected to more than double by the year 2000.

The ever-married woman born between 1900 and 1904 is likely to have had 2.5 children; in the year 1990, when she is 90 years old, her children are likely to be between 60 and 70 years of age. Assuming that her children lived to the age of 40, they would be approaching their own life expectancy of 69.2 years of age.[3] Inevitably, as she approaches her own extreme old age, her children face the increased probability of death, disability, or disease. Metroplitan Life (1977, cited in Bengtson and Treas, 1980:402) has estimated that a mother has a one-in-four chance of surviving her son.

While the younger adult child may face the dilemma of having to work or hire help, the older, retired adult child past age 65 may have neither the extra income to hire help nor the physical stamina to put forth the effort of providing care. Caring for elderly parents has been estimated to be equal to a full-time job (Newman et al., 1976). Yet it is members of the aging grandmother generation, who themselves may be ill or disabled, that are increasingly taking on the role of caring for the great-grandmother generation (Brody, 1985). About one-third of caregivers are 65 and over, and one-third also describe their health as only fair or poor (Stone, Cafferata, and Sangl, 1987). Patterns of mortality and morbidity also increase the probability that a caregiver will be involved in multiple caregiving roles: care of the disabled spouse *and* care of the extreme aged parent.

When planning for caregivers, attention must also be given to those who have neither the first line of defense (spouse) nor the second line of

---

[3]This demographic picture of children reflects the mother; data were not collected on fathers. Census data in this paper come from Table Series B 42–48, p. 53, and Series B 116–135, p. 56, in U.S. Bureau of the Census, *Historical Statistics of the United States* (Washington, DC: U.S. Government Printing Office, 1975). This analysis also assumes that there is no gene for longevity that would protect both the parent and the child. This is consistent with research by Palmore (1985); he found only a weak statistical relationship between the longevity of fathers and sons and no longevity relationship at all between mothers and sons and between either parent and daughters.

defense (surviving children). Here again, it is not a matter of family members shirking their responsibility; those family members on whom these obligations normally fall simply may not exist. Although only a small minority (6% in 1980) of women over 65 have never married, a larger number of women are not likely to have children available to them. For ever-married women born between 1900 and 1905, 20% had no children, and only 39% had three or more children (U.S. Bureau of the Census, 1975:53). Among the 43% who had one or two children, as they approach the age of 90, the odds decrease that an adult child will be available and able to help. Furthermore, other relatives and friends in their birth cohort are not likely to be able to function in a caregiving role even if they are still alive:

> Mrs. Frank was an attractive, witty, intelligent woman of 96 who had a career in the media industry that spanned the days from radio to TV. She still conducted a talk show on the local radio station and interviewed local personalities. She had been widowed since the age of 56 and had one daughter, who at age 74 had become terminally ill with cancer. Mrs. Frank managed a career and was caregiver to her daughter until the daughter's death, when Mrs. Frank was 95. Most of her closest friends were people of advanced years. She still maintained a strong support network among this group, but everyone recognized that if she had a need for intensive levels of personal care, she would have to receive assistance from the agencies and organizations in the community. A recent illness, which had abated after four weeks, made her acutely aware of her vulnerability.

Traditional Caregivers

Spouses and adult children are the traditional primary caregivers. The 1982 national caregiver survey found that 70% of all caregivers for the disabled oldest old were either spouses or adult children (Stone, Cafferata, and Sangl, 1987).[4] This is logical because spouses and adult children can most easily assume responsibility for the elder in all areas of care. No one would question a spouse-caregiver taking over tasks of money management. The physical intimacy involved in giving a bath is generally easier for a spouse or child to assume than for other relatives, friends, or

---

[4]These data are from the Caregiver Survey of the 1982 National Long Term Care Survey. The National Center for Health Services Research (NCHSR) has sponsored a preliminary analysis of this national survey of caregivers of the disabled elderly. Preliminary results can be found in Stone, Cafferata, and Sangl (1987), and in Cafferata, Stone, and Sangl (n.d.) and are available from the NCHSR.

neighbors. The spouse or child can enlist and coordinate help from secondary caregivers—friends, neighbors, and other relatives—and hire paid providers. Live-in arrangements are already in place for spouse-caregivers and are often put in place, when necessary, by child-caregivers. Other relatives, friends, and neighbors are less likely to assume a live-in caregiver role. A live-in caregiver can maintain a person with an extremely high level of disability. The Respite Demonstration Project of New York State, which offered respite services for live-in caregivers, found that more than 50% of the recipients were helping a person who could not be left unattended for more than a few minutes. More than 90% assisted an elderly person who could not be left un-attended for more than a few hours (New York State Department of Social Services, 1985).

For the oldest old, however, spousal care is often not available because the person has usually outlived a spouse and has little opportu-nity for remarriage. This predicament applies to both men and women after age 90, when a majority (62%) of men also are unmarried. Only 15.2% of caregivers of the oldest old are spouses (Stone, Cafferata, and Sangl, 1987). Furthermore, the presence of a spouse does not guarantee adequate care. If a spouse is also over 85, the likelihood of having the ability to care for a partner with severe physical limitations declines. Even for those aged 75–84, marriage effectively prevents in-stitutionalization; two-thirds of married persons with severe functional disabilities are cared for at home. Among those 85 and over, however, marriage is less of a protection. Only one-half of the severely disabled married oldest old are kept at home with their spouses.[5]

When a spouse is not available, adult children become the preferred source of caregiving (Cantor, 1979; Lipman and Longino, 1986). For the oldest old, more than half (55%) of all caregivers are adult children. The most common caregiver is a daughter (43.7%) (Stone, Cafferata, and Sangl, 1987). Among the female helpers of the oldest old, daughters provide nearly half (47%) of the helper days. The role of daughter as a female helper increases markedly from her provision of 27% of the female helper days for parents aged 65–74 to 47% for those aged 85 and over. The contribution of other female relatives, in contrast, remains almost constant, at approximately 30% of female helper days (Doty, Liu, and Wiener, 1985:Table 3). It is reasonable to assume that a substantial proportion of these other female relatives are daughters-in-law.

---

[5]These are estimates for 1980. A severely disabled elderly person was one who had five or six functional limitations in personal care activities of daily living. For the majority, eating was the only task possible (Manton and Soldo, 1985:Table 11).

Family Commitment to Caregiving

The intensity of the commitment to caregiving among adult children has been documented in many studies that have found children able to handle an elderly parent's needs even when confronted with functional disabilities in walking, toileting, and eating (Brody, 1981). Estimates are that one in three caregivers of functionally disabled women aged 85 and over are adult children who contribute nearly half of all the supportive service days needed (Manton and Soldo, 1985:Table 12). Blenkner (1965) has used the term "filial maturity" to describe this stage of life, in which dependencies between parent and child are reversed. The child "matures" by fulfilling this new role. Technically, the child caregiver role is not a life stage because the need for involvement in the life of a parent can be triggered by highly variable circumstances and can occur in a wide range of ages for both caregiver and care receiver. More and more in today's society, middle-aged people expect that they may one day be called on to help an elderly parent. Motivations for helping are not necessarily affection or a reflection of deep attachment; commitment may stem from feelings of duty. Furthermore, the availability of in-home formal services does not result in a lessening of the family's caregiving efforts (Harahan and Hamm, 1987):

> Mrs. Harris, age 62, had never been close to her mother. Mrs. Harris had actually been rasied by her maternal grandmother because her own mother had had an extremely immature personality and an alcohol problem. When her 86-year-old mother suffered from a stroke, however, Mrs. Harris felt a strong sense of duty to manage her mother's needs for services and to visit her mother on a regular basis. "After all, she is my mother. I would want my children to do the same for me."

Adult children, however, usually do not live with their elderly parents. The incidence of elderly people living with adult children is in sharp decline within the last 30 years. In 1950, for example, 32% of men aged 85 and over who lived in the community were living in an adult child's household. The proportion in 1980 was reduced to 9%. A similar trend is evident for 85-and-over women; in 1950, 47% of this group were living in an adult child's household, in contrast with only 18% in 1980 (Rosenwaike, 1985b:Table 7.4). The tendency for people of advanced years to live alone today may account for the continuing prevalence of the myth that adult children no longer care for their aged parents. These living arrangements, however, reflect the preferences of both parties. In the past, elderly parents and adult children usually lived together due to economic necessity, not choice. Today, adult children prefer to be nearby but not in the same household. One urban sample found that 70% of those 85 and over had a child living in the same urban area (Hays, 1984).

Living in the same household, moreover, may not be the best caregiving solution. A caregiver must respect the wishes of the care receiver as far as possible. Respecting the desire of the care receiver to stay in his or her own home may strain family care arrangements. In the case of Ms. Bongiovanni, a local program providing long-term care made it possible for her mother to stay in her own home until she died:

> In our particular case, my mother, being up in years at 92 and foreign born, Italian, raised us basically family-oriented. She became very modern in many ways, in many of her ideas, but she also clung to the old ways of the family taking care of each other. She said many times, "I do not want to go to anyone's home," meaning us. She knew that we would not put her in a nursing home.
>
> We received wonderful care from the visiting nurses, the homemakers, the doctors, everyone who was concerned with her care for the past year has been wonderful. But the home care has been cut back gradually to less and less. My mother lived alone. She would not go with anyone. She has five daughters and a son. She wanted to spend the rest of her days in her own home. There were five family members who lived further away than I do, but they all helped. They all had their own families, but we could not get help for more than 2 hours a day, 3 days a week, up until the last time, and that was going to be taken away. My mother prayed to pass away so that we would not have to be burdened, plus she saw how the cutbacks were coming. She had all her faculties right to the last moment, and it was sad because she was sad about what her children had to do. We are all senior citizens, her children. So we are not young. We all have ailments of our own. Everyone helped as much as they could.
>
> We spent 24 hours each under her roof, doing whatever came up, for a whole year.
>
> My mother's funds are exhausted, but we were willing to contribute and we did as much as we could. (U.S. Senate, Special Committee on Aging, 1984a:4–9)

Ms. Bongiovanni's story illustrates the potential for coordination of family care and community-based long-term care. In fact, effective coordination of family care and state-provided in-home help can forestall an undesirable move to an adult child's home or a nursing home. If such a move were to become necessary, 80% of one sample would choose to enter a "facility for seniors" rather than live with a child. For one-third of those who made this hypothetical choice, the primary reason was to avoid interfering or becoming a burden (Connidis, 1983). Provision of adequate help within the elder's own home may allow a postponement of this difficult choice.

Mr. Branagan, as he tells his story, demonstrates a strong commitment to caregiving but indicates that without home help, nursing home placement may be the only answer:

> I take care of my mother. She is 94 years of age this coming April. In December 1959, my mother broke her right hip and she was operated on unsuccessfully because bone absorption prevented the pin from holding. After that it went from one thing to another, arthritis, crutches, to a walker, then a wheelchair. With the help of her brother, who has since passed away, and good neighbors, and after hospital stays, with limited help of a visiting nurse and home health care services, we got by until November 1983, when my mother's other hip developed a hairline crack causing pain and another visit to the hospital.
>
> When she got home, we got help from the visiting nurses, therapists, a home health aide, which now, unfortunately, will terminate the end of this week. My mother is now confined to bed, which is very difficult for me, being a man, to handle since she must use a bedpan and requires frequent bathing, which I cannot do. I myself am 72 years of age and I am under treatment for a heart condition.
>
> We have attempted to get help from Title XX, and the answer I got there was they they have no funds and a long waiting list. Medicaid, we applied for. My mother seems to have too much income for Medicaid, but too little to pay for private help. Her savings are exhausted and she is on a very limited income, only from social security, and a small pension from my father's railroad retirement.
>
> From here I do not know where to go. . . .
>
> Right now she does not live with me, she lives alone. In the same apartment building, but in a different apartment.
>
> She at times feels bad and at times she cries sometimes when I take care of her, that I should have to do this because her being a woman and me a man. But on the other hand, she does say, "I think I should go to a nursing home, because I do not want to bother you this way." But I do not want to leave her. I know it would break my heart to send her to a nursing home because I know it would kill her right away. She loves her home. . . .(U.S. Senate, Special Committee on Aging, 1984a:7)

As Mr. Branagan's story suggests, it is often assumed that women fit more naturally into the caregiving role, especially in helping with the personal care activities of daily living—eating, dressing, bathing, and toileting (PADLs). Women are certainly not the only caregivers, however, and among spouse-caregivers, men and women appear to participate equally (Cantor, 1983). Adult children—sons and daughters—are equally involved as *helpers* (Rathbone-McCuan and Coward, 1985), but the role of *caregiver* is most likely to be a daughter who provides help in personal care tasks (Wilkinson, 1988). This is especially true for the oldest old, since surviving children are likely to be daughters, not sons.

The attitude of Mr. Branagan's mother illustrates that elders often express a preference for nursing home care when they live alone and need help (Béland, 1984). Elders do not wish to burden their children with heavy care responsibilities (Connidis, 1983). Of course, the nature of the burden and the precise point at which the burden becomes "too great" is different in each situation. Mr. Branagan's mother would probably have felt much less burdensome if her caregiver had been a daughter. Her expressed preference for a nursing home, however, may not result in a nursing home placement. She might well change her mind if faced with the reality of impending nursing home placement.

Dispersed Caregivers

The availability of family to help the oldest old is, of course, limited by proximity. It is believed that most elders have a child nearby in case of need. In fact, in an urban sample, only 8% of the oldest old had all their children living more than 50 miles away (Hays, 1984). Among these adult children and their parents, there is a higher risk of dependence for the elder. Once the elder needs help with shopping, for example, a greater effort is required for the child who does not live nearby. It is harder for the elder to reciprocate when a helpful shopping trip involves a six-hour round-trip drive. Some tasks, such as money management, can be handled at a distance (Litwak, 1985); other tasks, such as meal preparation, require daily attention. Even when the elder requires a caregiver, the dispersed caregiver function can often be managed by coordinating secondary caregivers—local friends and neighbors—or by arranging for paid caregivers. With dispersed caregivers it is also important to coordinate informal support with local agency services. If the elder is indeed dependent and requires a lot of help, a local case management service can take care of coordinating help and handling emergencies. Close relatives who live far away, however, often catapult their elderly relative prematurely into dependency. An adult child who is anxious about his elderly mother may precipitously assert his caregiver role, thereby depriving the elder of the responsibility for her own life. A typical reaction is to assume that the elder's own home will no longer suffice. In seeking out a "safer" housing situation, the adult child is often meeting his or her need "not to have to worry" rather than the elder's need for an independent or interdependent life-style:

> Mrs. Johnson is an 89-year-old woman who called the local social service agency requesting transportation. The intake worker quickly discerned that Mrs. Johnson was very depressed and that she wanted transportation in order to escape from a stultifying life-style. She was limited only by her failing eyesight and the need for a specialized, door-to-door transportation service, yet she was living in a board and care residence that was much too restrictive. This living arrangement was of three months' duration and was precipitated by a visit from her adult son and daughter-in-law. The children had made their annual visit to Mrs. Johnson and had become frightened that in light of their own aging process and the distance involved, they would not be able to respond to any immediate crisis or change in Mrs. Johnson's health. Out of their own fear, they became imperious and bullied Mrs. Johnson into giving up her apartment, which she had been renting for the past 40 years. They ignored her extensive social support network and interdependent life-style. Furthermore, they were unaware that the local senior service center provided all the assistance she needed to supplement her network. Mrs. Johnson was whisked into the board and care facility, where she felt estranged from her friends because she could no longer cook for them or invite them over for tea. She did not feel comfortable with the residents in the home, most of whom were functioning at a much lower level.

Other Caregivers

The national survey of caregivers for the functionally disabled oldest old found that 30% were neither spouses nor children (Stone, Cafferata, and Sangl, 1986: Table 2). Living arrangements of the oldest old suggest that relatives other than the child play a critical role in providing a home for the oldest old. Among the oldest old in 1985 who no longer lived in their own homes, 25% lived in the home of a child, but 18.7% lived in the home of a sibling or other relative.[6] In many of these situations, the

---

[6]The majority (53.4%) of those 85 and over who do not live in their own homes live in institutions. Of the 18.7% who live in the homes of other relatives, only a small number (2.9% of the total) live with a sibling. Living with a sibling is much more common at younger ages (65–84), especially among the never married (Lipman and Longino, 1986:Table 3).

other relative is likely to be a caregiver of the oldest old. This extended family responsibility no doubt makes a significant contribution to the total care, although limited evidence suggests that these other relatives do not provide the intensive care that spouses and children provide (Johnson, 1983). For the oldest old, more attention needs to be directed to these other relatives who are not the traditional child or spouse caregiver. Other relatives may provide critical family resources, and the dynamics of these family relationships need to be better understood. There is already some evidence that other relatives may be better able to manage the stress of caring for Alzheimer's victims (Wood and Parham, 1987).

Neighbors and friends rarely become live-in caregivers. But for the oldest old who live alone, a neighbor or friend caregiver can enable them to remain in their own homes. Indeed, as Cantor's (1983) research suggests, friends and neighbors may be an important overlooked resource. Although friends and neighbors are not likely to perform personal care tasks, they can assume caregiver responsibility for home management tasks:

> Mrs. Kahn was 96. She could prepare her own meals, but her vision and hearing were impaired. She relied on the paratransit service for mobility until she decided they were "against her" and could not be trusted. She had sufficient funds to purchase needed services, but her attitude of mistrust prevented her from negotiating the terms of the help she needed. Mrs. Kahn had no living relatives. A friend took on the role of caregiver; she bought groceries, performed errands, and provided transportation when necessary. This friend called regularly and served as advocate on behalf of Mrs. Kahn. The landlady of the apartment building also watched over Mrs. Kahn as a secondary caregiver. The landlady made sure that her refrigerator was stocked with food and that Mrs. Kahn was able to take care of her personal needs. With the help of these two caregivers, Mrs. Kahn lived out the rest of her life in her own apartment. Both the friend and the landlady relied on each other for emotional support when Mrs. Kahn's demands and/or suspiciousness caused them to feel stressed.

The research of Cantor (1979, 1983) suggests that friends, neighbors, and other relatives may experience the caregiving role more positively than do the spouse or child (cf. Wood and Parham, 1987). These caregiver groups are more likely to report that they get along well with, and are treated well by, the care receiver (Cantor, 1983:600). Of course, there is likely to be a self-selection element operating here because for these groups, the caregiving role is less one of duty or obligation and is more voluntary. In many of these caregiving situations, support from local community agencies is essential in order to ensure continued caregiving. In fact, community agencies can go one step further and organize potential caregivers. Project LINC in Los Angeles was one example, in which neighbors were organized to assume caregiver responsibilities in order to maintain dependent elders in their own homes (Pynoos, Hade-Caplan, and Fleisher, 1984). Tasks included transportation, shopping, meal preparation, and assistance with taking medication.

Caregiver Tasks

Avoiding premature institutionalization will require a caregiver; the oldest old are at highest risk of needing caregivers, not just helpers. Although the individual resources of many will sustain interdependence or even independence, a substantial minority will need to depend on a caregiver to avoid or postpone institutionalization. Trends in nursing home use suggest that there may be a lack of caregivers for the oldest old. In 1963, only 15% of the oldest old were in nursing homes, whereas in 1977, 22% were in nursing homes (Manton and Soldo, 1985:Table 16).

For many of the oldest old, the need for a caregiver is limited to the home management tasks of meal preparation, household chores, laundry, shopping, and/or money management. From a practitioner's perspective, limitations in performing home management activities of daily living (IADLs) may be as important as limitations in personal care activities (PADLs). Having someone available to help when needed in home management, though not basic to survival, is nonetheless essential to living alone. An unmet need in only one home management task can spell the end to an independent life-style. For example, the inability to use public transportation, coupled with limited financial resources and the absence of a community paratransit service, can prevent an individual from buying groceries. Inability to prepare nutritious meals can have a devastating effect on health. Fortunately, help in home management tasks can be managed by a wide variety of caregivers, including neighbors and friends. Furthermore, caregivers can organize the delivery of services by local agencies. Many communities may have good paratransit programs, meals on wheels programs, homemaker chore services, and case managers who can take over some of the responsibilities. Caregivers can be recruited from the family as well as from a broad-based nonfamily pool of neighbors, friends, and friendly visitors. Home management tasks require responsible and reliable assistance, but timing can be intermittent. Sometimes, a small fee paid to a neighbor will ensure the reliability of caregiving in such areas as transportation, help in taking medications, and meal preparation. With only home management limitations, there is usually no need for the elder to leave the house unless there are structural problems, such as too many stairs.

There is one home management task—money management—that presents serious problems for a nonfamily caregiver and can also lead to disputes within the family network. The need for help with money management affects 18% of all persons 85 years of age and over in the community (Feller, 1983:Table 5). The primary causes are probably cognitive impairment and poor vision. It is also true that even a healthy, normal 90-year-old may have short-term memory loss and forget to pay the bills on time. Some people who have relied entirely on a spouse for money management may find themselves unable to handle this task when they are widowed late in life:

> Mrs. King called, urgently requesting help with money management. At age 89, even with poor eyesight, she was managing the money well, but she feared that if she died, her 92-year-old husband would not be able to manage: "He was never good at it." She regretted that they had no children to take over this responsibility. She feared that distant relatives in the area would take over and exploit her husband.

Steinberg's "Staying at Home Project" demonstrated that many older people can maintain an independent life-style in most activities, yet have difficulty paying bills. Key informants and front-line practitioners frequently mentioned assistance with money management as the greatest gap in service. The Public Guardian Office of Los Angeles County found that of 118 cases referred since the beginning of 1985, 62% of the proposed conservatees had the need for money management as the presenting problem or as the unresolved issue. In the absence of a caregiver for this task, an individual will be at risk of premature institutionalization. The Social Security Administration is alert to this problem and has conducted experiments with Volunteer Payee programs. These programs are cosponsored by a senior center, which screens and supervises a volunteer caregiver, who deposits checks and pays bills. Unfortunately, these programs are often restricted because of the fear of lawsuits.

The need for help in the personal care tasks of bathing, toileting, grooming, dressing, and eating generally requires the caregiver to take more time and supervise more closely. With this kind of need, it is often more difficult to sustain a person alone in his or her own home. Community agencies are less likely to offer help in these areas. Friends and neighbors are rarely available for these tasks (Manton and Soldo, 1985:Table 12). Needing help with personal care tasks will probably result in a move to a relative's home, since a live-in caregiver is often necessary. Although the need for a bath can be managed on a less than daily basis, other tasks, such as toileting, require attention several times a day. A combination of three or more personal care deficiencies requires intense caregiving, including around-the-clock assistance. The advantages of a live-in arrangement are clear, not only in rendering assistance on a consistent basis but also in supervising any outside help. Hiring outside help to perform these personal care tasks, however, is extremely expensive, and for chronic care conditions, there is often only limited government help available. A caregiver handling three or more personal care deficiencies will not be able to manage many competing time demands from other family members. Spouses of the oldest old, as noted earlier, will be less physically able to provide personal care. As the oldest old subpopulation expands faster than any other age group, the numbers of available caregivers able to perform heroic levels of assistance may be small relative to the need.

Caregiver Burden

Generalizations about caregiver burden are difficult to make because the perception of a situation as burdensome is subjective and unique to each person. More than any other factor, negative feelings and stress may result in the decision to institutionalize a disabled elderly person (Zarit, Reever, and Bach-Peterson, 1980). Nevertheless, it is possible to identify different types of burdens, such as overall physical burden and restrictions on time and activities. These can be distinguished, in turn, from generalized feelings of burden involving emotional stress and strain. There is no clear relationship between feelings of emotional burden and the reported physical burden.

In those few cases of spouse-caregivers among the oldest old, the emotional burden of caregiving is often counteracted by feelings that caring for a spouse in extreme old age is both a highly appropriate and a very meaningful activity. For spousal care, the shift from reciprocity to a caregiver–care receiver relationship is likely to be smoother, since no shift in living arrangements is required. Furthermore, there is a sense of symbolic reciprocity. Explains one caregiver, "I know she would have done the same for me."

Spouse-caregivers are also more likely than child-caregivers to say that they understand the care receiver and are in turn understood by him or her (Cantor, 1983:600):

> By any standard, Mrs. Long had a high degree of objective burden. At the age of 79, she was caring for her 93-year-old husband, who had gradually become incontinent, could not walk, transfer, or bathe himself, and could feed himself only with assistance. Mrs. Long would balance her husband on her back and haul him into the bathroom, where he would occasionally manage to void and defecate in the toilet. She cleaned up the many "accidents" and assuaged his feelings of humiliation. They shared many good moments. He constantly praised her and was affectionate and loving. She received no outside help from the formal structure ("They won't do a good job"). Neighbors gave her rides to the grocery or sat with her husband when she had to do errands. Otherwise, she handled all the tasks and decisions on her own. Mrs. Long felt this experience was the "meaning" for her whole life—that she had "lived to take care of my husband when he needed me." When he died, she grieved for the loss and reminisced with fondness about their special relationship.

For the spouses of the oldest old, because of their own health problems, the burden most likely to result in institutionalization is probably the physical burden of caregiving. In these cases, a delay in nursing home placement of one spouse may result in the necessity to put both in a nursing home:

> Mrs. McDonald is 86, and she suffers from severe osteoporosis. Her back is permanently bent so that her head is parallel with her abdomen. She is physically frail. Still, she manages to drive her car and perform all the functions of keeping up a household. She has also been the caregiver of her 83-year-old husband, who has a moderately severe case of Alzheimer's. He can perform many of the activities of daily living, such as feeding and toileting himself, and he is completely ambulatory. His main symptom is loss of recent memory, which is evident in his repetitious questions. Basically, his care is not so difficult. He sleeps at night and most of the day. He is also content to sit in front of the TV, absorbing very little of the programs but making few demands on Mrs. McDonald. Until recently, this role gave her some pleasure. As long as she could get two days off per week while he was in a day-care center, she enjoyed "fussing over him like a baby." His total dependence on her was rewarding and seemed a loving response to her caregiving role. The caregiving role became burdensome, however, when her own health declined. As she has needed more assistance with physical care—something he is incapable of providing—she has

begun to resent everything about him. His disease has not progressed noticeably, yet she now sees him as being too much work. She states, "He belongs in a nursing home. Otherwise, I will go downhill too."

Spouse-caregivers do more for more impaired elderly than do other live-in caregivers (Soldo and Myllyluoma, 1983:608). Not surprisingly, the spouse-caregiver also experiences more physical and financial strain (Cantor, 1983:600). The situation of a child-caregiver is, however, less one of financial or even physical strain and more of emotional strain (Cantor, 1983:60; Kleban, Schoonover, and Hoffman, 1988).

For the adult child-caregiver, consideration must be given not only to the actual limitations of the care receiver but also to the emotional interaction of child and parent as well as the total family dynamics (Zarit, 1985). The family system context will shed light on each caregiver's unique intrapsychic reaction. Past character development, self-esteem, and behavior patterns shape the caregiving experience, as does the role played by the dependent person in the life of the caregiver and the way in which this role has changed. Some caregivers may find new depths in their family relationships; others may have old conflicts reactivated, leaving the caregiver feeling raw and wounded once again. Most important is the feeling generated by the situation of chronic care—it lasts for a long time, and the health-impaired person does not get better:

Miss Newman was the unmarried daughter in a family of three children. She had always believed that her mother favored the other two. Her youth had been spent in efforts to achieve perfection in all her endeavors in order to win the unattainable approval of her mother. This unresolved intrapsychic conflict had contributed to her many interpersonal difficulties and to her driving need to succeed in a career. She found employment that was 3,000 miles away from her mother and experienced relief in reducing the intensity of contact in this way. At the age of 93, the mother had a stroke that left her paralyzed, incontinent, and visually impaired. She was still mentally alert and feisty as ever, however. Since Miss Newman was unmarried and nearing retirement, the family selected her for the role of primary caregiver. They all agreed to contribute financially and to provide respite opportunities, but they expected Miss Newman to take on full-time caregiving of the mother. Miss Newman felt unable to refuse their request. She took the early retirement option at work, left her own support network, and embarked on what was for her a total reactivation of the childhood conflict. Her mother's calls for help were interpreted as constant criticism implying that Miss Newman did not "measure up." The family had adequate financial resources, so most of the personal care was provided by hired help. Miss Newman did not resent the tasks, however. It was the interpersonal interaction, the old conflict, that gave her the overwhelming, stultifying feeling of burden.

As is evident in the case of Miss Newman, the activities performed do not necessarily account for the feelings of stress. What may be an overwhelming, crushing, exhausting experience for one caregiver may be an opportunity to find fulfillment and meaning in life for another. The hopelessness of long-term care may be viewed by some as a time to share in the finishing of a life that has been lived to its fullest.

The emotional burden of a caregiver is often related to family dynamics other than those specifically involving the care receiver. A strong network can reduce feelings of stress, and conversely, expressions of burden can weaken a network. Assessment of perceived burden must be understood in a context of family dynamics (Zarit, 1985). How do family members help and support each other? What is their prior history of coping? What is the quality of family relationships? Although sibling studies are very sparse, there is some indication that daughters often denigrate the role of the sons, feeling that the sons do not do their share because they avoid personal care tasks. This dissension can produce feelings of burden on the part of both sons and daughters, thus weakening the caregiver network. In the national survey of caregivers, women reported more overall burden than men; specifically, daughters reported more overall burden than sons (Cafferata, Stone, and Sangl, n.d.). Interfamily dynamics can create additional emotional burdens. Old struggles for control can be reactivated. Sometimes other family members refuse to participate in caregiving activities because they do not agree with the way the primary caregiver has set up the situation:

> Mrs. Owen had always been "Mama's little helper"—the "hero" of the family. When Mama, age 85, became disabled following her stroke, Mrs. Owen "just naturally" brought her mother into her own home. The living room was transformed into a quasi-hospital room. No one in the family could bring friends into the house because "Mama would be disturbed." Family members became alienated from Mrs. Owen and refused to help out with Mama's care. Mrs. Owen's two brothers sided with her husband and refused to contribute any assistance. Mrs. Owen felt burdened because the family had "dumped" on her. Other family members felt burdened because there had been no consideration for their preferences and no mutual problem solving.

The case of Mrs. Owen also illustrates the great potential for emotional stress when the dependent person lives with the caregiver.

The oldest old are at high risk of developing Alzheimer's disease and other severe cognitive impairments. These impairments create special stresses for the caregiving family. Probably the most profound burden is the emotional strain on family members. The loss of personality experienced by victims significantly affects the potential helping network. To understand the effects of the dementia of Alzheimer's on a caregiver, it is essential to know what role the person played in the family prior to the onset of the disease:

> Mrs. Perry had been the "heart" of the family. It was she whom everyone turned to for support and understanding. She was the family communicator, making sure family members knew what was happening so that even the dispersed relatives felt they still had a strong family bond. Her advancing dementia was a serious loss to the entire network; there was no replacement for her role. Individual members grieved not only for the loss of contact with Mrs. Perry but for the loss of connectedness with each other that she had previously provided.

Wood and Parham (1987) investigated the caregiver burden for families caring for elders with Alzheimer's. The burden was less when the caregiver was not a spouse or child but some other relative. The loss of personality may be less burdensome to a sibling or grandchild. The caregiver burden was also less when the number of household members was large. Black families experienced less of a caregiving burden because their households were larger and the caregiver was more likely to be a relative other than a spouse or child.

For family caregivers, the greatest emotional burden generally results from neither the number of personal tasks required nor the general level of cognitive functioning. It is rather problem behaviors such as being suspicious, accusative, withdrawing, and noncooperative and disruptive behaviors such as striking family members, swearing, and disrupting meals that were key causes of stress (Deimling and Bass, 1986; Wood and Parham, 1987). These problem behaviors are often found in Alzheimer's victims.

Overall, these studies suggest that caregivers of the oldest old are less burdened by time restrictions on other activities; many of these older caregivers are themselves retired and/or widowed. This contrasts with younger caregivers, who are often engrossed in handling many competing demands on their time. They are sometimes called the "sandwich generation" because they are squeezed between the demands of adolescents and young adult children on the one hand and those of aging parents on the other. Add to this the demands of a marital relationship and a career and it is little wonder that feelings of burden erupt. Aged caregivers, in contrast, usually have fewer demands on their time. There may also be a greater resolution of parent-child conflicts at the older ages. Furthermore, men and women may be more likely to share the caregiver roles and to drop some of the gender differences when they are themselves more aged.

Deimling and Bass (1986) find that behavior of the care receiver—for example, anger (swearing) or depression (withdrawing)—can be very disruptive of family relationships. This can create an emotional strain that may affect the caregiver's willingness to help. The care receivers' own attitudes about their physical limitations and about needing more help than they can repay can frustrate adult children as well as other helpers. Even the oldest old person who still lives in his or her own home can become an emotional burden to the adult child:

> Into her advanced years, Mrs. Quinn had been an active person, contributing to her community on church committees, leading the university women's book review group, and participating in local political organizations. She had to give up driving on her 88th birthday because her coordination and vision were no longer reliable. As her physiological resources dwindled, her adult daughter, son-in-law, and granddaughters contributed more and more assistance in grocery shopping, home maintenance, transportation, and companionship. Mrs. Quinn was a vivacious individual and she attracted willing helpers. On her 90th birthday, however, she became depressed about aging. For the first time in her life, she dwelled on her lost spouse and friends. She feared her dependence and was terrified of becoming a burden to her children. Her former zest for life was replaced by an attitude of pessimism. The family caregivers began to resent having to help her because they did not want to hear her litany of gloom. With counseling for her depression, Mrs. Quinn's positive outlook was restored, and the family caregivers again enjoyed their filial involvement in her life.

Although emotional factors are the primary stress producers, the type of task can contribute to caregiver feelings of burden, particularly when the task is not part of the normal role expectation for the caregiver. When tasks reflect the family norms for appropriate caregiver roles, the activities seem less burdensome. Impersonal activities, such as handling finances, fixing up the house, shopping for groceries, and cleaning house are often perceived as a positive experience. For adult children, personal care that involves intimate body contact, such as bathing and toileting, may be perceived as a negative experience. This is likely to be the case when the caregiver is of the opposite sex and therefore feels that he or she is violating a family norm:

Mr. Robinson, a retired postal clerk, had never married and had lived with his mother all his adult life. She had been a young widow and had lived a glamorous life as a well-known artist. Mr. Robinson was a quiet person who helped with chores around the house, occasionally preparing meals and shopping for groceries. At the age of 92, his mother had a stroke that left her cognitively impaired and unable to handle most personal care. Mr. Robinson was humiliated and embarrassed to have to feed and bathe his mother. He was too ashamed to seek outside help, yet he neglected her and felt extremely burdened by this unexpected role. The mother's two younger cousins visited the household and were appalled by the condition of mother and son. They immediately placed the mother in a nursing home and sought counseling for the son.

Each caregiver–care receiver pair should aim at achieving a balance of caregiving activities that creates neither an extreme burden for the caregiver nor strong feelings of being a burden for the care receiver. The formal system should be available so that practitioners can step in before an extreme situation develops. The practitioner must be able to recognize when the care required exceeds the ability of the caregiver(s), for either emotional or physical reasons, to provide fully. The goal of keeping the oldest old at home must not contribute to situations of neglect, as with Mr. Robinson and his mother.

There is also the critical issue of preventing abuse. Kosberg's (1988) review of the literature indicates that the dependent oldest old may be at high risk of elder abuse. This risk is greater if the caregiver has economic, emotional, or cognitive problems. In the long run, preventing elder abuse of the oldest old will require programs that prevent or lessen dependency, including economic dependency. In the short run, policies and programs aimed at keeping the dependent oldest old at home and in the family's care need to be implemented with special attention to the risk of elder abuse (Kosberg, 1988). In some situations, preventing elder abuse may require moving the elder into a nursing home.

Caregiver Responsibility

There are four areas in which a caregiver's responsibility can be essential in preventing additional disability and preserving self-determination. These involve the prevention of falls; the prevention of acute illness, especially colds and flu; special attention to any behavioral change as a possible symptom of an unreported illness; and attention to the specific problems of drug intoxication.

Prevention is very important in reducing the risk of falls. Caregivers can evaluate and alter hazards in the home; exposed cords, loose rugs, improperly arranged furniture, out-of-reach kitchen items, and the like can be easily rearranged to lessen the risk of falling. In some cases, structural alterations are necessary—for example, handrails in the bathroom.

All caregivers should be aware of the high-risk of illness and should take precautions to avoid exposing the oldest old person to viruses and other diseases. Acute illness often leads to a downward spiral of hospitalization, convalescence at home or in a nursing home; recurrence of the illness or development of complicatons often results in readmittance. Moreover, the consequence of incomplete recovery from hospital episodes is often placement in a nursing home (Minaker and Rowe, 1985:343).

Both practitioners and physicians are aware of the underreporting of illness and its prevalence in the oldest old age group. The high prevalence of unreported illness, as discussed in Chapter Three, can be reduced by giving greater attention to any behavioral change. Caregivers may themselves contribute to the underreporting when they are misinformed about the aging process and believe that there is no need to seek help because the oldest old are "naturally" in a state of decline. Instead, caregivers should invariably seek out the diagnostic skills of a physician willing to take the care and attention that the oldest old require. The fear that a diagnosis will lead to institutionalization is a major motivation for underreporting illness. Caregivers can play an important role in reassuring the elderly person about the availability of both treatment and rehabilitation so that appropriate medical diagnosis and treatment can be obtained.

Caregivers can play an essential role in preventing the problems of drug intoxication while ensuring appropriate compliance with treatment. One-third of those 85 and over report needing assistance with the dispensing of their medications (Macken, 1986:Table 6). They also need help in monitoring any side effects of the drugs. Particularly when cognitive impairment is a complicating factor, a caregiver is required to alert each physician to the range and quantity of medications prescribed and reactions observed. Side effects could result in an increased risk of falls, cognitive impairment, and urinary incontinence. Caregivers can also organize the medication regimen—for example, by setting up a system of pill dispensing. Can the frail individual remove the pills from a childproof container? Can this person cope with more than three medications? Are the pills too large to swallow? A caregiver can make necessary adjustments in the medication regimen and thereby ensure compliance with a treatment program.

Respite Care

As the foregoing examples illustrate, the role of caregiver is not an easy one. Recent policy initiatives have developed the concept of *respite care,* care provided by the state in order to give some relief to the caregiver. Time off, even if only a few hours a week, can enable families to continue their efforts on behalf of the dependent person. Brief periods of emergency relief or prescheduled respite from the physical and emotional strain could re-energize a caregiver, renew his or her dedication to the role, and thereby delay or prevent institutionalization. There is a wide variety of possible respite care solutions. Some caregivers need in-home supportive service; others will want to place the dependent person out of the home in a day-care or temporary overnight facility. Other caregivers may be reluctant to use respite services because they do not believe that an impersonal outsider can "do it right."

Because much of the caregiver burden is emotional, there is a need for help with emotional stress. Previously troubled family relationships can erupt with great intensity. The potential for elder abuse may be high, particularly when family members have no release for their pent-up emotions. Mutual help groups of neighbors and other caregivers who share similar burdens can help ease the emotional stress. The availability of community services that are sensitive to the subjective burden issue and of psychiatric treatment programs can enable caregivers to reduce their level of burden and continue with their caregiving activities. In a midwestern community, respite services resulted in improved family relationships in two-thirds of the cases (Quadagno, Squier, and Walker, 1987).

Caregivers and care receivers may have little knowledge about how to locate available services other than hospitals or nursing homes. The research of Ward, Sherman, and LaGory (1984) showed that functionably disabled elders with strong family ties were less aware of formal services than were similar elders who had limited family ties. Family caregivers themselves are likely to restrict their social interaction and thus be less likely to hear of possible respite services. This lack of knowledge can become a serious problem in a crisis such as the illness of a caregiver. Local agencies and state-supported services need to maintain substantial outreach programs and community education programs to have the supporting resources highly visible in the community. Then, when such a crisis occurs, the affected individuals or someone within their network will know how to access resources other than nursing home care.

Conclusion

The picture of the caregiving burden presented here is certainly a pessimistic one. As Sarah Matthews (1988) has noted in her critical assessment of the recent literature on caregiver burden, most research is based on systematically biased samples of agency populations. Agencies, after all, are geared for people who have difficulties, who are not coping well, and for whom a breakdown in the caregiver network has occurred. People who are managing well do not tend to come into the agency system. The national caregiver survey found that "only 10 percent of all caregivers use formal services in caring for the disabled [elderly] person" (Stone, Cafferata, and Sangl, 1987). Caregivers most likely to use the services had fewer economic resources and cared for the more severely disabled elderly (see also Bass and Noelker, 1987). Expansion of programs for respite care will not cause families to limit their care of the disabled elderly; on the contrary, it might prevent or postpone institutionalization.[7] This is especially critical for the oldest old, who have the highest risk of institutionalization. Special attention to caregivers of the oldest old may be the most effective way to keep elders in their own homes or in relatives' homes. The problem to be confronted by policymakers, service providers, and individuals aged 85 and over is the limited availability of traditional caregivers. In the oldest old age group, spousal care is tenuous or nonexistent. Adult children, often the linchpin of the network, are themselves aging and in short supply or even disabled. To prevent the social and psychological costs of unnecessary

---

[7]These conclusions come from the Long-term Care Channeling Demonstrations, which contained two experimental groups and one control group. The program was carried out in ten states to see whether the provision of community-based services could postpone or prevent institutionalization. The results thus far indicate no change in either nursing home use or hospital use after 12 months. There was, however, no evidence of a substitution of formal services for family care. In one of the experimental groups, friends and neighbors did reduce caregiving efforts, but families did not (Harahan and Hamm, 1987).

institutionalization, emphasis must be placed on enhancing caregivers' capacity to continue in the role. Willingness of caregivers to assume major responsibilities has been well documented in the literature. Policies and programs need to address instead the issue of caregiver ability and to find ways to strengthen existing networks.

Front-line practitioners working with the oldest old should make a comprehensive assessment of the informal support network, highlighting both existing and potential caregivers and other helpers. Particular attention must be paid to feelings of emotional burden because this dimension makes the greatest contribution to "caregiver burnout." Care plans, always highly individualized, can be tailor-made for each caregiver's special needs and physical abilities. Respite care options can be made available to lessen the physical and/or emotional burden. Case managers can look at the social environment in the broadest sense and search for potential secondary caregivers who could be enticed into becoming part of the network.

Agencies and organizations serving the oldest old must take a hard look at their mission statements and develop a broad model of social care. Most programs are characterized by a more limiting medical model. With this population of advanced years, the medical model is inadequate for assessing people whose needs are primarily chronic rather than acute and who often require the help of another person on a regular basis. Eligibility criteria for services based only on the medical needs of a client identified as frail often are not useful. The agency must expand the whole concept of "client" to embrace the psychosocial context of the individual's needs as well as the abilities of his or her potential support network. The caregiver's needs should have equal weight with the care receiver's needs, and the overall responsibility that the primary caregiver has assumed for the care receiver should be recognized. Meeting this objective is problematic because no single agency has the capacity to provide for the full range of services required. It will become necessary for agencies to drop the rigid boundaries of mutually exclusive services and to find ways to work with other organizations as part of a collaborative community of care. Policies designed to shift more of the burden onto the caregivers could be self-defeating. Without supportive services, potential caregivers, especially relatives other than spouses and children, may be more reluctant to become part of the caregiving network.

Chapter Six

Economic Resources of the Oldest Old

In extreme age, as in earlier life, the worlds of the rich and the poor differ. Although the health problems of extreme age fall on the rich as well as on the rest of us, the rich are, by definition, able to purchase everything to make their later life one of comfort and dignity. Long-term care needs can be managed at home with a staff of servants and trained medical personnel. Family and friends need only oversee the process and provide affection and emotional support. The elder, although physiologically dependent, need not fear becoming a burden on friends and family and also need not fear the dreaded move to a nursing home. During the last year of her life, before her death at age 89, the Duchess of Windsor needed long-term care. A close friend describes her last visits to the duchess, who was confined to the bedroom of her home of more than 50 years:

> A nurse was with her. Her hearing was excellent, and she turned her head and smiled. Our eyes held for a moment before she turned back for want of something to say, and I was choked by the great difference in her. The hair around her face was white, due to not having been dyed in a long time. . . . Her bed had been replaced with an adjustable hospital one. . . .She was looking at me, and her face had a sweet, almost timid expression. Placing her hand on mine, she asked, "Who are you, my dear?"

I saw that it embarrassed her that she did not know. I said, "I'm Aline."

"Oh, Aline dear, forgive me." She patted my hand. "Look at the way the sun is lighting the trees. You can see so many different colors. Tell David to come in. He wouldn't want to miss this."

I walked down the stairs slowly, consciously delaying my departure, certain that this was the end of over thirty years of friendship. Although I was depressed, I reflected upon my friend's good fortune. At least she was in a sort of dream world that allowed her to have her dear husband near. At least she was no longer alone.

I made another visit about a year and a half ago. It was almost identical to the one before. Her beautiful violet eyes were no longer sad, and she looked amazingly well. . . .Obviously her dreamlike existence had given her peace, and she was being cared for with affection. She had her favorite flowers, pictures of her husband, the Porthault sheets. . . .(Aline, Countess of Romanones, 1986:123; used by permission).

This picture of peace and dignity in spite of severe mental and physical disabilities contrasts markedly with that of a similarly aged, disabled, and childless widow who is poor. A widow who is poor and childless is likely to live out the last days of her life in a nursing home. There will be no trusted servant or child to look after her needs or even to protect her from abuse. She will have little choice in nursing home placement because few nursing homes accept patients who have no resources. As a poor woman who can afford only what Medicaid will cover, she may have to choose a nursing home quite a distance from her home neighborhood.[1] Thus, it would be more difficult for close friends and neighbors to visit and keep an eye on things. Furthermore, nursing homes with a high percentage of Medicaid patients have been found to provide poorer quality care than nursing homes where most patients pay from their own resources (Elwell, 1981, 1984).

There is another dimension to the contrast, however. The poor widow's nursing home costs will be paid by taxpayers, since Medicaid is a public program that provides nursing home care for the needy poor. As the 85-and-over population grows, the projected increase in public expenditures for this program worries budget analysts looking for ways to cut corners. In contrast, there is never any questioning of the enormous

---

[1]As part of the federal and state government's cost-cutting strategy, the Medicaid payment has been kept so low that many nursing homes actually lose money in accepting Medicaid-only patients (Freudenheim, 1988). Recent changes in some states' Medicaid reimbursement policies have increased the incentives for accepting the heavy-care patients.

expenditures made by the duchess or by others equally wealthy. Yet the ability of the rich to provide elaborate care for their very old is no less a function of government policies than are Medicaid and cash assistance to the poor. The British government would not allow any members of the royal family, even the controversial Duchess of Windsor, to live out their days with any less care, no matter what the price. Both the wealth and the poverty among the oldest old are the result of explicit government decisions in areas such as Social Security and pension regulation, as well as implicit decisions such as taxing of assets in the form of home ownership but not stock ownership. It is these policy decisions, rather than individual motivations to "save for old age," that largely determine the distribution of income the proportion of rich and poor among the oldest old.[2]

Government Policy

The impact of government policy on the distribution of income is dramatically illustrated by comparing the situation in the United States with that in Sweden for persons 75 years of age and older. The most obvious comparison shows that in Sweden, there is no poverty among those 75 years of age and over; indeed, in Sweden, there is no poverty among the elderly at all, either by the official U.S. poverty standard or by a standard that is significantly higher (Smeeding, Torrey, and Rein, 1986). By contrast, in 1985 the official U.S. poverty rate among noninstitutionalized persons aged 75 to 84 was 15.3%, and the rate for those 85 and over was 18.7% (U.S. Senate, Special Committee on Aging, 1987a:Table 2-4). Clearly, Sweden has made the elimination of poverty among the elderly an explicit government policy; compared with other Western nations, it has achieved outstanding success. In addition, the Swedish government provides extensive assistance in housing, medical care, and long-term care.[3]

---

[2]Government regulation of pension policy, as well as general economic and fiscal policy, affects the distribution of income (Dowd, 1980; Crystal, 1982; Phillipson, 1982; Estes, 1983).

[3]Sweden is far ahead of the other nations in this study (Germany, Norway, United States, United Kingdom, and Canada) in the complete elimination of poverty among its population 65 and over. Comparable income data from these six nations provided by the Luxemburg Income Study shows that poverty is most prevalent among the elderly in the United Kingdom. Using the U.S. official poverty line, the elderly are twice as likely to be poor in the United Kingdom as in the United States. The risk of poverty is similar for the elderly German and the elderly American. The Canadian elderly have only one-fourth the poverty risk of the American elderly (Smeeding, Torrey, and Rein, 1986:Table 2).

While there is a lack of poverty among the elderly in Sweden, there is also a lack of very affluent elderly: overall, there is great equality of income among Swedes who are 75 years of age and older. Although in each age group in Sweden, income generally is distributed more equally than it is in the United States, it is most equally distributed among those 75 and over. This is in direct contrast to the United States, where the overall distribution of income is more unequal than in Sweden but is most unequal for residents who are 75 and over. This means that the 75-and-over population has the greatest disparities in income compared with any other age group (Smeeding, Torrey, and Rein, 1986). There are many poor and near poor and a substantial minority who are well off among Americans aged 75 and over.[4] Those who are well off, moreover, are not so because of hard work or prudent savings but because of pension benefits and a range of government policies relating to taxation and inheritance.

The great disparities in income among those 75 and over create problems in planning services and determining how they will be paid for. While Sweden can plan programs for the old old with average incomes and know that nearly everyone will be able to participate, program planners in the United States must always confront the problem that a set fee could be too costly for many elders who might wish to participate. A free service, however, raises questions about affluent elders being subsidized by taxpayers. For poor elders, transportation costs alone may limit participation; for example, in New York City, a round-trip bus ride to a senior center six blocks away cost $1.00 in 1987.

Economic Resources and Dependence

Affluence can effectively protect against dependence by enabling an elder to afford suitable housing and pay for needed help. An undesirable move to a dependent situation in an adult child's household can be avoided by purchasing the house next door and remodeling it to suit the elder's needs. In urban areas, those who are unable to use public transportation can hire a cab, reserving their social support network for other needed tasks. Assistance with household chores, the area of greatest unmet need according to Stoller and Earl (1983), is a form of help that can be purchased. Indeed, it is probably easier to find a friend who will

---

[4]The definitions of poor and near poor are provided in the following pages.

chauffeur you around than to find one who will gladly scrub your kitchen floor. Poverty, on the other hand, probably precludes hiring help or even using a cab. Furthermore, poverty is a good predictor of the need to live with relatives, although the actual arrangement may be one of interdependence among family members sharing a household rather than dependence of the elder.

The Income of the Oldest Old

The most common measure of limited economic resources is an income that is below the official U.S. government poverty standard for a period of one year. In making this determination, data are collected on family income, that is, income from all sources—pensions, Social Security, public assistance, interest, rents, annuities, wages, and self-employment—for each family member. The economic value of a family's total income varies by the number of family members it must support. In 1985, most observers agreed that a family income of $10,000 was adequate for most individuals 65 and over but represented an inadequate income for a family of four or more.

Determination of government poverty line takes into account the various minimum income needs of families of various sizes. Below the poverty line, families are classified as having too little income to meet minimal needs for food, housing, and everything else. For example, an elderly person who lived alone needed at least $5,160 in 1985, whereas an elderly married couple was poor with less than $6,510. Clearly, the poverty line criteria are based on an assumption similar to the old motto "two can live almost as cheaply as one." Duncan, Hill, and Rodgers (1986) define the affluent as those who have incomes more than five times as high as a poverty-level income. So, in 1985, an affluent elderly person would have had an income of at least $25,800, and an affluent elderly couple would have had an income of at least $32,550.

The situation of the oldest old, however, is more complex because such a large proportion of them live with relatives other than a spouse. Although they themselves may have only a poverty-level income, if they are living with a son or son-in-law at the peak of his earning career, they may be a member of an affluent family. Thus, a family consisting of a son aged 60, his elderly mother, and his employed wife could easily have an income of $42,850, or five times the poverty level of $8,750 for a three-person household in 1985. If the son retires or becomes disabled, however, and his wife has to quit her job to care for her mother-in-law, the income of this family could diminish rapidly. The actual extent of poverty among the oldest old is therefore obscured by the fact that many live with their more affluent children.[5] For some of these, living with an adult child was a choice they had to make because they could no longer afford to live alone. Mollie Orshansky estimated in 1978 that 30% of all persons 65 and over had too little income to live by themselves (cited in Binstock, 1983). The poor oldest old·may be an additional economic burden on the families of their adult children when these families also have poor or near-poor incomes; this is likely to occur among black and Hispanic families.[6]

The official government poverty standard has been used to measure inadequate income for more than 25 years. This measure has been criticized as being too high by those who claim that, for example, taking into account assets of the elderly, many would have adequate incomes because they own their homes free and clear. Others criticize the measure as being too low because it is less than half the median income, which is a measure of being poor relative to what others have (cf. Schulz, 1985).[7] The official government poverty line also ignores the special market basket needs of the elderly for medical care, housing, convenience foods, and hired help, as well as the extremely rapid inflation in areas of rent and medical care (Borzilleri, 1978).

Given the debate over the official government poverty line, it is important to understand the background of this measure. It was developed by pricing the cost of the cheapest food budget determined by the Department of Agriculture for *emergency* or *temporary* use. It is therefore assumed that this food budget is nutritionally inadequate in the long run. This budget requires thrifty shopping and careful and efficient meal preparation. In the final choice of a poverty line, the amount required for the food budget was multiplied by three. Food expenditures were assumed to be one-third of the budget; all other

---

[5]For oldest old women who live in family households (very few of which are married-couple households), the poverty rate in 1979 was only 8% as compared with a poverty rate of 40% for those living alone (Taeuber, 1987). Persons 72 years of age and older living in a relative's household are less likely to be classified as poor than are persons 72 years of age and older living with a spouse or alone (U.S. Bureau of the Census, 1987).
[6]Blacks and Hispanics aged 65 and over living in households of other relatives are more likely than whites to be living in poor households (U.S. Bureau of the Census, 1987). Oldest old black women living in families had a poverty rate of 23%, in contrast to the overall rate of only 8% for all oldest old women living in families (Taeuber, 1987).
[7]A poverty standard of less than one-half the median income, if applied to persons 65 and over in 1981, would have increased the percentage of poor in the United States from 11.7% to 17.4% (Smeeding, Torrey, and Rein, 1986:Table 2).

expenses, including rent, utilities, clothing, and so on, would comprise the remaining two-thirds of the budget.[8]

Since 1959, the official poverty line has increased each year along with increases in the consumer price index. In order to get a sense of how the poverty budget assumptions can be applied, one can work backward from the official poverty line of $6,510 in 1985 for an elderly couple. One-third of this amount is meant for food, which works out to $5.95 a day, or $1.98 for two people at each meal. This budget clearly does not allow for prepared convenience foods, which an oldest old person might need in order to cope with the task of meal preparation; it does not even allow for purchase of two "kiddie meals" at McDonald's at a cost of about $2.00 each. These budgets make subsidized meals at senior centers look very attractive.

The official 1985 poverty line allowed for two-thirds of the $6,510, or $83 a week, to take care of all else. In addition to rent, this amount would need to cover transportation, telephone, and toothbrushes, over-the-counter medications and other out-of-pocket health care expenses. Thus, the official poverty line represents hardship. Even for homeowners, the $83 a week or $362 a month must cover taxes, utilities, and repairs. The hardship of the poverty standard is acknowledged by the widespread use of the near-poverty standard (Binstock, 1983). The near poor are above the poverty standard, but not by much. A person is near poor if his or her income is less than 125% of the poverty standard. In 1985, an elderly couple with an income of less than $8,138 would have been classified as near poor.

How widespread is poverty and near poverty among the oldest old? Almost one-fifth (18.7%) of those 85 and over living in the community were poor in 1985. The noninstitutionalized oldest old have the highest poverty rate of any adult age group. When the rates of poverty and near poverty are combined, the oldest old have the highest rate of any age group; 31.2% of the oldest old were poor or near poor in 1985 (U.S. Senate, Special Committee on Aging, 1987a:Table2-4), in comparison with the next poorest age group, children under 18, who had a poverty–near poverty rate of 26.6% in 1984 (U.S. Bureau of the Census, 1987). In addition, almost one-fourth of the oldest old are institutionalized, and long stays in nursing homes result in impoverishment. The institutionalized oldest old had a median income in 1980 of less than half

---

[8]The estimate that one-third of the budget is spent on food comes from a 1950s survey of average expenditures. Mollie Orshansky, who helped develop the original poverty line, estimates that if the same formulas were applied today, the poverty line would increase by 40% (cited in Binstock, 1983).

the official poverty level (Rosenwaike, 1985b). It is therefore reasonable to assume that the extent of poverty and near poverty among those 85 and over, both institutionalized and noninstitutionalized, is greater than that of any other age group. This picture of high poverty rates among those 85 and over contrasts sharply with recent reports of declining poverty rates among those 65 and over.[9]

Why Is There So Much Poverty Among the Oldest Old?

Poverty can be understood primarily as a condition of those who are not able to obtain a decent living through paid employment. In a social system like ours, the highest priority is placed on rewarding paid work, and a low priority is placed on providing adequate incomes for those who do not work. In such a market economy, persons who do not have direct or indirect access to income derived from working will probably be poor unless, as in Sweden, the government makes a special effort to transfer or redistribute income.

One reason why the young old have low poverty rates (10.6% in 1985) is that many of them are still working (Schulz, 1985). Those aged 65–71 who had worked at all during the previous year had less than a 4% risk of poverty in 1985 (U.S. Bureau of the Census, 1987). As individuals pass the age of 75, however, their chances of being able to earn money through work decrease dramatically. This is due partly to their increasing likelihood of being disabled and partly to age discrimination. For many of the functionally able oldest old who live alone, the simple tasks of daily living have been estimated to require as much as six to eight hours a day (Rosenwaike, 1985b:94). Furthermore, there are frequent visits to the doctor; those 85 and over are more likely to have visited a doctor in the past month. These activities may leave little time for working. Indeed, less than 4% of the oldest old are actively working or looking for work (Rosenwaike, 1985b:Table 6.7); only 8% received any wage or salary income in 1980 (Torrey and Taeuber, 1986). Those who do have employment, however, are probably better off in a number of ways:

> Miss Stewart, at 87, describes herself as "in good health." Her limitations mainly involve fatigue and the need for help with heavy housework. She

---

[9]Since 1983, the poverty rates for those over 65 have been slightly lower than the rates for those under 65. This reflects the serious problem of child poverty as well as the improvement in income of young old married couples. In 1985, the poverty rate for the over-65 group was still higher (12.6%) than the rate for adults aged 18–64 (11.3%) (U.S. Senate, Special Committee on Aging, 1987a).

receives food from the local meals on wheels program. Her income is above the poverty level but still very modest; Social Security is her primary source of income. However, for the past decade she has filled the position of apartment manager in her apartment building. She collects rent and handles maintenance problems. For this work, she gets a significant reduction in her rent. The irregular and intermittent hours suit her at-home life-style and also provide an important social activity. She is now planning to hire a cleaning lady to help with the heavy housework. Her good fortune in having such suitable work is important because she has very limited social-familial resources. She has no friends outside the apartment building; a niece, who lives two hours away, visits only occasionally. Miss Stewart, however, is quite content with her life-style and can manage effectively with her modest income.

The Lotteries

For the majority of the oldest old in the United States, there are two critical lotteries: the pension lottery and the marriage lottery. The lucky minority will be winners: married persons with adequate pensions. The majority will be losers: widows and widowers with minimum Social Security benefits.

The Pension Lottery

For the vast majority of elderly who no longer work, it is the presence or absence of a private pension from a previous employer that most often spells the difference between adequate and inadequate income. "The typical private pension recipient is male, white, and retired from a relatively well paying position in a private corporation" (Crystal, 1982:119). In contrast to countries like Sweden, where nearly everyone gets a pension, the United States' pension lottery provides high benefits only for the lucky minority.[10] This lucky minority is restricted primarily to white men and their wives. But even among this elite group there are losers of the pension lottery, such as Mr. Ronald Sprague, a registered professional engineer and a member of the Institute of Electrical and Electronic Engineers:

---

[10]In addition to Sweden, Germany, France, and the Netherlands, all have high rates of coverage. In these systems, however, the benefits are less relative to previous earnings (Crystal, 1982:121).

. . . I have pursued a mobile career in engineering, having an average time per employer of approximately 5 years, not including the self-employment periods or my current employer. Unfortunately, the price my wife and I have paid for my mobility is a forfeiture of opportunities to accrue substantive retirement benefits by remaining with an employer who provided a company-sponsored pension plan.

In fact, during this period of my employment career, my wife has also had eight different employers in her nursing career, none of whom offered her a pension plan. Even if she had been able to participate, it is unlikely that she would have been able to vest because of my mobility.

In summary, my wife and I have had a collective total of 15 employers since my engineering career began. We currently have only our IRA investments to depend upon for retirement income. (U.S. Senate, Special Committee on Aging, 1985b:9)

Mr. and Mrs. Astoria were also losers in the pension lottery. Mrs. Astoria, a bank clerk, tells their story:

. . .My husband's company, Hooven Letters, Inc., went out of business, and with it went my husband's 27 years of service and his pension; he got nothing.

Now I am nearing retirement age, and we are both afraid that there will be little income for us to account for in our final years.

I have to tell you I feel so cheated by the company. I see other employees with far fewer years than I have, retiring with benefits just because they worked a few more hours a week than I did.

Considering that I worked for a company longer than almost anyone else, and I was always there to fill in for other positions when I was needed, I feel I should have been in the plan, too. I cannot tell you how many times I would work full-time hours when I was asked, filling in for those people on vacation, or perhaps when they had a busy period, but then I would be told after another time that I must soon return to my part-time hours; otherwise, complications would arise, and I would have to be eligible for benefits.

This shows how arbitrary the policy is. In my case, working "too many hours" would mean that I work on an hourly, not a salaried, basis. The pension plan says that anybody working on a hourly basis—and that means all the part-timers—can be excluded. But this does not really make any sense to me. Doesn't ERISA say that employees who work 20 hours a week, or 1,000 hours a year, which I do, should be included in the plan? I was told that my employer took advantage of certain exceptions to the rule that allows him to exclude all the part-timers as a class.

Now, let me ask you, why should employers be getting big tax breaks to set up plans if they are allowed to leave out whole categories of employees?

In my case, they have excluded employees on an hourly basis even if they do meet the 1,000-hour rule. I even heard of another woman who was excluded because she was a secretary, and the only woman in the firm. I think this is very unfair. (U.S. Senate, Special Committee on Aging, 1985b:7)

Miss Boley was left without any pension because of a practice called "integration." She describes this practice as it happened to her:

After 20 years, I hoped that at least I would get some sort of a retirement pension, but instead, I got a letter which said that I would not get a dime. What it said was that if the Social Security benefit meets the pension plan's retirement income goals, then no benefit is payable from the plan. Since Social Security meets the plan goals, there is no pension payable to me.

I really did not understand what this meant. A friend of mine explained that the plan used Social Security to wipe out the pensions of lower paid workers like me.

What is so strange about all this is that I received statements from the company each year, telling me that I was fully vested. I guess I was vested in zero.

I should mention that I have heard that J. C. Penney changed the pension plan after I retired so someone like me would not completely lose out. Under the new plan, someone in my position would get a few dollars a month. But the question is, why should a company be able to take away any of a person's pension by subtracting Social Security?

This is completely unfair. I always thought that the reason a company had a pension plan was to make sure workers can get more than Social Security at retirement. After years of work with the company, they certainly owe us something. (U.S. Senate, Special Committee on Aging, 1985b:4)

While legislation in the 1980s will end some of the problems of the workers' pension lottery mentioned above, the oldest old did not even have the protection of the Employee Retirement Income Security Act of 1974 (ERISA), which was in effect in all of the situations discussed above.

The Marriage Lottery

The other lottery that determines the income situation of the oldest old is the "marriage lottery." Winners keep their spouse or remarry after a spouse's death; losers become widows or widowers. The marriage lottery is especially critical for women. If they worked, as was the case with Mrs. Sprague, Mrs. Astoria, and Miss Boley, they are not likely to have adequate pensions, due to part-time positions, job changes, and low-wage jobs. In the generation of the oldest old, however, the vast majority of married women never worked. Their pension income therefore is dependent on their spouse's pension coverage. Losing the spouse can mean loss of all pension benefits. In addition, the new widow will lose one-third of the couple's Social Security benefit. Only 11% of all widows received any income from a pension, theirs or their deceased spouse's, in 1982 (Andrews, 1985, cited in Myers, Burkhauser, and Holden, 1988:3). Women who are 85 and over did not have the benefit of more recent pension laws requiring a survivor option that provides for the wife after the husband's death. But as recently as 1978, 62% of married workers chose no survivor option.[11] Legislation now requires that the wife sign in case her husband chooses no widow's benefit in his pension plan.

The hypothetical situation of John and Mary Doe illustrates the dramatic fall in income that could follow the death of the husband. If John has a pension of $1,000 a month for his lifetime only, plus a Social Security benefit of $500 a month and a Social Security dependent's allowance for his wife, Mary, of $250 a month, the total monthly income of this married couple would be $1,750. On John's death, however, Mary loses his pension income of $1,000 a month and the Social Security dependent's allowance of $250. Without any income from stocks or savings, she will now be near poor with only $500 a month, less than one-third of the couple's former income.

Social Security is more evenhanded when it comes to widows and widowers. In both cases, the original benefit for the worker and his or her spouse is reduced by one-third. If John and Mary had been receiving only his Social Security benefit of $500 a month and a spousal benefit of $250 a month for a total monthly check of $750, the death of either would reduce the income to $500 a month. Social Security favors married couples. In the case of John and Mary, the death of either would leave the surviving spouse with a near-poor income (Warlick, 1983). Although men, too, can be losers in the marriage lottery, the greater life expectancy of women means that they are more likely to be the losers. Furthermore, men are more likely to be able to remarry and thereby increase their Social Security check by 50%. In 1984, the average income of couples aged 80 and over was $13,190, or more than twice the

---

[11]While this refers to both married men and married women, it applies primarily to married men; see Robert J. Myers, Memorandum No. 25 to the National Commission on Social Security Reform, cited in Schulz (1985:156). The no-survivor option provides higher benefits during the pensioner's lifetime; the survivor option provides lower benefits for the joint husband-wife lifetime.

poverty standard of $6,275 for an aged couple. Women are more likely to lose both the pension lottery and the marriage lottery. The average unmarried woman aged 80 or over had a 1984 income of only $5,850 (Grad, cited in Atkins, 1988); she would be classified as near poor because her income was less than $6,223 in 1984.

The economics of aging for most women means not only a doubling of the risk of poverty from age 65 to age 85 but also an income level close to the poverty standard as a widow at age 80. Although at 65, as part of a married couple, a woman's income was likely to be four times greater than the poverty standard, at 85, as a widow, her income is likely to be below the poverty standard.[12] For unmarried women, who do not experience the shift to widowhood in the years from 65 to 85, poverty remains high. If a woman is widowed by age 62–64, her chances of being poor are already nearly one in four. Even for the woman who never married and is likely to have earned a pension of her own, the risk of poverty is one in five after age 71 (U.S. Bureau of the Census, 1987:Table 11). By the age of 85 or over, if a woman lived alone, her risk of poverty was 40% in 1979 (Taeuber, 1987).

When Social Security Fails

When the Social Security Act was passed in 1935, it established two tiers. The first is a social insurance tier, in which those who have made contributions into the system get their Social Security retirement check as a "right," irrespective of their assets or of most other income.[13] This tier is based on a modified insurance principle; the retirement check amount is related to past earnings. The problem is that when earnings are low, the Social Security check is even lower; also, losers of the marriage lottery lose the additional income of the dependent's allowance. More than half (58%) of women aged 72 and over living alone who rely only on a Social Security check are poor (U.S. Bureau of the Census, 1987).

---

[12]Women who are now 85 and over were probably less well off 20 years ago, when they were 65 and married, than unmarried women aged 65 are now. Nevertheless, their average income when married was certainly far above the poverty standard. Given the increases in Social Security checks and the advantage to married couples, future generations of married women will also see their poverty risk escalate as they become widows between the ages of 65 and 85.

[13]Recent tax reform does make part of the Social Security income taxable when the total income reaches a specified amount.

It was not the goal of the original 1935 legislation that Social Security would be a program to help the needy. So the original legislation included a second tier, Old Age Assistance, a welfare program to help old people who were destitute. Old Age Asssistance, which was a state program rather than a federal one, embodied all the stigma of the old "means test." One state required the recipient to have not a penny. Many states allowed the elderly to continue to live in their homes but put a lien on the home so that when it was sold, the state would recover any payments. In seventeen states, the adult child's income was taken into account, and the state would refuse to pay even if the adult child would not provide (Schulz, 1984:23).

In 1975, the state Old Age Assistance programs were replaced by Supplemental Security Income (SSI) for those 65 and over. This was a euphemism, since those receiving SSI may not have any other income to supplement. This new federal program established the right to benefits in all states irrespective of adult children's incomes. It also ensured a minimum benefit for all elderly persons irrespective of the state of residence. One goal of the program was to reduce the stigma of this welfare payment by administering the program through the Social Security Administration offices, not the old welfare offices. SSI provisions (1974, 1976, and 1982), moreover, exclude from the asset test the entire value of the home and $1,700 in savings. Elderly homeowners could now get help without running the risk of turning their homes over to the state.

The SSI program was created to help the needy elderly. How successful is the SSI program in preventing poverty among the elderly? First, the federal minimum standard was never set above the poverty level. Second, as with Social Security benefits, married couples do better, with a federal minimum guarantee at 90% of the 1984 poverty level, whereas for individuals the minimum is only 76% of the 1984 poverty level. Some states with high costs of living do supplement above the official poverty level, but this supplementation is certainly not generous, considering the high cost of living in these states. Furthermore, more states supplement a couple's income to an amount above the poverty standard. In 1984, 13 states provided elderly couples with SSI payments at or above the poverty level, but only four states provided individuals with SSI payments at or above the poverty level (Schulz, 1984:Table 3).

How successful has the SSI program been in helping the oldest old? There are a number of indicators that the oldest old have fared less well than the young old under SSI. Clearly, married couples obtain more adequate poverty protection than do persons living alone, but the oldest old are very unlikely to be part of a married couple; only 22% of oldest old persons living outside institutions are living with a spouse, and 39% are living alone. The oldest old are further disadvantaged by the SSI provision that if an individual receives food and shelter in someone else's household, the SSI payment is reduced by one-third. Since 26% of the noninstitutionalized oldest old live in a relative's household, this provision strikes especially hard. This regulation is especially difficult to justify for the oldest old; when they do move in with relatives, they are likely to do so for reasons of failing health or limited income or both (Soldo, Sharma, and Campbell, 1984). This provision also disadvantages black and Hispanic oldest old persons, who are both more likely to be poor *and* more likely to be cared for in a relative's household. These relatives are likely to be poor or near poor themselves and yet must make do with a one-third reduction in the SSI benefit for their oldest old member. These provisions also disadvantage women, who among the oldest old are most likely to be living in their own or a relative's household and very rarely (8%) form part of a married couple household. Overall, women who were 72 and older, receiving SSI, and living alone had a poverty rate of 78% in 1985 (U.S. Bureau of the Census, 1987). There is little or no poverty protection for unmarried women in SSI. Yet, of course, women are most likely to have to resort to SSI because their other income is too low; three-quarters of all aged SSI participants are women (Schulz, 1984:29).

It is reasonable to assume that many of the oldest old do not participate in SSI because of the stigma of welfare and fears concerning the old laws that gave the state title to the home or required family support. It is estimated that 35–50% of those eligible for SSI do not participate (Hollonbeck and Ohls, 1984: The Commonwealth Fund Commission, 1987b:30). Furthermore, the older the eligible elder, the less likely he or she is to participate. One reason for this is that the oldest old are also less aware of the program (Warlick, 1982:251).

Command Over Resources-In-Time

The foregoing discussion has focused only on the dollar amount of yearly income among the elderly and specifically on patterns of poverty at a single point in time. The use of income as a critical measure has been extensively criticized, however, because income clearly fluctuates and people can move in and out of poverty from year to year. Furthermore, what about all those assets that the elderly are known to have hidden away? Don't they own their own homes? Perhaps these contain substantial value. And what of all the benefits they get, such as tax breaks, senior citizen's discounts, subsidized housing, and free medical care? Some ambitious budget cutters are suggesting that the elderly are getting more than their share (Hudson, 1978). Titmuss (1962) was the first to stress that yearly income was an insufficient measure. Total resources over time are represented by the reliability and stability of income as well as the assets an individual has to fall back on. If the value of pension income is eroded by inflation, and if pension income disappears on the death of a spouse, it is neither stable nor reliable in terms of future budgeting. Furthermore, budgeting for some items is almost impossible. A key item of uncertainty in the budgets of all the elderly, and especially of the oldest old, is medical expense. Here a system of national health insurance would provide an essential command over a critical resource-in-time. Without it, the budgets of the oldest old may be devastated by out-of-pocket medical costs.

Assets

The major asset of the elderly is the home. In the early 1980s, nearly 75% of all aged persons owned their own homes, and 80% of these homeowners owned their homes "free and clear" (U.S. Bureau of the Census, 1984a; U.S. Bureau of the Census, 1983). The widespread prevalence of home ownership, even among the poor (Struyk and Soldo, 1980), suggests that state and local tax breaks on property taxes for the elderly may offer significant help. However, home ownership declines with increasing age. For persons 72 years of age and over living alone, only 60% had wealth in the form of home ownership (U.S. Bureau of the Census, 1987). The oldest old are likely to have the smallest amount of this form of wealth (Atkins, 1988). They are also likely to experience difficulties in maintaining their homes. Many of the oldest old who had owned homes have had to give them up and move into the home of a relative or a nursing home.

Other than home equity, the average person 80 years of age and older has one-third less assets—savings, stocks, bonds, and so on—than the average person aged 75–79 (Atkins, 1988). Those 80 and over are most likely to have little or no assets (other than home equity), in comparison with younger age groups (Atkins, 1988). For all assets combined, the elderly experience the greatest disparities in wealth and have the highest concentration of top wealth holders of any age group (Greenwood, 1983, as cited in Atkins, 1985:407).

Another way of understanding the concept of command over resources-in-time for the oldest old is to examine their resources—after-tax income, assets, and Medicare—relative to their potential needs. The after-tax income of single and married householders 80 years of age and over is only three-fifths of the after-tax income of single and married householders aged 65–69 (Atkins, 1988). Clearly, they have to make do with less, about $2,000 per person per year less than in households of persons aged 65–69. But the 80-year-old householder is spending as much on health care as is the 65-year-old householder, in spite of significantly lower income (Atkins, 1988). This means that the 80-year-old who needs help with household chores is less likely to be able to pay for that help. Yet the 80-year-old is more likely to need the help. Overall, the income of the 80-year-old household is less, but medical expenses are the same and the need for additional help is greater. Clearly, Medicare does not relieve the 80-year-old householder of the financial burden of health care or of the special needs created by functional disability.

Of course, the health problem that breaks the budget of the oldest old is long-term care. This is most likely to be care in a nursing home, but it also includes at-home care. There is no state or federal program that insures against the cost of long-term care. The elderly must "spend down" their assets, becoming impoverished so that they can become eligible for Medicaid assistance in their state. For example, a Massachusetts study assumed Medicaid eligibility in 1984 when an individual's savings were $1,000 or less and his or her income was $4,000 or less. This study predicted that almost half of those 75 and over living alone would become impoverished "after only 13 weeks of nursing home care. Only one of four . . . would escape impoverishment in the first year following nursing home placement" (Branch and Freedman, 1985:53). The impoverishment of the oldest old often includes the placement of liens on their homes so that the state is reimbursed its costs on the death of the elder or the sale of the home. It is not surprising, then, that nursing home residents aged 85 and over are poorer than individuals of the same age who reside at home (Rosenwaike, 1985b).

Paying For Medical Care

The economic situation of the oldest old, then, is marginal, not only because of their low incomes and limited assets but also because of their high cash outlay for medical care and their high risk of impoverishment due to nursing home care. This picture contrasts sharply with a popular view of the elderly as affluent and adequately protected against health care costs through Medicare, the federal health insurance program for the elderly. Although only 2% of the oldest old have no health insurance, 25% have only Medicare (Harris and Associates, 1986). Because of the limited coverage of Medicare, these oldest old are at special risk of having to pay high out-of-pocket medical costs. In fact, the out-of-pocket financial burden of health care for all of the elderly is greater now than in 1965, before Medicare came into effect. And the costs of medical care are rising rapidly. Edward R. Royal, chairman of the House Select Committee on Aging, summarized the committee's findings thus:

> Elderly out-of-pocket health care costs in 1980 were $966. Since that time, these costs have risen rapidly to a 1985 level of about $1,660 per elderly person. Out-of-pocket costs will increase even more rapidly at least through 1990 when the average out-of-pocket health care cost will be $2,583 per elderly person. Elderly out-of-pocket costs in 1990 will be over two and one-half times higher than they were a decade earlier. (U.S. Congress, House Select Committee on Aging, 1985:39)

Although the expansion of Medicare coverage in 1989 will help reduce this high out-of-pocket expense, elders will still have to pay for their long-term care (Tolchin, 1988). Furthermore, the deductibles are large—$600 for prescription drugs. The poor and near poor with only Medicare coverage suffer the most. Half of the poor and near poor aged 75 and over have Medicare only (U.S. Senate, Special Committee on Aging, 1984a:Table 13). Furthermore, the additional Medicare premium of $4 a month beginning in 1989 is likely to cut severely into these poverty-level budgets. Seventy-eight percent of the higher income elderly, but only 50% of the poor and near poor, have supplemental medical insurance (U.S. Senate, Special Committee on Aging, 1984a:Table 12). Good supplemental insurance, however, is that obtained through a former employer. This insurance coverage, like pension coverage, is less available to the oldest old, and if available, it often dies along with the covered spouse. The oldest old are least likely to have any form of supplemental health insurance (Harris and Associates, 1986:41).

What About Medicaid?

The Medicaid program was put into effect in 1966, at the same time as Medicare. It was designed to provide the needy with medical care. The poor elderly could thus have coverage under Medicare and be covered for most other health care costs under Medicaid. This program does help, because poor and near poor on both Medicaid and Medicare averaged an estimated $157 in out-of-pocket medical expenses in 1981; whereas those poor and near poor covered only by Medicare faced out-of-pocket expenses of $522 (U.S. Senate, Special Committee on Aging, 1984a: Table 16). The most urgent problem with Medicaid is that it does not reach all of the elderly poor. Only five states cover all of the poor and some of the near poor; 21 states cover less than half of their poor populations (Grannemann and Pauly, 1983, cited in Harvard Medicare Project, 1986:18). The Commonwealth Fund Commission estimates that two-thirds of the elderly poor are not eligible for Medicaid (1987a). This is because states have a lot of discretion in establishing eligibility standards; they may, for example, limit eligibility to those elderly receiving SSI. The Harvard Medicare Project (1986:18–19) recommends a uniform standard making all poor and near-poor elderly persons eligible for Medicaid in all states. Of course, even this reform would still leave the elderly faced with a means-tested program in which there would be strict limits as to assets and income.

Medicaid is, however, the only program that provides for long-term care in a nursing home. The expansion of Medicare coverage under the Catastrophic Coverage Act of 1988 will still leave the risk of impoverishment due to nursing home care. For the oldest old this risk is highest, since "an 85 year old is two and one half times more likely to enter a nursing home than is a 75 year old" (Cohen, Tell, and Wallack, 1986:790). And, as if in final irony, the oldest old often have no other choice but to enter a nursing home and to risk becoming destitute because they have outlived their family support network.

Cash Versus Services

There has been a long-standing debate in the field of social welfare as to the priorities that should be given to cash in contrast with the provision of services or in-kind benefits. In general, the provision of cash is the choice of persons who would leave to the client the decision as to how to spend the money. This approach is supported by those who believe that the individual should be able to choose in a marketplace that provides a full range of choices. This involves the assumptions that the marketplace does provide a full array of services and that the individual can wisely purchase those most suited to his or her needs with a little more available cash.

There are several possible examples of the choice between cash and services. At the lower level of simplicity, we can discuss whether to provide extra cash or a free or subsidized meal. Those in favor of services would argue that the meal service could provide better or at least more reliable nutrition than the individual might; if cash were provided, the individual could spend the extra money on soft drinks, sugar snacks, or possibly alcohol. Although provision of services may be viewed as paternalistic by the nonelderly—who often prefer cash—there is an entirely different set of issues for the elderly, especially the oldest old. For example, shopping and preparing nutritious meals may be a very burdensome chore, even for those 85 and over who can still manage to do so. Alternatives within their price range, such as fast food restaurants, may provide less value for the money and even pose nutritional problems, such as too much salt. Then, for the oldest old person who lives alone and has no functional disabilities, the social atmosphere of the senior center dinner may provide an extra incentive for maintaining good eating habits, in contrast to a meal alone in a fast food place or a bowl of cereal at home. The added service of the meal delivered to the home may be especially needed by the oldest old. In fact, provision of this service may be more important in preventing dependence than an equivalent cash grant. This may be the case for services such as meals on wheels programs.

Although free-market economists like to think that the private market will provide the best alternative at the cheapest price, there is evidence indicating that for health and long-term care services, this is not the case (Titmuss, 1971; Lubben, 1987). Especially for the oldest old, the provision of appropriate services may be the most effective way to prevent dependence. Although the SSI levels should be raised to the poverty line, the addition of a few more dollars in cash each day would be inadequate for purchasing needed help. The "right" to purchase their own food for a few extra dollars would not meet the needs of many of the oldest old who need help with shopping and/or meal preparation.

The hiring of help in the private market, furthermore, poses problems even for those who have the money to pay for these low-wage jobs. As one social worker commented about an upcoming home visit for an 86-year-old, "I hope this is not just another domestic help problem." Social workers should not be involved in arranging household help and negotiating disputes between employers and employees; yet clearly, in this case the unregulated private market was not providing adequate help. The issues involved in these jobs are the same as in other domestic jobs: low pay, dead end, no benefits, no employee protection from capricious employers, no employer protection from employee theft, and so on. Given the working conditions, it is not surprising that many workers pose problems for their employers. If workers feel, as they often do, that the pay is too low, they may steal, using the "logic" of the wage-theft system. No third party is available to arbitrate disputes. There is no sick leave, no vacation pay: why not quit? This free-enterprise marketplace leaves both employer (the oldest old or the caregiver) and employee in a vulnerable position. In this case, more bureaucracy, or at least more bureaucratic standards, will be needed in order to provide consistency and reliability for both parties.

The Future Economic Status of the Oldest Old

Gerontology textbooks are filled with optimistic predictions about the future economic status of those past the age of 65. First, poverty levels are now low in this group; in 1983, only 12% of those aged 65–74 were poor, and each succeeding generation will have better education and better pension and Social Security coverage. Age discrimination is now illegal, so those past the age of 65 can more easily obtain earned income. In addition, more and more women are working and earning Social Security and pension rights based on their own incomes.

Although each optimistic statement above is certainly true, the fact is that none of these factors offers a significant promise for improved economic status of the oldest old. Again, the most significant demographic fact is that the oldest old are two-thirds women. Warlick's (1983) analysis of the situation of elderly women still applies: there is no predicted change in the poverty levels of unmarried women. Aged couples may do better, but once the men die, significant pension benefits are likely to die with them. The 1984 legislation requiring a wife to sign in the case of no survivor benefits, together with extensive education programs, may mean that some widows may fare better in the future. A woman can, however, still sign away her right to survivor benefits; in fact, she may be encouraged to do this so that the couple has the extra money while both are alive. Furthermore, future generations of women will have higher proportions of divorced women. Compared with widows, divorced women tend to have fewer economic resources and fewer pension rights in their ex-spouses' pension plans.

The major trend that will limit possible future pension income for both men and women is the number of jobs that actually have pension coverage. In 1983, among nonagricultural workers, 41% of the men and 48% of the women were not covered. Workers most likely to be covered are those in large firms with a union (Andrews, 1985:128–130). In the eighties, most new jobs have been in nonunion small firms. Jobs in nonunion small firms are also likely to be low-wage jobs, so even the Social Security earnings-related benefit will be low. Women are more likely than men to hold these low-wage jobs.

What about the two-earner couple? As the traditional unionized manufacturing jobs are lost, both husband and wife often work in the lower paid sector to put together an adequate family income. In spite of an almost doubling of work hours, the net result for the husband and wife will be lower benefits under Social Security. The widow will also suffer. Schulz (1985:126) offers the following example, developed by a Department of Health, Education and Welfare task force. The Social Security benefit in 1979 for a couple in which the man earned $12,000 a year would have been $7,640 a year—that is, a $5,093 benefit for him and a spousal benefit of $2,547. In contrast, a couple with $12,000 total earnings shared equally would get $3,173 each or a total of $6,346 a year, nearly $1,300 less than the family with one earner at a higher wage. On widowhood, moreover, the widow of the single earner would get his full benefit of $5,093 a year, whereas the widow in the two-earner family would be much worse off at only $3,173 a year. She would have been classified as poor in 1979. Currently, the Social Security system favors married couples and widows of high-earning men. The women who are increasingly entering low-paying labor market jobs are unlikely to see any substantial increase in their Social Security benefits or their own private pension benefits. Social Security will not aid the average working wife when she becomes a widow.

Although the future economic prospects for aged couples with pension coverage is bright, the prospects for future generations of oldest old, composed largely of unmarried women, are dim. Their high risk of poverty and near poverty is not likely to diminish. Such limited resources can push the oldest old into dependence even with only minor health limitations. Housing problems, as discussed in the next chapter, will no doubt become more pervasive as rents and taxes increase faster than the incomes of these widows. Much more can be done to protect the incomes of those who lose the pension lottery and the marriage lottery.

Chapter Seven

Formal Services

Beverly Sanborn and Sally Bould

Introduction

Formal services for the elderly can be distinguished from informal services in that the former are provided by an employee as part of his or her job, while the latter are provided by family, friends, and neighbors on a voluntary basis. In the case of complex services involving, say, housing or medical care, many different employees are involved within one of several bureaucratic structures. For example, health services may be provided by doctors, nurses, physical therapists, social workers, and nurses' aides. These individuals may be employees of a bureaucratic structure such as a community agency, a hospital, or a home health care organization, or they may be self-employed. Except for privately arranged domestic help, the self-employed person is also subject to the larger bureaucracy of the state or local licensing departments and subject to government review as to qualifications and quality of care.

The salaries of employees who provide care can be paid in various ways. They may be employees of a bureaucracy: the hospital or the home health care organization. The money to pay their salaries may come all or in part from general public funds (i.e., taxpayers' money), as in the case of a public hospital, which could also be funded partly by philanthropic funds (charity). The money could come from both public funds (taxpayers) and contributors (beneficiaries) such as the special insurance fund for Medicare, as in the case of Medicare reimbursement. Payment may come all or in part from private sources, including private insurance funds and/or out-of-pocket payments by the person or family receiving the help. For example, the funds to pay for a private nurse could be entirely out-of-pocket for those elders whose income permits.

Although medical care is the formal service most familiar to everyone, there are many other services that provide help to the elderly. For the oldest old, who are most likely to need some kind of help, it is often those other services that can enable them to live an independent or interdependent life-style in the community. These other formal services include meals delivered to the home (meals on wheels programs), housing assistance, special door-to-door transportation (paratransit services), and help with household chores. For the oldest old who are dependent, there is also respite care to help the caregiver. Respite care may be provided in an adult day-care center or at home. In either situation, the caregivers get some time off with the assurance that their relative will be well cared for in their absence. The dependent oldest old are at highest risk of using the ultimate formal service of a skilled nursing home.

For the oldest old living in the community who require the assistance of others, a mixture of formal and informal services is possible (in the nursing home, all services are provided by the institution). The oldest old who have abundant economic and social-familial resources can often make the choices themselves. For example, they might hire a housekeeper for cleaning and cooking (formal services) but go shopping with a daughter. By hiring help in some areas and using public services in others, they can maintain an interdependent life-style in spite of limitations.

The Substitution of Formal for Informal Care

There is a widespread belief that if the formal system provides a service without cost, the family will reduce its efforts to help the elder (Brody, 1985). This is called the "substitution effect." Fear abounds that elders will be dumped on the publicly supported formal system. Yet even when the helping tasks require a caregiver, only one caregiver in ten makes any use of the formal system of care (Stone, Cafferata, and Sangl, 1987).

In the most extensive study to date, involving ten states, it was found that family caregivers did not reduce their efforts even when a full array of services was available at no charge (Harahan and Hamm, 1987). Although concern today is focused on the potential costs of health and social services for the elderly, this study suggests that costs will not become inflated due to the family's turning over the care to publicly funded programs, agencies, and/or institutions simply because such care is available.

Among friends and neighbors, however, a substitution effect was found in the ten-state study noted above. Friends and neighbors did reduce their helping activities when formal services became available. Nevertheless, there is evidence that the substitution effect could be prevented by active case management (Harahan and Hamm, 1987; Gutkin et al., 1987). Especially when an elder's needs increase, a case manager can take on the overall responsibility for care, encouraging friends and neighbors to continue with their usual helping tasks. Any extra help needed can be provided by formal services so that friends and neighbors are not overwhelmed by escalating needs.

The major expense for formal care is found in nursing home use. Even among the oldest old, however, there are two severely disabled (three or more PADL limitations) persons maintained at home for every three who are maintained in a nursing home (Manton and Soldo, 1985). Furthermore, when the elder does move into a nursing home, the patient and/or family collectively pays half (49.8%) of all nursing home costs on admission. Public funds from Medicaid pay 40%, and Medicare pays less than 5%, of the total expenditures on admission. The remaining 5% comes from other sources, including private insurance (National Center for Health Statistics, 1987b). For the oldest old, however, the eventual public costs are higher because they and their families are less likely to have the economic resources to pay for the extended stays that are often required (National Center for Health Statistics, 1987a). The growth of the 85-and-over population raises fears as to their "public expense," since they have a high probability of needing nursing home care for longer than six months. There is, however, a broad, growing consensus that the elderly should not have to impoverish themselves in order to obtain needed nursing home care (Brody, 1987).

Long-Term Care

A large proportion of the oldest old are at risk of needing long-term care before death. This is because they have a high risk of developing diseases and disorders for which there is no cure. These chronic conditions need continuous management with some combination of family help, medical services, and social services. These conditions may require modifications of the home or a move to alternative housing; in severe cases, a move to a nursing home is required. Unfortunately, what most people mean by long-term care is nursing home care. But the majority of long-term care takes place outside the nursing home and is managed by the elder and/or the family. Medicare provides only very limited help because it is oriented around acute care, not long-term care:

> Mr. Thomas, age 86, needs long-term care. He has severe Parkinson's disease and cannot get out of bed or even turn over. His wife turns him with the help of a mechanical lift, but she cannot do this more than twice a day. Consequently, he gets bedsores. These severe health problems do not qualify him for assistance from Medicare. When Mr. Thomas gets pneumonia, however, he can be admitted to the hospital, where all his bills will be covered. Following the hospitalization, he qualifies for home health care for three weeks. After that, any help must be paid for out-of-pocket. Only the acute care episode of pneumonia qualifies him for Medicare; the long-term care of his Parkinson's disease must be paid for out-of-pocket because the couple's income is too high for them to qualify for Medicaid. There are no other available services in their community.[1]

If the caregiver is not a spouse and does not wish to institutionalize the elder or live with the elder, there is often a very high cost to providing care:

> Mrs. R. [Ray], age 90, spent $21,600 in 1985 for her long-term care at home. Her sons arranged for two students to obtain room and board at a cost of $400 a month in extra grocery bills plus $150 a month in extra utilities. Long distance calls to her sons to manage her affairs cost $50 a month. There was a housekeeper during the week at $250 per week. She needed to rent a hospital bed at $50 per month. Taxis cost about $50 a month. In addition, medical insurance and out-of-pocket medical care costs were very high.[2]

Mrs. Ray is able to remain in her own home, avoiding both a nursing home and her sons' home, because she has the economic resources and the family resources—her sons—to arrange and manage her long-term care needs.

The types of care required by Mrs. Ray and Mr. Thomas are examples of long-term care. The need for long-term care really began at

---

[1]This case was provided by a colleague.
[2]The case of Mrs. R. was presented in detail by Torrens (1987).

age 82 for Mrs. Ray, when she had to give up driving and began to need help with shopping. A couple of years later, she also needed someone to manage her money and provide supervision in the evening. At age 90, she ended up in a nursing home. Long-term care includes a range of care, both medical and social, for the functionally disabled elderly. It is not acute care, and the individual is not expected to get well. Indeed, it can often happen, as with Mrs. Ray, that the individual gets progressively worse over the years. In a recent analysis of the Longitudinal Study of Aging (LSOA), only 7% of those 70 and over receiving help with any PADL limitations at the time of the first interview were free of limitations two years later, at the second interview (Kovar, 1987). Long-term care can be provided by family members and friends or through the formal system. It can be paid for by the person herself, as in Mrs. Ray's case, by other family members, or by public or philanthropic financing.

Linkages

In the United States, the provision of long-term care for the oldest old is hampered by a lack of linkages. As in Mrs. Ray's case, there may be a lack of linkages within the informal system: her sons lived at a considerable distance, and most of her local friends had died or were disabled. Furthermore, there was the additional problem of the lack of a good linkage between the formal and informal systems. These lacks meant that help often was not delivered in time because the sons did not realize quickly enough that help was needed. When they saw that she needed help, moreover, there was no place to turn for advice as to how to provide the help. Fortunately, Mrs. Ray had considerable economic resources, which, when managed by her sons, could provide her with adequate help in her own home as long as possible (Torrens, 1987).

There are, of course, some components of the formal care system that are linked. Hospital care is linked to placement in a nursing home; the hospital will locate a nursing home and arrange for the transfer. The nursing home will also link to a home health agency for certain personal care services. These services will be covered by Medicare and provided for a limited time. But after a hospital stay, the oldest old person living alone is likely to need personal care services for longer than Medicare provides, even if the prognosis is good. If the elder has adequate income, he will often be on his own in the private market trying to hire help.

The community may offer a range of services. Home-delivered meals are often provided by a church-related agency; a specialized transportation service with door-to-door assistance may be available through the local senior center. For elders with limited economic resources, there may be homemaker chore services operated through the local department of public assistance as well as special housing designed for the elderly operated by the housing department of the local government. In many communities, more than four different organizations may be involved, each with its own set of procedures and qualifying rules. The oldest old senior must be a very good manager to put together an appropriate service package.

Even when a needed service does exist and the elder is effective in locating it, the elder may not qualify because his or her income, although modest, is too high. Even if the elder qualifies, as is often the case with special subsidized housing for seniors, there may be no unit available in the community. The elder is then put on a waiting list and meanwhile must cope with the hazards of his or her current apartment for a year or more.

Since these services are not formally linked, the responsibility rests with the elder. Without an active caregiver, an elder could be overwhelmed. If, as is often the case, there are additional medical problems, such as fatigue due to arteriosclerosis or mild cognitive impairment due to a previous stroke, the elder could end up back in the hospital.[3] The lack of any coordinated system of care often results in the "911 cycle" for the elderly who live alone. Dialing 911 will bring help in the form of an ambulance and a trip to the hospital for treatment. When released, and, it is hoped, linked with a home health agency, the elder will manage for a few weeks, especially if friends and neighbors provide a lot of help. But without effective follow-through and long-term care supplementing that provided by friends and neighbors, the elder (or his or her anxious and overwhelmed neighbors) will again dial 911 and begin the cycle anew.

The foregoing examples point to the need for a linkage service. This can be provided by a case manager. The case manager acts as a master programmer for each client; needs are assessed and economic, social-familial, and community resources are analyzed. The help of friends and neighbors can be coordinated with formal services, thereby preserving these informal helping networks as the elder's functional ability declines (Gutkin et al., 1987). The client's preferences are taken into account and a plan for service delivery is designed and arranged. The case manager follows through to determine quality of care and client

---

[3]Preliminary studies support this effect with the implementation of the diagnostic related groups (DRGs). Among the elderly, hospital services, including length of stay, were reduced the most for the oldest old (Gay and Kronenfeld, 1987).

satisfaction. Unfortunately, case managers are still rare. As a result, the array of long-term care options continues to operate as discrete services. The only widely built-in linkage is that provided through acute medical care. If the initial problem had not resulted in hospitalization, it would have been difficult to get even the limited Medicare payment and assistance with home health care. The only coordinated linkage in the formal system—hospital to nursing home to home health care agency—would be unavailable to an individual with arteriosclerosis who was gradually able to do less and less but who had no acute episode such as a broken bone or pneumonia to qualify him or her for entry into the system.

A Continuum of Care

Ideally, long-term care should be provided in the context of a continuum of care, available to all those who need help of any sort. One definition of a continuum of care is "an integrated, client-oriented system of care composed of both services and integrating mechanisms that guides and tracks clients over time through a comprehensive array of health, mental health and social services spanning all levels of intensity of care" (Evashwick, 1987:23).

One could enter the continuum at any point—say, at the need for housing—and be linked with all other services. There would be no time restrictions; the care would be provided as long as needed. Desires of the client as to housing and home help would be responded to by provision of a flexible system. The most appropriate roles of family and friends would be worked out with the client's desires in mind. Self-determination with respect to physical rehabilitation, choice of living arrangements, and choice of helper would be enhanced. Working with the client's preferences, case managers would be available to provide the "integrating mechanism" for service coordination.

One element that needs to be added to this continuum of care is the role of the elder in helping others or even contributing to the community. Special attention is needed to involve family, friends, and neighbors in interdependent, reciprocal arrangements. No one aspect of the informal helping network should be overburdened if at all possible. Elders, where possible, can be shown how to limit any burden on family and friends. The cultural ideal of independence often obscures the important role of interdependence in long-term care; many elders can give in return for what they receive. Self-determination does not necessarily mean having to do it all yourself but involves being able to negotiate the terms of the help received. Rather than merely attempting to relieve "the effects of illness and to maintain or enhance functional capacities to maximize personal independence" (Vogel and Palmer, 1985:v), long-term care should aim at enhancing the person's ability to negotiate the terms of the help needed and should encourage interdependence within the family and community context, so far as is possible.

Although it is important to keep in mind the broader goals of a continuum of care to meet both acute and long-term care needs of the elderly in a client-oriented, integrated system, it is also important to examine the necessary components of such a system of formal services. The following array of programs has been proposed by Estes and Harrington (1985:253–254) as those that could provide a continuum of care for both acute and long-term care needs:

> Basic acute care [hospital based]:
> > acute care
> > ambulatory care
> > drug coverage
> > [health promotion and disease prevention]
> > other health-related services
>
> Institutional care (licensed health facilities):
> > rehabilitation
> > skilled nursing services
> > intermediate care services
> > psychiatric services
>
> Residential care (homes without nursing care):
> > group homes
> > family homes
> > personal care
> > boarding care
> > foster care
> > congregate living
> > [assisted living]
>
> Community services:
> > hospice care—for terminally ill
> > respite care—short-term care to relieve caretakers
> > day health care—health and rehabilitative services
> > day care—social programs without health services
> > sheltered workshops—supervised work settings
> > community mental health
> > legal services

protective services
information and referral
transportation
case management—coordinator of care
home health nurse/aide
homemaker chore services
meals
housing
combination of the above programs

Gaps in the Continuum

Some communities offer all of the services listed above; others offer many of these services, but there may be significant gaps, such as in the provision of specialized transportation (paratransit) services. For the oldest old, a gap in either general public transit or specialized transit could prove highly detrimental to an independent or interdependent life-style (Thomas, 1985b). Furthermore, since many of the oldest old have problems of mild cognitive impairment, limited energy, low level of education, or limited fluency in English, they are especially in need of assistance in coordinating and managing the services that are available. Unfortunately, case management, which provides this type of service is not often available. For many of the oldest old, the only services easily accessible are those that can be termed "medical" and are thereby provided in the basic acute care or the institutional care categories noted above.

Federal Programs for a Continuum of Care

The major federal programs that provide health and social services for the elderly were passed by Congress in 1965. These include two programs targeted directly toward the needs of the elderly: the Older Americans Act (Title III) and Medicare. Two additional programs—Medicaid and Title XX of the Social Security Act (the Social Services Block Grant Program)—were targeted for persons "at risk" or "in need" in all age groups. Together with federal housing programs, these four legislative acts form the bases of government provision for the elderly.

The Older Americans Act

The Older Americans Act of 1965 (OAA) outlined the following broad objectives at its initial passage:

1. An adequate income in retirement in accordance with the American standard of living.

2. The best possible physical and mental health which science can make available and without regard to economic status.

3. Suitable housing, independently selected, designed and located with reference to special needs and available at costs which older citizens can afford.

4. Full restorative services for those who require institutional care.

8. Efficient community services, including access to low-cost transportation, which provide a choice in supported living arrangements and social assistance in a coordinated manner and which are readily available when needed.

9. Immediate benefit from proven research knowledge which can sustain and improve health and happiness.

10. Freedom, independence, and the free exercise of individual initiative in planning and managing their own lives. (U.S. Senate, Special Committee on Aging, 1985a:1–2)

These objectives appear to have been written to meet the requirements of a continuum of care. Although the emphasis is on independence and individualism, the objectives are compatible with interdependence as well. Meeting these objectives would be especially relevant in preserving self-determination among the oldest old. Adequate income, suitable housing, and efficient community services are essential ingredients for sustaining an interdependent life-style and making the most effective use of social and familial resources for the oldest old.

Congress further modified these objectives in later amendments to OAA. These modifications made them even more relevant to attaining a continuum of care in terms of both acute and long-term care. Specifically, the need to provide help in the home was recognized as critical, and objective 4 was modified to require "a comprehensive array of community-based, long-term care services adequate to appropriately sustain older people in their communities and in their homes." Opportunities for self-determination were to be expanded, and premature dependence in a nursing home was to be avoided. There was to be "a continuum of care for the vulnerable elderly." (U.S. Senate, Special Committee on Aging, 1985a:2). These amendments laid a basis for the development of a wide range of services to help elders in their activities of daily living, both in home management needs and in personal care needs. It also provided a rationale for helping families who were caring for their elderly relatives, through providing a range of respite services.

Even the need to avoid the role of the passive, dependent service recipient was acknowledged by a later amendment, which required full participation by the elderly "in the planning and operation of community based services and programs provided for their benefit" (U.S. Senate, Special Committee on Aging, 1985a:2). As amended, objective 10 recognizes the need to avoid dependence in all forms. The fulfillment of these objectives would provide for much greater self-determination among the oldest old. Such programs are critical for the oldest old because today's medical knowledge, while promising a long life, cannot promise freedom from functional disability.

Unfortunately, OAA has provided neither the level of funding nor the administrative authority required to attain these broad objectives. A wide range of community-based services has been developed, however. These services include information and referral services; outreach assistance; transportation; legal services; protective services; counseling; recreation; education; congregate and shared housing; ombudsman services for nursing home patients; nutrition services; meals on wheels; senior center meals; adult day care and other respite services; in-home care, including home health aides as well as homemaker chore services; and case management. This broad array of services exists, however, primarily in principle. In practice, about 60% of the modest services budget ($669 million in 1985) went for nutrition and food programs (O'Shaughnessy and Price, 1987:204), which in the vast majority of cases means meals for seniors at the local center. Only 10% of the service budget paid for meals on wheels, a program that is more likely to serve the oldest old than would meals at senior centers (O'Shaughnessy and Price, 1987:205).

In the 1987 reauthorization of OAA, a strong statement was made urging provision of nonmedical in-home services, including homemaker and home health aides, chore maintenance, and in-home respite care for families. However, the amount of special extra funds authorized for these services in fiscal year 1988 was a modest $25 million. That amount is less than one-sixteenth of the $414.7 million authorized for meals at senior centers (U.S. Senate, Special Committee on Aging, 1987b:Table 1). Furthermore, only $4.8 million of the $25 million authorized for the extra services was actually made available to area agencies on aging for service delivery. Although the 1987 reauthorization stressed the importance of in-home services, all funds available under Title III were still very limited relative to the growing need.

Although the objectives of OAA include *medical and social services,* there is no broad jurisdictional authority to provide a link between these two. Clients can easily get lost in moving from acute medical care to available social services because they do not hear about these services from their doctor or nurse. Reimbursement of medical care under Medicare is administered directly by the Health Care Financing Administration (HCFA); reimbursement of medical care under Medicaid is administered by the state medicaid agency, which is monitored by HCFA. Neither program is linked directly to the federal Administration on Aging or the state agencies on aging that administer the programs of OAA. Furthermore, total funding for all services under OAA was only $669 million in 1985.

The limited funding for OAA programs, together with the lack of a broad authority, has meant, in practice, that they are more likely to be in the form of discrete services—for example, provision of nutrition services rather than a linkage service for all programs for the elderly. Under OAA, case management programs could form a critical link between health services and other social services for all of the functionally disabled elderly. This case management service could be especially important for the oldest old in coordinating in-home services provided by family, friends, and neighbors with privately purchased formal services and those provided by the government. All elderly persons are eligible, and there is no limitation on how long the elder can receive the service. Yet with such limited funding, little case management is available, and in many areas there are few in-home services as well, except for the meals on wheels programs.

To date, the major accomplishment of OAA has been to provide opportunities for a continuum of care to be developed (Binstock, 1987). Under this program, attention has been directed toward the needs of elders and, more recently, toward the need for in-home long-term care. OAA has been critical in establishing what is called the "aging network." The legislation set up the Administration on Aging (AOA), which provides money for state agencies on aging; these state agencies then fund 664 area agencies on aging (O'Shaughnessy and Price, 1987:203). The objective of these agencies is to plan, coordinate, and link to other programs. A broad network is in place, but with neither funding nor authority, its role in improving the delivery of formal services to the elderly has been restricted.

Title XX—Social Services Block Grants

Title XX of the Social Security Act (the Social Services Block Grant Program) was passed by Congress in 1965, the same year the Older Americans Act was passed. It could have filled many of the gaps in OAA programs, as one of the primary goals of this legislation was to provide services to prevent or reduce "inappropriate institutional care by providing for community-based care." Here is a program that would seem to be targeted for the oldest old population, with their high risk of institutionalization. The eligibility criteria include being "at risk" or "in need," but there are no longer any federal requirements as to income limits or payments according to income.

Although this program also sounds excellent in principle, its implementation has been limited in terms of both funding and eligibility. States have instituted a wide range of income tests by which many of the oldest old would not qualify or would be reluctant to claim benefits. Some states restrict eligibility to those who are receiving SSI payments. Funding is limited ($2.7 billion in fiscal year 1985), and the program has, in the past, emphasized services to families on welfare (AFDC) in order to help them become self-supporting. In 1983, only 11% of all Title XX recipients received home-based services, and, although data on the age of recipients are unavailable (O'Shaughnessy and Price, 1987:203), it is estimated that only $309 million was spent under Title XX on providing services to the elderly in fiscal year 1986 (U.S. Senate, Special Committee on Aging, 1987a:105).

The federal government provides grants to states for funding Title XX services. These services, however, are most likely to be administered by the state and local departments of public assistance, which serve primarily families on welfare (AFDC). Some funding may be channeled through the state or area agency on aging, but in general there is little coordination between OAA programs and Title XX programs. Furthermore, the potential recipient usually has to deal with the "welfare bureaucracy," which in many areas has a reputation for being chaotic, unfriendly, and confusing. In Los Angeles, which has one of the largest Title XX homemaker chore programs in the country, it is difficult even for case managers to process the red tape necessary for the delivery of service to their clients.

Medicare and Medicaid

Title XX and the Older Americans Act contain the appropriate objectives to develop a broad array of community-based services and to link those services in a continuum of care. Limited funding, however, has severely hampered the ability of these programs to develop long-term community-based care. In contrast, the two other programs, Medicare and Medicaid, are spending billions, not just millions, of dollars. These services, however, tend to be highly restricted, with a predominantly medical component. They are targeted for either acute care (Medicare) or long-term institutional care (Medicaid). Estimated expenditures in 1986 were $64.4 billion under Medicare and $8.9 billion under Medicaid. If all federal funding for health and social services for the elder is totaled, [4] including $4.8 billion for housing, the outlay was $87.6 billion in 1986, of which 89% was spent on medical and health services (U.S. Senate, Special Committee on Aging, 1987:104–105). In many communities, the only services available to all of the elderly are those that are paid for by Medicare—doctors' visits and hospital stays. Home health care is generally available under Medicare, but only under an acute care model—that is, if the person shows signs of getting better—not under a long-term care model, in which the prognosis is uncertain at best and further deterioration is expected at worst. In the case of Mr. Thomas discussed earlier in this chapter, his Parkinson's disease did not qualify him for in-home care. He could obtain help under Medicare only when he suffered from pneumonia, an acute illness from which he could be expected to recover.

For more than two decades acute medical care, funded by Medicare, has dominated the delivery of services to the elderly. In fact, 73% of all federal expenditures for formal services to the elderly were funded by Medicare in 1986. In 1965, when the legislation was passed, the service system of doctors and acute care hospitals was already in place. Furthermore, these medical authorities were allocated a large measure of control over the distribution of services. In spite of an initial reluctance, these professions and institutions were in a key position to benefit by a rapid expansion of their services. Furthermore, this expansion of acute care services to the elderly—including an increase in their costs—was never really questioned until the budget crisis of the 1980s. Acute medical care had become a right of our senior citizens; eligibility was defined as broadly as possible, and many of those who would not have been covered initially were included under special provisions if they had reached the age of 72 by 1968.[5] The federal government would insure the

---

[4]This total excludes all cash payments, such as Social Security, SSI, and veterans' compensations; it also excludes state matching funds.
[5]These are cases in which the individual had not accumulated sufficient credits of Social Security coverage to qualify.

elderly against impoverishment due to large medical bills. The expansion of Medicare coverage proposed for 1989 similarly reflects a belief that the elderly should not have to worry about impoverishment due to acute health care costs (Tolchin, 1988).[6]

The American value of independence and self-help was stretched in the case of the elderly. The elderly citizen would no longer have to exhaust his or her own economic resources or the family's resources in order to obtain medical care. The fact that the elderly were facing a large risk of high medical costs on a fixed income prompted this move to societal interdependence and a social right to medical care (Brody, 1987). Like Social Security, Medicare is built on the interdependent model of social insurance. The government collects the payments: Part A contributions for hospitalization are made when the individual is working and contributing to the Medicare fund; Part B coverage for doctors' visits is a voluntary deduction from the elder's Social Security check.[7] Medicare is not provided to everyone but is available only to those who have contributed. Nevertheless, the rules of eligibility are generous.

Another important influence encouraging public provision of acute medical care was the assumption that adult children should not be responsible for either the cost or the provision of this care. Adult children should not themselves be impoverished by their elder parents' illness, but neither should adult children attempt to provide medical care directly. Unlike other services, such as housing, transportation, and personal care, families are not expected to provide medical treatment or advice. Furthermore, because of the expert nature of medical care, there was already a built-in gatekeeping authority in the role of physician. The physician could determine the need for help and delineate the responsibility of the family. No cash need be given to elderly individuals or their families; physicians, respected authorities in our society, would

---

[6]These changes in Medicare include expanded hospital coverage, physician care, home health care, and respite care. There is to be some coverage of prescription drugs by 1991. Nursing home care would still be limited to a skilled nursing home for only 150 days (Tolchin, 1988).

[7]Part A is the Hospital Insurance (HI) program, which covers hospital stays plus limited nursing home care and home health services. Payments by contributors (employees and employers) covered 84% of expenditures for this program in 1983. Part B, the Supplemental Medical Insurance (SMI) program, covers "physician care, outpatient hospital visits, home health care and other services." In 1983, insurance premiums covered only 26% of expenditures. The balance of Medicare expenditures is paid for by general tax revenues (Rabin and Stockton, 1987:81). The 1988 amendments that expand Medicare coverage will be financed by premiums deducted from Social Security checks plus a surtax on beneficiaries' income (Tolchin, 1988).

be paid directly for services provided to the elderly. Therefore, in terms of medical services, it was easy to implement the Medicare program. Physicians were already functioning as gatekeepers for delivery of medical help, either in or out of the hospital. With such a respected gatekeeping authority in place, it is not surprising that a social right to medical care quickly became established.

In 1965, when Medicare was passed, it was also recognized that the poor needed medical services that they could not afford. The principle is not one of social insurance composed of contributors and beneficiaries but of government largess offered to those who could prove themselves to be poor. The intention of Medicaid, therefore, was to provide the poor with acute medical services. Participating states were to provide such services to their low-income elderly; many states provide Medicaid *only* to their elderly SSI recipients.[8] The Medicaid legislation (Title XX), as amended, did contain provisions to pay for nursing home care for those who could qualify as poor. The program is funded by both the federal and state governments; states are required to provide matching funds. In 1984, the states put up 22-50% of the funds for all Medicaid expenditures (Rabin and Stockton, 1987:82).

At the time of passage, there was little concern that payments for nursing home care would become so large, since the potential of a growing need for long-term care in the aging population, and especially among the old old (those 75 and over), had not yet been recognized (Brody, 1974, as cited in Brody, 1987). The unanticipated preponderance of funds for nursing home costs in Medicaid federal and state budgets has led to some limitations in nursing home placement. Concern with the costs of nursing home care under Medicaid finally led, in 1981, to the creation of a special authority, 2176 Waivers, to provide a range of long-term community care services in order to prevent or forestall placement in a nursing home. This program, however, is available only in selected communities and only to those who qualify as poor.[9] This is the only program in which acute and long-term medical services are integrated with social services, such as case management, homemaker chore services, adult day-care services, and respite care.

Medicare and Medicaid predominate in the delivery of formal services, and within that framework there is a strong institutional bias.

---

[8]Other SSI recipients and AFDC recipients usually qualify as "categorical needy."
[9]States may define income and asset tests by the more liberal standards used for nursing home payments. The cost of services, however, was not to exceed the cost of nursing home care. "As of June 30, 1985, HCFA had approved 107 waivers in 46 states" (O'Shaughnessy and Price, 1987:200).

About three-quarters of the funds cover institutional care in hospitals or nursing homes. The vast majority of the remainder goes for doctors' fees. "Less than 2% of either Medicare or Medicaid funds were spent on home care" in 1978 (Lubben, 1987).[10] The institutional bias of both acute and long-term care was bolstered by the Hill-Burton Act, which was to stimulate hospital construction and later, nursing home construction. The institutional bias reflects primarily the bureaucratic operation of the programs and their funding. The major type of government-provided formal service to elders who need help in personal care occurs in an institutional setting and is structured along medical lines. The terms "skilled nursing facility" (SNF) and "convalescent hospital" point to this medical bias. There is little recognition within the system that SNFs are actually residences where the average person will live for two years or more. The residents do have extensive health-related needs, but it is their personal care needs that consume most of the institution's resources.

Townsend (1981) has called this system "structured dependency." This care model endorses the form of a total institution with a hierarchical system (Goffman, 1961). In this system, doctors and administrators are at the top; aides, who give 90% of the personal care, are at the bottom. The patient is dependent on having an aide who is a caring person; there is often no recourse when an aide is uncaring or even abusive.[11] Patients have forfeited any chance of negotiating for their personal choices. They are at the most restrictive level of care.

The Medicalization of Help

Under Medicare, the fact that the physician was available to serve as gatekeeping authority was critical in the process of the medicalization of formal services. When a service could be labeled "medical," the problem of who would function as gatekeeping authority was easily resolved. Society has taken responsibility primarily for those whose need for help

---

[10]Recent efforts to cut hospital stays under Medicare Part A have no doubt contributed to increases in expenditures on home care under Medicare Part B. The overall increase in expenditures under Part B has resulted in a 35.8% increase in the Part B insurance premium (Callahan, 1987).

[11]Concern over conditions in many nursing homes has resulted in a special OAA authorization of $20 billion for fiscal year 1988 for ombudsmen—persons whose job is to check out all complaints about the quality of care in a nursing home.

can be defined medically and can be delivered either in a hospital or by a physician. It is possible to obtain such help as a right, as long as the help needed is medically defined. The physician can deter those whose need for formal services is not truly medical and who therefore should receive help informally, from the family.

The government steps in and provides additional help only when social-familial resources and economic resources are exhausted and the need for help escalates to the point at which institutionalization is necessary. Provision of custodial care in a nursing home is not under the direct control of the physician; here the gatekeeping function is performed by the institution. The individual must first spend his or her own assets; only after those assets are mostly spent can the patient qualify for government assistance in terms of Medicaid nursing home payment. This service, which often comprises primarily help with activities of daily living, is provided in a medical facility. Medicare, which provides for acute care hospitalization, offers only limited help for nursing home payment; government help is available only for those who are institutionalized and needy under Medicaid. In order to get publicly provided help in managing their daily lives, individuals must become dependent on the institution for care *and* qualify as poor and become dependent on the state for paying for that care. Caplow (1977:xiv) notes the serious problems of "the imposition of an inappropriate medical model on old age institutions as a condition of receiving public funds" and "the increasing unresponsiveness of these institutions to residents' preferences." The options now available for the oldest old severely restrict self-determination.

Furthermore, requiring institutionalization in order to get help often forces on the elder the harsh choice between surviving at home without help, imposing on an adult child's family, or submitting to the control of an institution. Help is provided by society only when it is incorporated into society's mechanism of social control (Clark, 1983). For those needing help with their daily activities, not much has changed in the options society offers since the days of the poorhouse (Townsend, 1981). In-home help permits self-determination, but there is no effective gatekeeper to deter those individuals and families who might "abuse the system."

States, which must bear the front-line responsibility for provision of formal services to their elderly populations, respond according to fiscal incentives. Monsignor Charles J. Fahey, director of the Third Age Center at Fordham University, makes the following point:

> State Government's first principle has been to maximize Medicare (no state money being involved). The second has been to maximize Medicaid

(open-ended federal matching). Virtually every human frailty has been defined as a medical problem to capture federal Medicaid funds. It is questionable whether this policy has resulted in the most humane and economic technique of meeting human need. (Fahey, 1984:8)

Although the acceptance of this social right to receive help for the elderly has given them much-needed access to acute medical care and institutional care, it has also meant that the medical model has dominated the form of help delivered. The medical model has been characterized as individualistic and mechanistic; a central component of this model is the analogy of the body as a machine (Rossdale, 1965). The body-machine analogy implies that the task of medical science is to understand how the machine is structured and how it operates so that physicians can intervene and readjust the faulty mechanism. Surgery and drugs tend to be the dominant treatment forms. Those who deliver this service, of course, must be physicians or their designates, and the setting is the doctor's office or hospital. The medical model emphasizes providing active treatment, doing something to the patient in order to achieve the anticipated recovery.

The medical model is based on the expectations that the condition is acute and that procedural interventions by physicians will promote the patient's recovery. Yet the oldest old are more likely to have chronic conditions, such as Alzheimer's, for which there are no clear medical procedures and there is no expectation of recovery. For other chronic health problems of the oldest old, surgery (i.e., hip replacement) (cf U.S. Senate, Special Committee on Aging, 1985c) or drug therapy may be inappropriate due to concurrent health problems. Even with acute conditions such as hip fractures, the consequence for the oldest old is most likely to be long-term disability. A major medical need among the oldest old, however, is for thorough diagnostic examinations, because of the common occurrence of multiple diseases (some of which may be treatable) and the underreporting of symptoms (Rowe, 1985a). Yet time spent in determining a diagnosis, which may take more than an hour for the oldest old, is not reimbursed by Medicare at the same rate as are specific procedures. Medical care is only available within the constraints of the medical model, which is less applicable to the special medical needs of the oldest old.

Even more critical, however, is the fact that much of the help that the oldest old need because of their chronic health problems is not medical at all. Oldest old persons with chronic conditions often need help in simply managing their daily lives. They need to be exempted from some normal responsibilities, such as, for example, bathing themselves, because they no longer have the necessary ability and the risk of severe injury is too great. Therefore, they must assume what Parsons (1951) calls the "sick role." Other persons, notably family members, are expected to take over these responsibilities. This sick-role behavior and family assistance are assumed by Parsons to be temporary, however; it is expected that the person will get well and manage for himself. But for the oldest old, the need for this help is likely to be permanent. It is clearly the expectation of the government that families can and should step in and provide help. Yet even though a family may be able to do so on a temporary basis, a need for permanent help may easily overwhelm the family and put the elder in a nonreciprocal, dependent role. In addition, reliance on the family as backup for this kind of care is based on the assumption that the oldest old person still has family members able to provide help.

The legitimation of social responsibility for medical help in the past two decades, although critical for medical needs, has constrained society's approach to the elderly. If the help needed is not medical, responsibility ultimately rests with the oldest old individuals and their families. Yet this medicalization of help will be far from adequate to meet the minimum needs of this population in the near future. In examining the public provision of help to the elderly, it is clear that the process of medicalization has been a dominant trend. The medicalization of a number of perceived social problems has an involved history. It determines the manner in which "solutions" are proposed and help is delivered. Illich (1976) claims that the process has encompassed a "medicalization of life." More recently, McKinlay (1987) has described the "medicalization of aging." Medical authority, then, becomes necessary in order to manage everyday life. This process creates unnecessary dependence, especially among the oldest old. They are most likely to need help in their everyday life but are not provided with viable options, such as suitable housing or in-home help, that could enable them to manage their own lives.

In developing the concept of the medicalization of deviance, Conrad and Schneider (1980:23) note specifically the role of law and medicine in terms of labeling illnesses and developing appropriate treatment. This labeling involves the medical profession, lawmakers, and the current administration's interpretation and enforcement of the law. With joint state-federal programs such as Medicaid, it also involves state legislators and administrators. The medical profession, however, is the key in defining problems as medical (Clark, 1983). Policymakers are also careful to define entitlement to care within narrow medical constraints, fearing that a broad provision for publicly funded care will lead to an abdication of individual and family responsibility; the assumption is made that individuals and families will dump their elderly on the state because they couldn't be bothered to care. A strict definition of medical need would restrict such widespread potential abuse of the system. Nevertheless, many lawmakers, as well as the general public, do feel that families are, in fact, abusing the system by "dumping" their elderly relatives in institutions (Brody, 1985). New ways of preventing "abuse" involve simply restricting the number of beds available under Medicaid.

Recent proposals to expand Medicare in order to limit out-of-pocket expenses among the elderly only suggest a further medicalization of help. Furthermore, the emphasis on utilizing Medicare funds does not serve the special needs of the oldest old for noninstitutional care. Although the oldest old are at a much higher risk of developing chronic health problems, they are not heavy users of Medicare Part B (SMI) for doctors' visits. In fact, the usage in 1984, calculated at $704 per year per person 80 years of age and over, is not much higher than the $559 per-person-per-year expenditure on those aged 70–74. This is not surprising, since Medicare often does not provide the kind of in-home help the oldest old are likely to need. Furthermore, it does not fully support their special needs for diagnostic attention, even when they can manage the logistics of getting to the doctor's office.

Indeed, the only sure way of having the government provide help for the oldest old in their activities of daily living has been for them to qualify for institutional care, which can be labeled as medical care and which occurs within a medical facility. Those 80 years of age and over are heavy users of Medicare funds for hospitalization (HI). Federal benefits for this group in 1984 were $1,781 per person, in comparison with $995 for those aged 70–74.[12] Similarly, those aged 80 and over are very heavy users of federal Medicaid funds; their usage is estimated at $864 per person per year, in contrast with only $60 per person per year among those aged 70–74 (Torrey, 1985:379). Although help provided in a medical facility, hospital, or nursing home is an essential component of a continuum of care, this form of help does not meet the wide-ranging needs of the oldest old for noninstitutional help, nor does it respect their right to self-determination.

---

[12]See Torrey (1985:379). However, Medicare expenses in the last year of life decline sharply at age 85. This is, no doubt, due in part to a substitution of nursing home care for hospital care (Riley et al., 1987).

Other, Noninstitutional Government Services

Could more help be provided by the government for long-term care at home? Recent concern over the rising costs of Medicaid incurred by nursing homes, as well as the personal economic catastrophe of nursing home placement, has led to initiatives for government insurance coverage of long-term care and especially at-home care (Brody, 1987; *The New York Times*, 1987; AARP, 1987). Demonstration projects have shown that case managers can effectively mobilize existing services for clients living at home and for their families. These projects, however, are targeted for the elderly who are already at high risk of being institutionalized (Harahan and Hamm, 1987). Although these recent initiatives have broadened the concept of the elder's right to receive help beyond that which is strictly medical, they have concentrated on those elderly whose need for help is so great that they are probably already dependent an probably already have a caregiver. More attention needs to be paid to the elderly whose limited physiological resources put them at risk because they need another's help, yet who still have sufficient resources—including economic and social-familial resources—to be interdependent if appropriate government services are available. The two kinds of formal services most often needed to prevent dependence for this at-risk group of oldest old are housing and transportation. Unfortunately, these two essential services are often the area of the greatest gaps in a continuum of care for the oldest old.

Transportation

A survey conducted by the U.S. Department of Transportation showed that nearly half of the urban "transportation handicapped" were elderly persons. They were not homebound but had difficulty in using public transportation because of a health problem. Primary problems involved "needing a seat," difficulty in getting "on and off," and difficulty in getting to the bus stop (Thomas, 1985b:464–466). These problems are most likely to occur in the oldest old population. Oldest old persons who have social-familial resources can rely on family and friends for a ride; those who have economic resources can use taxis. But use of taxi services can consume limited economic resources, and reliance on friends and relatives can exhaust social-familial resources, making the elder prematurely dependent. In rural areas, moreover, taxi services often are unavailable and automobile ownership is limited (Thomas, 1985b:468).

Transportation services are subject to the same problems as are the other services in terms of fragmentation. There are multiple funding sources. Besides the programs discussed above, there are special services available from the Department of Transportation (DOT) for urban mass transit for the elderly and handicapped. Some communities, however, have no specialized transportation, and other communities have found themselves with a rash of programs:

> In 1975, Pinellas County, Florida had 26 different [transportation] projects serving the elderly and handicapped. Among all the projects there were 40 vehicles (not including taxis and cars driven by volunteers) and "26 separate budgets, maintenance bills, drivers and administrations." (U.S. House of Representatives, Select Committee on Aging, as quoted in Thomas, 1985b:468–469)

The availability of transportation and other services can also be constrained by strict geographic restrictions. Living four blocks outside the city limits, for example, can often result in a person's not being eligible for services:

> Mr. and Mrs. Young and their adult daughter urgently needed transportation as well as other in-home services. Mr. Young, at age 86, was dependent because of a stroke. His adult daughter and wife shared the caregiver role. But his wife, now 82, had her own health problems and had the use of only one arm; the adult daughter was in a wheelchair. The family could no longer manage using the available public transportation, but they were not eligible for the door-to-door service of the special van. The van could only serve persons within the city limits. This family lived four blocks outside the city limits.

This family's situation illustrates the need for more than a bus system that makes regular stops. In the DOT survey of the transportation handicapped, the majority preferred a paratransit system that goes door-to-door, meeting the needs of each individual rider. This type of system could meet the special needs of 42% of the elderly transportation handicapped who need the help of another person while traveling (Thomas, 1985b:474–475). In New York City, even those who have the money to pay for a taxi may find that "cabdrivers do not want to stop for fares who need help getting in and out," (Rimer, 1987). It is essential that the oldest old conserve their limited economic and social-familial resources in order to prevent dependence. Paratransit services can be a central factor in prevention of dependence, yet there appear to be few hopeful signs for future improvement (Rich and Baum, 1984:177).

Housing

The objective of the Older Americans Act of 1965 of providing suitable housing for all of the elderly has become more remote with each passing year. In this area, so critical to self-determination, the decade of the 1970s provided much rhetoric but limited housing assistance for those in need. In the 1980s, money for the special housing needs of the elderly at risk of dependence has dwindled further. Meanwhile, the cost of housing in the private market has soared. Now the housing problem has reached the point at which some of the elderly are joining the ranks of the homeless. Housing needs, especially for the oldest old, will grow rapidly (Newman, 1986), and a crisis management approach can only result in more of the very old seeking refuge in temporary shelters or nursing homes. Adequate housing cannot be provided on an emergency basis. Indeed, even the short term is too short to construct or rehabilitate housing units appropriate to the needs of the oldest old. And yet, without appropriate housing options, the oldest old are at highest risk of losing their self-determination and becoming dependent on their families or on institutions.

The Need for a Continuum in Housing

Housing is an essential service component in a continuum of care providing for the long-term care needs of the oldest old. This component itself should form a continuum ranging from services for the functionally able elderly home owner through institutional care for the most severely functionally disabled (Thomas, 1985a). A comprehensive array of housing units should be available at affordable prices for all of the elderly, especially the oldest old. Instead of a continuum, however, only the extremes of the spectrum are supported. At one extreme, institutional care is provided, primarily through Medicaid funding from HCFA, and the construction of nursing homes is supported by construction loans under the Department of Housing and Urban Development (HUD). At the other extreme, functionally able elderly home owners are supported by a variety of favorable tax benefits at the federal level (mortgage interest deductions and one-time capital gains exclusions) as well as a range of state and local tax benefits. Government funding for these two extremes of a housing continuum has experienced substantial increases since 1980 (Turner, 1986:50).[13] Yet the oldest old are most in need of programs in the middle of the continuum in order to preserve their independence and/or interdependence. The oldest old are least likely to benefit from policies favoring home owners and most likely to need financial assistance and/or special services for their special housing needs.

Congress has recognized these needs in setting forth legislation for low-income public housing, low-income rental assistance (Section 8), and direct loans to nonprofit agencies for construction of special housing for the elderly and handicapped (Section 202). These efforts, however, have been very limited by low levels of funding. As a result, there are simply not enough units, and the waiting lists are long. For the most successful program serving the elderly and handicapped, Section 202, "the average wait is over one year and nearly one in four applicants is forced to wait five or more years" (U.S. Senate, Special Committee on Aging, 1984b:3). Public housing, the least successful program, has been plagued by maintenance problems (such as malfunctioning elevators) and high crime rates, making this form of housing especially unsuitable for the oldest old. In 1987, Congress passed the first housing bill since 1980, indicating a renewed awareness of the problem. The level of funding, however, remains low, with $1.68 billion provided for low-income rental assistance (Section 8) and $1.71 billion allocated for special elderly housing (Section 202) (*Congressional Quarterly Inc.*, 1988).

In addition to the need for suitable, affordable housing, Congress has also recognized the need to link in-home formal services directly with housing. The Congregate Housing Service Program (Title IV of the 1978 Housing Act) was passed in 1978. This program ideally would back up the other programs, providing a continuum of housing to meet long-term care needs. But again, funding has been very limited, and the services offered have been largely restricted to food programs (Thomas, 1985a:404). Overall, total expenditures under the HUD housing programs to meet the needs of the noninstitutionalized low-income and functionally disabled elderly were $4.9 billion in 1984; in that same year, an estimated $5.1 billion was spent by HCFA for nursing home care under Medicaid (U.S. Senate, Special Committee on Aging, 1987a: 94–104).

---

[13]Tax losses from the one-time capital gains exclusion probably amounted to more than $950 million in 1985 (Turner, 1986:51), more than funding for all programs under OAA.

Without a change in emphasis, the majority of the oldest old are likely to fall through the large cracks in the middle of the housing continuum. The lack of suitable housing, furthermore, can directly increase the risk of future dependence, as is the case with Mrs. Miranda, a 90-year-old widow living in New York City:

> To get to the bus, Mrs. Miranda, arthritic and nearly blind, painfully makes her way down the four narrow flights of stairs in her tenement. "I hold on to the bannister and count the steps," she said, describing her descent . . . matter-of-factly. . . . "Going down, it's like a slope." There are 57 steps.
> Mrs. Miranda, who has outlived her only child, a son, as well as her husband, is trapped in the three room apartment. . . .
> Lately, she has started losing her balance without warning. She has fallen twice on her building staircase but somehow escaped injury. (Rimer, 1987)

Housing is an integral part of any system of long-term care (Thomas, 1985a; Struyk, 1986). It includes a range of special needs, such as affordability and safety, in terms of both crime and other hazards. The availability of formal services, and especially of transportation, can be critical. Also, however, there are important neighborhood considerations for needs such as convenient shopping and friendly neighbors to lend a hand with informal services (Pollack and Newcomer, 1986; Litwak, 1985).

Conclusion

This review of formal services indicates a growing future need in all areas for the oldest old. Housing needs may well head the list, followed by the need for in-home services and a case manager to coordinate the services. Transportation is also high on the list. Currently, these efforts are severely limited by lack of funds and by lack of coordination when funds are available. Housing officials often do not realize that providing in-home services to the elderly is part of providing suitable housing (Thomas, 1985a:408), and Medicare does not fund transportation to the doctor's office or to the rehabilitation center. Even medical services, which account for substantial government funding efforts, still result in high out-of-pocket expenses, which are likely to increase. Yet it is clear that the oldest old will have neither the economic resources nor the social-familial resources to fully manage their long-term care needs themselves. This realization has prompted concerned policymakers to develop demonstration projects and lawmakers to explore alternatives to the current haphazard array of long-term care opportunities.

Chapter Eight

Epilogue: The Future

Laura Reif

This book focuses on the oldest old—those 85 years of age and over. The resource limitations and problems faced by this group throw into graphic relief the strengths and weaknesses of current programs and policies for the elderly. By examining the circumstances of the oldest old, it is possible to evaluate more effectively the impact of future trends in the organization and financing of health and social services. The experiences of the oldest old dramatically illustrate the serious shortcomings of a health care system that is almost exclusively oriented around disease and medical intervention. Such a system fails to provide adequate assistance to growing numbers of persons with long-lasting functional impairments that are the result of chronic conditions for which there is no "medical fix." The result is unnecessarily high levels of dependency and a great loss of self-determination for the oldest old, as well as for other groups facing similar problems related to poor health. This is a particularly lamentable situation, since it is now apparent that even those with grave deficits can achieve higher levels of functioning and maintain themselves outside institutions if appropriate supportive services are made available (Brody and Ruff, 1986; Brody, 1987).

If the goal is to prevent unwarranted dependency in the oldest old, it is necessary to provide sufficient assistance so that members of this group can manage their lives despite any resource constraints they must deal with. As has been amply documented in preceding chapters, many among the oldest old are faced with multiple, long-lasting limitations in personal resources. In Chapter One, building on a model proposed by Hendricks and Hendricks (1986), we noted that the oldest old may experience resource limitations in four different areas: physiological, social-familial, personal-psychological, and economic (see Table 8.1). In the oldest old, constraints stem from (1) physical and cognitive disorders, and an accompanying increase in the number and severity of functional limitations; (2) a significantly diminished social support network; (3) decreased effectiveness of personal and interactional coping strategies; and (4) a progressive decline in economic resources (under circumstances in which income and assets were often inadequate to begin with).

Assistance supplied from the outside can supplement or shore up the limited personal resources of many of the oldest old. Such assistance, when appropriately matched to an individual's needs, can help preserve maximal functioning and prevent unwarranted dependency on either formal service programs or on help donated by family and friends. Table 8.1 outlines the kind of assistance that needs to be supplied for each of

Table 8.1. Resource Limitations and Types of Assistance Needed

Type of Resource	Resource Limitations	Assistance Needed
Physiological	Multiple chronic conditions; impairment of ability to carry out activities of daily living (IADLs and PADLs)	Broad range of health and social services, provided in least restrictive setting possible
Social-familial	Diminished social support network; remaining family members and friends are too ill or impaired to help	Paraprofessionals to provide assistance that would ordinarily be provided by family
Personal-psychological	Magnitude and long-lasting nature of problems have outstripped the individual's ability to cope; physical or cognitive deficits have eroded the person's adaptive strategies	Help from a case manager to plan, arrange, and coordinate formal services and to identify and mobilize informal caregivers
Economic	Impoverished, medically indigent, or surviving on very marginal income	Income and housing subsidies; long-term services covered under entitlement programs

the four different types of resource limitations commonly faced by the oldest old.

For those with physiological limitations, a broad range of health and social services needs to be provided, preferably in the least restrictive setting possible. Because the oldest old frequently have very diminished social support networks, paraprofessional workers must supply services that would otherwise be donated by family members or friends. Among the oldest old, there are many persons whose coping strategies have been eroded by physical or cognitive deficits. For others, the sheer magnitude and duration of their problems have outstripped their ability to manage. These persons could greatly profit from the help of a case manager—a professional who assumes responsibility for planning, arranging, and coordinating both formal services (help that is paid for) and informal caregiving (help from family, friends, and neighbors).

Economic problems are very prevalent among the oldest old. Of all the age groups, the oldest old have the highest percentage of persons living in poverty. Many among this group are medically indigent; that is, they cannot afford to purchase needed health services beyond those paid for under social entitlement programs such as Medicare. To prevent impoverishment or severe financial hardship among the oldest old, there is a critical need for income supplements, housing subsidies, and reimbursement for services under a public or private insurance program that covers both health and long-term care.

Mismatch Between Service Need and Available Help

There currently exists, however, a grave mismatch between the types of services needed by the oldest old and those services that are presently available to them through public programs (see Chapter Seven). The current service system is deficient in a variety of areas:

1. The *range of services provided by existing programs is excessively narrow*, rarely approaching the full continuum of care necessary to sustain the oldest old. Moreover, much of the available help is medically oriented; by contrast, the main services required by the oldest old are nonmedical in nature. The oldest old primarily need services that support functioning and that supply assistance when physical or cognitive capacities are compromised.

Much of this needed care can be provided by paraprofessional workers who have little or no medical training.

2. *Financial coverage is very restricted,* paying for only a fraction of the multitude of services needed to ensure that the oldest old avoid unwarranted dependency. Financing, like services, is oriented around acute medical and institutional care. Because there is usually no money to pay for a suitable alternative, many of the oldest old are placed in an unnecessarily restrictive setting, such as an extended care facility. Others become a heavy burden to family and friends because financial restrictions greatly limit available choices.

3. Services are mainly targeted toward two groups of elderly: those who can be self-sufficient (except for occasional episodes of acute illness) and those who are so impaired that they need to be in a nursing home. This means that *the majority of oldest old are underserved* because they fall outside these two categories.

4. *Both provision and financing of services are highly fragmented.* Funding comes from different jurisdictions, each with a different set of rules and regulations governing eligibility and coverage. Care is delivered by different organizations and in a variety of settings, each with a specialized focus. Case managers and service brokers can often supply the necessary "glue" to paste the pieces together, but this sort of help is not easy to obtain. During times of serious illness or impairment, the oldest old require a comprehensive range of services, careful coordination of care, help in moving through a variety of settings as their situation changes, and access to many different sources of funding. At present, it is very rare to find all the necessary service components provided by a single "umbrella" organization. Coordination of the different sources of payment for services is even rarer.

5. The current system of health and social services depends heavily on the family as a source of regular assistance for those elderly who have limited individual resources (physical, functional, or economic). Many of the oldest old do not have family or friends who are capable of providing assistance. Social support networks may be greatly depleted because of death and disability; competing commitments and physical distance may prevent relatives and friends from assuming full caretaking responsibilities. Since existing service systems usually supply very limited help from homemakers or other family surrogates, *formal services are often*

inadequate for those individuals who do not have family and friends to sustain them.

An Alternative Model for Service Delivery

Based on a close examination of the resource limitations and needs of the oldest old, it is possible to identify the essential features of a model service system capable of addressing the requirements of this age group. The goal of such a system would be to reduce unwarranted dependency among the oldest old and other populations facing similar restrictions of individual resources. In this discussion, we will refer to this new service paradigm as the "dependency-reduction" model. Its key features are listed in the right-hand column of Table 8.2. It should be noted that a care system based on the dependency-reduction model can effectively serve not only the oldest old but other groups of functionally impaired individuals as well. Among the groups that might benefit from such a care system are children with crippling birth defects; young adults who have sustained traumatic head or spinal cord injuries; middle-aged persons who have survived a catastrophically disabling event, such as a severe stroke; the chronically mentally ill; and persons with debilitative, progressive, and incurable diseases, such as Alzheimer's-type dementia, multiple sclerosis, and AIDS.

The elements of our existing health care system are profoundly different from those that characterize the dependency-reduction model. Our current system is based on a "treatment-oriented" model. The key features of this system are depicted in the center column of Table 8.2. In the current treatment-oriented system, the focus is on the individual and acute illness. Eligibility for funds and services depends on there being a high probability that the disease can be corrected and that the person can be rehabilitated—generally, within a relatively short time frame. The goal is to cure the illness. It is assumed that the individual will be able to return to normal functioning once the disease has been eradicated.

By contrast, in the dependency-reduction model, the focus is not solely on the individual but is rather on that individual in the context of the family unit or some other type of social support network. The problem focused on is functional impairment, regardless of whether it is a physical or mental condition that causes the loss of self-sufficiency. The goals to be accomplished are multiple. Assistance is provided in order to restore the person to optimal functioning, to ensure that help will be

Table 8.2. Contrasting Models for Organizing Help for Oldest Old

	Treatment-Oriented Model	Dependency-Reduction Model
Locus of intervention	Individual	Individual/family/community
Focal problem; basis for service eligibility	Acute illness that is amenable to correction or rehabilitation	Functional impairments that are chronic, multiple, and/or severe
Goals	To cure the underlying disease and return the individual to independence	To maximize functioning; care for residual deficits; support self-determination; avoid unwarranted dependency; assist family caregivers; and protect the individual from poverty
Main forms of assistance	Medical intervention; skilled, acute care	Broad continuum of health and social services; housing; transportation; help with care management; training and respite help for family; income maintenance; insurance coverage for health and long-term care
Key persons supplying help	Physicians; health professionals	Paraprofessional workers; family caregivers; wide range of professionals or interdisciplinary teams; case managers
Duration of services	Short-term/episodic; intermittent	Long-term; continuous
Dominant care setting	Hospital; nursing home	Individual's home; non-institutional setting

provided in areas in which functioning is compromised, to support self-determination or individual choice (as much as possible), to assist family caregivers who may supply regular daily assistance, and to protect the person and his or her family from becoming impoverished as a result of having to pay for needed services.

Under the treatment-oriented model, help consists largely of medical interventions and skilled services provided by doctors and other health professionals. Care is short term and intermittent. Services are usually institution based—they are provided in acute-care hospitals or nursing homes designed to deliver skilled, medically oriented care.

In contrast, under the dependency-reduction model, a broad spectrum of health and social services is provided. Sheltered housing, special transportation services, training and respite for family caregivers, and assistance with care coordination are all regarded as necessary components in the service continuum. Paraprofessional workers, case managers, and family caregivers figure prominently in the range of persons who supply help. Care is expected to be long term and relatively continuous. Services are mainly provided in the individual's home or in noninstitutional settings. Institutional care becomes necessary only when health status or functional ability is too compromised to permit the person to live safely or comfortably in the community.

Key Issues: The Need to Expand Services and Funding

By comparing the two different models for service systems listed in Table 8.2, it is possible to identify the key issues that need to be addressed in order to improve existing programs for the elderly. Program redesign can ensure that the oldest old will not suffer unnecessary hardship or be forced into unwarranted dependency. In order to create a system that has the characteristics outlined in the dependency-reduction model, services and funding would both have to be substantially increased.

Expansion of Services

If services are to be significantly expanded, attention must be given to the following areas:

1. There is a great need to *increase the range of services available to those with functional impairments* that prevent them from independently carrying out activities of daily living. Particularly essential are homemaker services, rehabilitation for physical impairments, sheltered or modified housing, and specially designed transportation for persons with mobility limitations. Support and respite for family caregivers is also critical, since relatives will undoubtedly continue to provide a significant amount of help to the oldest old.
2. The *period of time over which help is given needs to be lengthened* significantly. At present, services are often prematurely terminated, based on evidence that the illness has stabilized. Care

should be extended beyond this point, particularly when functional impairments do not allow the individual to perform necessary activities of daily living.

3. *Mechanisms for ensuring continuity of care need to be improved.* The oldest old and other groups with long-lasting disabilities often move between settings and levels of care, utilizing a wide variety of providers and service modalities. Coordination of care, as well as a smooth transition between service sectors, can only be ensured when specific responsibility is assigned for case management, when service personnel operate as a multidisciplinary team, and when there is coordinated record keeping to ensure adequate communication among a very diverse group of care providers (Vladeck, 1987:7–10). Services provided by a professional case manager can often be extremely valuable to the oldest old, who may lack the physical or cognitive ability to orchestrate services for themselves or who may lack a local caregiver able to take on this responsibility.

Expansion and Redirection of Available Funding

If appropriate resources are to be made available to the oldest old, the way in which services are funded also needs to be reformed. Among the areas that need attention are the following:

1. *Funding needs to be expanded and redirected.* Nearly 90% of public expenditures for services for the elderly go for health care (U.S. Senate, Special Committee on Aging, 1987a). Funding sources need to be expanded so that a broader spectrum of health and social services can be delivered to the elderly. At present, services are dictated by available funding. Existing eligibility and benefit structures are so narrowly defined that they have resulted in serious gaps in services. As a consequence, many of the oldest old cannot obtain critically needed care. Funding programs must be expanded to cover these needed services.

   The imbalance between expenditures for institutional care and those for noninstitutional care also needs to be corrected. In 1986, more than 54% of personal health care expenditures for *all age groups* went for services delivered by hospitals and nursing homes (Health Care Financing Administration, 1987:15). For persons over the age of 65, fully 67% of all personal health expenditures go to hospitals and nursing homes (Davis and Rowland, 1986:34). Moreover, public funding for *long-term care* is mainly directed toward institutional care. Approximately 90% of the total money spent for long-term care under Medicare and Medicaid goes to nursing homes (Doty, Liu, and Wiener, 1985). This funding pattern results in underfunding or absence of funding in such critical areas as prevention of disease and disability, rehabilitation, long-term care provided in an individual's home, and a variety of related noninstitutional services that are essential in order to keep those with functional impairments from becoming unnecessarily dependent.

2. *Mechanisms need to be put in place to ensure more value for the dollars spent on services,* and more cost consciousness on the part of service organizations. Financing programs have long been plagued by reimbursement structures that provide disincentives for cost control and responsible fiscal management. Until recently, many service organizations (most notably, health care institutions) could pass the cost of services directly on to various third-party payers, such as private insurance companies, Medicare, and Medicaid. However, some dramatic changes in health care financing, set into motion in the early 1980s, have begun to affect the way public programs pay for services.

   Among these recent reforms are *prospective payment systems,* under which a set fee is paid in advance for an agreed-upon set of services. This sort of financing mechanism encourages the provider of services to be more cost conscious. Under this type of payment, providers cannot merely pass along the cost of care to the third-party payer. Rather, a preestablished payment (with a fixed ceiling) is all that will be paid for services. Providers that exceed this ceiling must absorb the loss; providers that can deliver services below that fixed fee may keep the extra revenue. However, these sorts of innovations in the financing of services are relatively new and are not very widespread. More experimentation with new methods for financing and cost control needs to be undertaken, so that service systems will assume more responsibility for avoiding unnecessarily high expenditures and so that consumers and third-party payers will get the best value for their dollars.

3. *Diverse funding streams need to be better coordinated* so that money from multiple sources can be pooled and used more flexibly to finance the broad range of assistance needed to sustain the oldest

old and other populations who face problems related to poor health and low functional capacities. At present, fragmentation of funding sources is very prevalent. Health and social services are paid for by separate entitlement programs. Payment for acute and long-term care are under different jurisdictions. There exists no single authority to oversee funding for all services delivered to the aged (as was pointed out in Chapter Seven, the Administration on Aging lacks sufficient funding and authority to assume this role). As many as 80 different federal programs pay for various types of assistance for persons such as the oldest old who require long-term care (O'Shaughnessy and Price, 1987:196).

Recent Trends in the Organization and Financing of Services

Of particular importance to the oldest old are some recent changes in the organization and financing of services. Many of the most significant changes have occurrred in the health care arena, so that is the focus of this discussion. Reforms in health services are likely to have widespread effects on the organization and financing of other types of services for the elderly. As will become apparent from material presented in subsequent pages, health care institutions (especially hospitals) are assuming an increasingly prominent role in the care of the aged. In fact, large hospital-based systems are quite likely to become the hub around which services for the elderly revolve.

Recent Revolution in Health Care Financing

As previously mentioned, there have been a number of major revisions in the way government programs provide reimbursement for services. The most radical and consequential changes were initiated with the introduction of Medicare's prospective hospital payment system (based on diagnostic related groups or DRGs), mandated by the Tax Equity and Fiscal Responsibility Act of 1982 (TEFRA) and the 1983 Social Security amendments. In addition, home care benefits provided by Medicare and Medicaid were liberalized (under the 1980 and 1981 omnibus reconciliation acts) and Medicare reimbursement policies were modified to encourage the enrollment of more elderly persons in health maintenance organizations (through provisions of TEFRA).

The above changes were prompted largely by concern about the alarming increase in service utilization (particularly hospital use) and by the rapidly escalating costs of care (Davis and Rowland, 1986; Harrington, 1985a, 1985b; Reif, 1984). Services delivered to the elderly caused the most worry because of the high expenditures for services for this population. The aged represented only 11% of the population in 1980 but accounted for 31% of the total personal health expenditures in that year (Fisher, 1980). The rapid increase in expenditures by this age group continues to be a source of concern. Medicare expenditures more than doubled over a six-year period, increasing from $35 billion in 1980 to $79 billion in 1986. Medicaid expenditures for the elderly have almost tripled; increasing from $6 billion in 1977 to $15 billion in 1984 (Davis and Rowland, 1986).

Prospective payment systems for hospitals were intended to curb the use and costs of expensive institutional care by limiting admissions of patients, curtailing a patient's length of stay, and setting a limit on the payments hospitals could receive for the care of a specific type of patient (based on that patient's diagnosis). Public financing innovations related to the expanded use of home health care and health maintenance organizations were also intended to curb health care costs by shifting expenditures into care modalities viewed as less expensive or more cost effective. These innovations in health care financing are beginning to dramatically change the pattern of health service delivery and utilization in this country.

Restructuring of Health Care Delivery for the Elderly

A restructuring of the service delivery system is occurring. Among the most important changes are the following:

1. Hospitals are diversifying and expanding their range of services (Brody and Persily, 1984). About two-thirds of hospitals contacted in a recent survey reported that they were expanding services for the elderly (Hospital Research and Educational Trust, 1986). In just the past five years, the number of hospital-based home health agencies has grown to ten times what they were in 1981. This dramatic growth in provision of home care by hospitals is largely the result of the introduction of prospective

payment for inpatient services (Reif, 1984; Sanker, Newcomer, and Wood, 1986).

Hospitals, fearing loss of revenues from decreased numbers of admissions and shorter lengths of stay, are beginning to provide services to patients *after they leave the hospital.* Some hospital administrators believe that continuing contact with patients will promote their use of other hospital services. For example, patients who use the hospital's home health services may more easily be referred back to the hospital when they are in need of other types of care, such as physical therapy, laboratory services, or outpatient care. It is also anticipated that such a patient may return to that hospital should he or she have another acute illness that requires inpatient services.

2. The total number of home health agencies has more than doubled since 1981, when home care benefits were made more liberal under Medicare and Medicaid (Reif, 1984). The rapid growth of home care providers was also triggered by the implementation of hospital cost containment. Patients are now being discharged from hospitals "sicker and quicker," and the need for posthospital services is increasing (Wood, 1986; Pesznecker et al., 1987).

3. Most important, there has been a major change in the structure of organizations that provide care for the aged, with the emergence of new types of providers, referred to variously as managed-care systems, consolidated care organizations, and integrated service systems. These new types of providers are designed to deliver a full spectrum of services from acute to long-term care. In many of these new systems, care is financed under a prospective payment system (Kodner and Feldman, 1982; Zawadski, 1984; Collins and McDonald, 1984; Greenberg et al., 1985; Harrington, 1985b). Among these new types of providers are health maintenance organizations specifically designed to serve the elderly; newly developed social/health maintenance organizations; consolidated care organizations for dependent adults (patterned on On Lok Senior Health Services in San Francisco); various types of vertically integrated, hospital-based, comprehensive service systems; and life care communities for older adults.

Health maintenance organizations (HMOs) are a special type of health care organization that is designed to provide comprehensive medical services for a fixed fee, paid in advance. Older persons who enroll in an HMO can obtain all the services they are entitled to under

Medicare. Moreover, by simply paying a nominal monthly premium to belong to the HMO, older adults can avoid the high and often unpredictable out-of-pocket expenditures for services not fully covered by Medicare. HMOs are now accommodating increasing numbers of elderly persons (Iversen et al., 1986). More than 1.1 million older adults (nearly 5% of the total elderly population) currently receive health care through an HMO. There has been a doubling of the number of Medicare enrollees in HMOs in just the past two years.

Moreover, as a result of provisions in the Tax Equity and Fiscal Responsibility Act of 1982, Medicare can pay HMOs a set fee per month for providing health care to beneficiaries (this fee is equivalent to 95% of the average per-person expense paid by Medicare for beneficiaries who receive services under the traditional fee-for-service system). By 1987, most elderly HMO participants were enrolled in a plan under which Medicare pays a set fee for each enrollee (McMillan, Lubitz, and Russell, 1987). This is significant because under such a reimbursement system, the HMO has an incentive to manage care in the most cost-effective way possible.

Although HMOs use an innovative organizational model and reimbursement system, they do not far surpass conventional health care providers when it comes to offering an expanded range of services; for example, HMOs fail to provide any sort of long-term care for their members. However, two other new model systems, the social/health maintenance organization and the consolidated care organization for dependent adults, do offer long-term care.

The social/health maintenance organization (SHMO), a new model currently being tested in four different sites nationwide, attempts to extend to long-term care the HMO concept of prepayment for care. Both well and disabled elderly can enroll in the SHMO, which provides a wide range of integrated services. The SHMO attempts to transcend the conventional service delivery distinctions that separate social from medical services, acute from long-term care, and institutional from noninstitutional services. Services are financed by periodic prospective payments, with monies coming from Medicare, Medicaid, and elderly enrollees themselves (payments made by individual enrollees range from $25 to $50 per month, depending on the SHMO). SHMOs assume the financial risk for providing covered care and thus have an incentive to ensure that services are delivered efficiently and in the least costly manner (Leutz et al., 1985; Harrington and Newcomer, 1985).

From the standpoint of the individual consumer, the SHMO offers a way to obtain coordinated health, medical, and long-term services under the sponsorship of a single umbrella organization. However, a major disadvantage of SHMOs is their limit on expenditures for long-term care (the cost of these services cannot exceed a fixed amount—$6,500 to $12,000 per year, depending on the plan). A further problem is the inaccessibility of this type of new service system. Only four SHMOs were in operation in 1988 (in Minneapolis, Minnesota; New York City; Portland, Oregon; and Long Beach, California). The oldest old and other groups that have high rates of functional impairment are likely to find it particularly difficult to join a SHMO, since SHMOs strictly limit the numbers of high-risk patients they enroll (current SHMOs restrict the percentage of disabled elderly to 5–7% of the total enrollees).

Another model, the consolidated care organization for dependent adults (CCODA), is specifically designed for those who require long-term care. This type of service delivery system was developed in 1973 by On Lok Senior Health Services, an organization created to serve nursing-home-eligible elderly in a section of San Francisco where residents are primarily Chinese and Filipino. On Lok participants receive a full spectrum of services, from acute to long-term care. On Lok even offers special sheltered housing for its participants. A single monthly fee paid in advance covers the cost of all services the person may require, including hospital and nursing home care (Zawadski, 1984, 1985). Money to cover this set monthly fee currently comes from Medicare, Medicaid, and premiums paid directly by program participants. Special federal legislation (signed October 21, 1986) waives a number of usual Medicare and Medicaid requirements so that a service system based on On Lok's CCODA can be duplicated in as many as ten different sites across the nation. In 1988, On Lok was providing technical assistance to several different organizations so they could replicate the CCODA model.

Two other innovations in service delivery are worth discussing: vertically integrated, hospital-based service systems and life care communities. Hospital-based comprehensive service systems are becoming increasingly more prevalent. Limits imposed on inpatient services by Medicare's prospective payment system have forced hospitals to consider other ways of delivering care to the increasing numbers of the aged they serve. Although it is diffucult to know precisely how many hospitals are developing a broader range of services, there is evidence that a large percentage of these institutions are moving in this direction (Hospital Research and Educational Trust, 1986; Davis and Rowland, 1986). It is clear that most hospitals are going beyond delivering acute care and are now expanding into noninstitutional, long-term health and social services, such as home health care, day care for older adults, hot meals programs, and case management. These efforts are specifically designed to attract a larger proportion of elderly patients to the hospital (Brody and Persily, 1984). Although the new hospital-based systems have the potential for delivering more comprehensive and coordinated care to the elderly, at present many of these organizations still fall far short of the goal of total "vertical integration"—that is, their different service components still function quite separately.

The life care community, or continuing care retirement community, is another relatively new concept in long-term care. The community is a total living environment that provides housing, meals, housekeeping services, and social activities to older persons for the duration of their lives. Although medical and hospital services are not covered, many life care communities do offer nursing home care, personal care, and other supportive services, such as home nursing and physical and occupational therapy—all available on the grounds of the facility. Persons who join the community are required to pay an entrance payment and monthly follow-up fees. While payment structures vary widely, entrance fees are often as high as $40,000–$100,000, with monthly payments as high as $600–$800 per month. According to estimates made in 1984, between 300 and 600 life care communities were serving some 90,000 elderly people (Winklevoss and Powell, 1984). It is estimated that about 2% of all elderly will reside in life care communities by the year 1990 (Alpha Center, 1984).

Life care communities are not unlike an insurance system, offering to provide lifetime protection for the person who contracts for services. Since experience with life care communities is limited, data about the costs of managing such an organization are still quite inadequate. Some communities have experienced financial problems, partly because of their inability to accurately predict the longevity and service use patterns of their residents. For some communities, costs have exceeded the revenue generated by entrance fees and monthly charges, leading to the threat of insolvency. This has resulted in an increased interest on the part of federal and state officials in providing more regulation and oversight of this new type of service provider (U.S. Senate, Special Committee on Aging, 1983).

The reorganization of service systems described above is a particularly important trend to consider when planning care for the oldest old. These new systems have some features that make them especially well equipped to deliver care to this age group as well as to other populations that face equivalent limitations in personal resources. Among the innovative features that characterize these systems are the following: (1) these service systems not only attempt to treat disease, they also try to pay some attention to the functional impairments that accompany illness;

(2) a large range of services is provided and coordinated, through a *single* service organization; (3) services are delivered over relatively long periods of time; moreover, the organization assumes responsibility for maintaining continuing contact with the persons it serves; (4) care is provided in the least restrictive setting possible, partly because this is seen as a way to lower the high cost of institutional care; and (5) the organization is paid a set fee per month, in advance, and is expected to stay within that fee while providing a relatively comprehensive range of services for the individual client.

From the standpoint of the oldest old, these new service systems have a number of advantages: (1) help can be obtained for functional impairments as well as for medical problems; (2) "one-stop shopping" is possible, since a large range of services can be obtained from a single provider; (3) it is possible to deal with the same service organization over long periods of time rather than being moved from provider to provider as needs change; (4) there is a greater likelihood that the person can remain at home while receiving health services rather than being moved to a hospital or nursing home when the need for help increases; and (5) out-of-pocket expenditures for health care can be kept lower and more predictable.

A few of these new systems have features that are quite similar to the dependency-reduction model of care described earlier in this chapter. The consolidated care organization for dependent adults (CCODA), in particular, approximates this model. The CCODA provides a broad continuum of care delivered under a single auspice. Coordination of services, information, and funding is managed by a single service organization. The goals, types, and duration of services, range of personnel delivering care, and predominant care setting are quite similar to that described in the dependency-reduction model. Moreover, the CCODA is specifically designed to sustain persons whose individual resources have been severely eroded.

It is important to note that the CCODA is not only sound in design but effective in practice as well. This model, as implemented by On Lok Senior Health Services, has been quite successful in maintaining very frail and old persons in the least restrictive setting possible. The average age of On Lok participants is 81 years. Moreover, all participants are so disabled that they have been certified as eligible for nursing home care under the Medicaid program. Despite this, rates of institutionalization, and particularly of nursing home use, are dramatically lower than for a comparable group of nursing-home-eligible elderly who are receiving care from traditional health and social service organizations (Zawadski, 1988). Nursing home utilization—acknowledged to be an unambiguous indicator of dependent status—accounts for less than 5% of the total days of care provided to On Lok participants (Zawadski, 1988). This compares with 40% of days spent in a nursing home by a comparably old and disabled group that is served under the traditional fee-for-service system (Zawadski, 1988).

On Lok participants spend *less* than 1% (0.7%) of their days in the hospital. This compares with a rate of about 3% among a group of comparably disabled and old persons served outside of On Lok, and a rate of 1% among the general elderly population (Zawadski, 1988). In addition, hospital expenditures account for less than 20% of the total service costs at On Lok. This contrasts sharply with the traditional pattern of health care expenditures for the elderly, in which 70% of current benefit payments under Medicare go to hospitals. It seems apparent that the CCODA, as implemented by On Lok, has succeeded in sustaining very old and disabled persons through the use of largely noninstitutional services. Indeed, this new service system appears to be capable of achieving dependency reduction even for those persons assessed as appropriate for placement in a nursing home.

Increasing Interest in Expanding Financing for Long-Term Care

In the past several years, there has been mounting concern on the part of the public, professionals, and policymakers about the alarmingly high cost of long-term care. One leading analyst has described expenditures for long-term care as "the third economic catastrophe" to be faced by the American family (Brody, 1987). Brody describes how the first two economic catastrophes (the potential for impoverishment in old age because of inadequate retirement income, and poverty caused by lack of coverage for medical care) were partially resolved by the development of the Social Security and Medicare programs. Brody argues compellingly for application of this same approach—initiation of a public program to protect families from poverty—to ensure that the costs associated with long-term care do not also lead to financial catastrophe for the elderly and/or disabled and their families.

By now, there is no doubt that expenses associated with long-term care can quickly lead to impoverishment of the aged and often of their families. Medicare is a monumental failure when it comes to covering the cost of long-term care. In 1985, Medicare paid for less than 5% of the total cost of nursing home care (National Center for Health Statistics, 1987a,b). Ironically, the "catastrophic coverage" that was added to Medicare in 1988 does not protect individuals from the catastrophic costs of long-term care provided in nursing homes or in the home. The major aim of this coverage is to insure against the high costs of acute, high-technology care provided in the hospital. Private health insurance policies designed to supplement Medicare (commonly known as "medigap" insurance) are also woefully inadequate in covering long-term care. First, these policies cover only about 1% of the cost of nursing home care. Second, 34% of the elderly do not have such a policy and so need to pay out-of-pocket for Medicare coinsurance and deductibles (Davis and Rowland, 1986).

Reimbursement for long-term care becomes available if the individual and family are sufficiently impoverished to qualify for Medicaid; as a result, most families initially pay out-of-pocket for long-term care. Only when they have exhausted their economic resources do they qualify to receive long-term assistance from Medicaid (and then, funding is available mainly for nursing home care, *not* in-home services). Recent evidence suggests that the high costs of long-term care can impoverish older persons at a surprisingly rapid rate. Three out of four adults over the age of 75 and living alone would be reduced to poverty within a year of their being placed in a nursing home (Branch, 1985:53).

For the oldest old, the threat of economic catastrophe is very real. Recent research conducted at the Brookings Institution shows that persons over 85 years of age exceed any other group in their use of long-term care, yet the oldest old have the fewest economic resources to pay for the high cost of these services (Hanley, 1988). Although those over 85 currently represent only about 11% of the total elderly population, they account for 26% of all aged who use home care and 42% of those elderly residing in nursing homes. Brookings' analysts estimate that 30 years from now, the oldest old will account for fully half of all expenditures on long-term care, consuming services worth a total of $46 billion in a single year. By that time, the oldest old will have doubled in number. Yet, although they will account for only 14% of all older Americans, they will represent 34% of those elderly who use home care and 52% of those aged who reside in nursing homes (Hanley, 1988; Rivlin et al., 1988).

The oldest old are the age group least likely to be able to afford to pay for long-term care; the average income for this group is lower than that of any other group of elderly. Moreover, the oldest old will experience the smallest growth in income of any group of elderly. Average annual income for this group was a scant $11,000 in 1987 and is predicted to increase by only 50% in the next 30 years. The average family income for other groups of elderly is expected to double in that same period (Hanley, 1988). This means that most of the oldest old will have incomes too low to pay for long-term care.

Since 1984 there has been an increasing movement in the direction of expanding coverage for long-term-care expenses (U.S. General Accounting Office, 1987; Meiners, 1983; Wiener, Ehrenworth, and Spence, 1987). A considerable amount of this activity has occurred in the private sector. By early 1986, about 50% of all private insurance companies were offering some form of long-term care insurance. By 1986, 200,000 policies had been sold. That number had more than doubled by early 1988, so it is estimated that approximately 500,000 long-term-care policies were in effect in that year (Wiener, 1988).

Unlike conventional health insurance, Medicare, or medigap policies (all of which pay for nursing home stays of less than 150 days), most of the new long-term-care policies cover nursing home care for three years or more. Under most policies, benefits are paid as an indemnity; that is, a fixed daily rate is paid directly to the policyholder when that individual becomes eligible for benefits. Rates of payment vary from $10 to $120 per day, depending on how much the individual pays in premiums. In general, however, the average policy pays $50 to $60 per day. It is important to note that this benefit rate may be too low to adequately cover the actual cost of care, since in many urban areas nursing home costs already exceed $100 per day. Moreover, 97% of the policies currently being marketed are not indexed for inflation; that is, indemnity levels remain the same for the duration of the policy. Yet it is common for many years to elapse before the individual has occasion to use the benefit. Benefits paid at that time are likely to be woefully inadequate. For example, if an individual purchased a $50-per-day policy at age 40, by age 85 that individual would need an indemnity payment of $800 per day to cover the cost of nursing home care (assuming an inflation rate of 6% per year for the cost of that care) (Wiener, 1988).

From a consumer's standpoint, private long-term-care insurance policies have a number of disadvantages:

1. The cost of these policies is very high, especially if the person is over 75 years of age at the time of initial purchase. Premiums vary widely, and there is no guarantee that a more expensive policy will provide better coverage. In 1988, the cost of an adequate policy ranged from $35 to $80 per month for an individual 65 years of age.

2. Many companies exclude high-risk individuals by setting an upper age limit (usually 80 years) on would-be purchasers. Individual health screening is also required. This allows the company to disqualify persons who have chronic conditions (some

companies report their rejection rates to be as high as 30%) (Consumer Reports, 1988).

3. Home care and other noninstitutional long-term services are still not adequately covered by most policies. In fact, in 1987, only half of the policies being marketed covered home care. The range of benefits provided to persons at home is very narrow (very few policies cover hospice care or adult day care; many fail to cover homemaker services or other supportive services in the home). Home care benefit payments are usually only 50% of the amount that would be paid by that policy for care in a nursing home. Home care coverage typically extends only half as long as would nursing home payments under the same policy.

4. Persons with Alzheimer's-type dementia and other long-lasting but medically stable illnesses may find it difficult to qualify for benefits. In 1987, 72% of the policies required a three-day prior hospitalization before long-term care would be paid for. Such a requirement effectively excludes from coverage about 60% of persons who enter a nursing home, since they do so directly from the community. Organic mental illness, such as Alzheimer's disease, may be covered only if it can be established that the person has this illness. This may present problems, since Alzheimer's disease can only be conclusively diagnosed through examination of brain tissue obtained during an autopsy.

From the standpoint of public policy, private insurance initiatives are unlikely to solve the problem of providing adequate funding for long-term care. A "second generation" of insurance policies is emerging, offering better coverage, more liberal eligibility requirements, and even access to a few group policies that waive individual underwriting (most policies now screen applicants on a case-by-case basis). Nevertheless, recent research reveals that only a small fraction of the nursing home expenditures in this country will be paid for by private insurance. It is estimated that 30 years from now, such insurance will be paying for only 7–12% of the total cost of institutional long-term care and will reduce Medicaid payments to nursing homes by only 5% (Spence, 1988). For people with only modest income and assets, private long-term care insurance is not currently affordable. Moreover, the oldest old and others with severely limited economic resources are likely to impoverish themselves very quickly and thus will have their nursing home costs paid for under the Medicaid program.

In addition to private sector activity, there has been considerable interest on the part of state governments in developing programs that can protect their residents against the catastrophic costs of long-term care. Since the mid-1980s, state initiatives have largely focused on two areas of activity: (1) performing regulatory review to ensure protection for consumers, while encouraging experimentation by the insurance industry in the development of long-term care insurance products; and (2) providing incentives for the expansion of private long-term care insurance by giving tax credits to consumers; subsidizing the cost of premiums, so low-income consumers can purchase this type of protection; and providing tax relief and reinsurance for insurers (Meiners, 1988). By 1988, half the states had passed legislation that regulates the type of long-term care insurance that can be offered to consumers. A number of states, such as Washington, have encouraged the development of improved insurance products by mandating broader service benefit structures.

Because payment for long-term care under Medicaid represents a very high proportion of state expenditures, state governments are interested in seeing that financing options for long-term care are expanded. A number of states have developed initiatives that would provide substantial benefits to consumers who choose to purchase private long-term care insurance. For example, Massachusetts, Connecticut, and California have proposed using a combination of public and private funding to pay for the cost of long-term care insurance. Massachusetts is considering subsidizing premiums for the low-income elderly as well as eliminating the spend-down requirement under Medicaid. The latter provision would allow persons who purchase private long-term care insurance to qualify automatically for Medicaid-funded nursing home care when their insurance runs out. Such persons need not exhaust their remaining assets before Medicaid will pay.

Connecticut has proposed a stop-loss provision that would allow an individual who purchases long-term care insurance to protect assets equal to the amount of the policy. Under such a plan, an individual who purchased $50,000 worth of long-term care insurance and then used all the benefits under that policy would be allowed to keep as much as $50,000 in assets and still be eligible for Medicaid nursing home payments. An initiative proposed in California would mandate that all private insurance companies and health maintenance organizations be required to offer long-term care coverage. Under this proposal, the state could also develop its own insurance plan. In addition, the state could partially subsidize the cost of premiums for low-income individuals, using monies derived from a half-cent increase in the sales tax.

The federal government has been much slower to come to terms with the problem of how to pay for long-term care. By mid-1988, coverage for catastrophic illness had been added to Medicare. However, this expansion of Medicare mainly benefits the small percentage of persons who stay a long time in the *hospital*. Long-term care in a nursing home or at home is still not covered under Medicare. However, an encouraging sign is that in 1987 and 1988, an increasing number of bills that proposed expanded funding for long-term care were introduced into Congress. Among these legislative proposals was a bill to expand Medicare so that this program covers comprehensive, long-term home care for persons of all ages. Eligibility for services would be based on impairment in two or more activities of daily living. Another recent proposal would expand nursing home coverage under Medicare. Under this proposal, the cost of long-term care in an institution would be paid after the individual had paid for the first three years of nursing home care (presumably, private insurance could also be used to cover these initial costs). The proposed source of revenues for each of the above expansions of Medicare would be the same: money would be obtained by lifting the wage cap on Social Security payroll taxes (currently, only income below $45,000 per year is subject to this tax).

Congress' preoccupation with the federal deficit makes it unlikely that funding for long-term care will be significantly expanded in the near future. Nevertheless, there is evidence of growing public pressure on the federal government to avert this newest "economic catastrophe" for families: impoverishment caused by the high cost of long-term care. It is noteworthy that long-term care became a major issue during the 1988 election year and that groups such as the American Association of Retired Persons are becoming an increasingly potent force in shaping both public opinion and legislative action.

The Future: The Need for Continuing Innovation and System Reform

Despite the progress that has been made, there is a pressing need for continuing innovation and system reform. Revisions in the organization and financing of care have barely begun to change the character of services for the elderly. Even less progress has been made in addressing the needs of those among the elderly who are most vulnerable—the oldest old.

The emergence of managed-care and consolidated service systems has resulted in some notable gains: (1) these organizations are beginning to bring together health and social services, acute and long-term care, and institutional and noninstitutional services; (2) coordination of diverse service personnel and care components is now possible through case management; and (3) some of these providers are starting to take more financial risks by agreeing to provide a comprehensive range of services for a set fee, paid in advance. However, only a small percentage of the population is currently being served by these new organizations.

A particularly troublesome problem is that a medical orientation still prevails in many of these new managed-care systems. Ironically, the government's attempts to limit inpatient expenditures and encourage expansion of in-home and outpatient care have had the unexpected effect of solidifying the hospital's dominance over the delivery of services. Hospitals are now expanding into noninstitutional and long-term care. As a result, the hospital is becoming even more firmly established at the center of the service network. This may result in some significant benefits for groups like the oldest old, who now can obtain a broader continuum of services from a provider that previously concentrated on acute care, delivered largely in an institution. However, there is a real danger that many hospital-based, vertically integrated systems will not expand beyond the narrow goals and services that characterize the treatment-oriented model outlined earlier in this chapter (see Table 8.2).

HMOs and SHMOs also tend to concentrate on medically oriented care. With both of these new systems, expansion of services has been very modest. HMOs, faced with progressive decreases in the amount of revenues they receive under prospectively paid rate structures, have largely confined themselves to the traditional range of health services. Moreover, long-term care has never really been provided as a service benefit by these organizations. Even SHMOs, which are specifically designed to offer a broader range of services, have had to greatly restrict their long-term care benefits in order to keep premiums and service expenditures down.

Only the CCODA, in which the central goal is to provide long-term care, has truly gone beyond the confines of a treatment-oriented service model. Although the CCODA is now being replicated in a number of different sites nationwide, it is still too early to say whether this approach to service delivery can serve as the best model for providing long-term care to the oldest old and other populations with equivalent levels of disability. Up to this time, the CCODA has focused on those elderly with the most severe functional impairments and the greatest limitations in individual resources. This type of managed-care system is probably most effective for those whose physiological and psychological resources have been very substantially eroded—at that point, there is a very high chance that the person will become dependent on formal services or on help from family or friends. Under these circumstances, a broad range of services, carefully case managed, is very beneficial and probably cost saving.

A potential problem with a number of the new managed-care systems is their continued reliance on the family as the primary source of regular help for the functionally impaired. For example, HMOs and SHMOs still take for granted that the family will supply the bulk of care. Despite the fact that these organizations depend on informal caregivers to keep services affordable, few programs provide adequate training for family caregivers, and even fewer offer respite care. These types of assistance can enable families to sustain caregiving over longer periods of time, thus lowering the chances that the individual will be placed in an institution.

Recently, a great deal of attention has been focused on the need to improve funding for various forms of assistance for the aged. However, progress on this problem remains painfully slow. Financial barriers still keep the majority of elderly from obtaining necessary services, particularly help in the home and long-term care. Underfunding of many essential service components severely limits the range of available alternatives and often seriously jeopardizes the quality of care. Financing still supports a pattern of service delivery that is focused on medically oriented, institution-based care. Federal and state governments have not yet taken any bold steps to reform financing so that services can be brought into better alignment with the needs of the oldest old and others whose resource limitations might force them into dependency. Concerns about the cost of expanding services has virtually stymied efforts to address the problem.

Private sector initiatives, such as the development of long-term-care insurance policies, have done little to ensure that the majority of elderly, and in particular the oldest old, will be protected from poverty should they require extended services for grave functional impairments. Private long-term care insurance is currently very expensive and still does a better job of covering care in nursing homes than in the home. The vast majority of oldest old and others with low incomes cannot afford to buy these policies. Moreover, recent projections indicate that private financing is likely to pay for less than 12% of this country's total expenditures for long-term care (Spence, 1988).

Much more progress needs to be made if our goal is to prevent unwarranted dependency among the most vulnerable in our population—the oldest old and other groups who suffer from multiple and severe limitations in individual resources. What is needed is a service continuum that spans the conventional boundaries between acute and long-term care, health and social services, and institutional and noninstitutional settings. Such a comprehensive, coordinated care system can only be achieved by expanding services and financing and by transcending the narrow confines of a treatment-oriented model of care. The benefits of such a system would be great: appropriate, more humane care would be available to persons of all ages who suffer from serious impairments caused by one or more chronic conditions. Services need to be provided in a manner that preserves maximal functioning and self-determination for the individual. By considering the special circumstances of the oldest old, it is possible to identify problems with the current service system and to explore new organizational models. An understanding of the oldest old can help point the way to needed system reforms.

References

AARP
1987 "Long-term care social insurance program initiative." Unpublished proposal by AARP, OWL, and The Villers Foundation, Washington, DC.

Adams, B. N.
1968 "The middle-class adult and his widowed or still-married mother." *Social Problems* 16 (1): 50–59.

Aline, Countess of Romanones
1986 "The dear romance of the Duke and Duchess of Windsor." *Vanity Fair* 49 (6): 62–80, 118–123.

Alpha Center
1984 "Long-term care alternatives: Continuing care retirement communities." *Alpha Centerpiece* (January): 1–6.

American Academy of Opthalmology
1982 *Eye care for the elderly.* San Francisco. American Academy of Opthalmology.

Andreoli, K., et al. (eds.)
1986 *Health care for the elderly: Regional responses to national policy issues.* New York: The Haworth Press.

Andres, R. O.
1987 "Tests of balance performance in the elderly: A review." *Danish Medical Bulletin* 34, Gerontology Special Supplement Series Number Four (April): 18–21.

Andrews, E. S.
1985 "Coverage under employer-sponsored retirement and capital accumulation plans." Pp. 112–135 in U.S. Senate, Special Committee on Aging, *The*

Pension Gamble: Who Wins? Who Loses? Hearings, June 14. Washington, DC: U.S. Government Printing Office.

Atchley, R. C.
  1980 "Age and suicide: Reflection on the quality of life?" Pp. 141–162 in S. G. Haynes and M. Feinleib (eds.), *The epidemiology of aging.* Rockville, MD: National Institutes of Health.
  1985 *Social forces and aging.* Belmont, CA. Wadsworth Publishing Company.

Atkins, G. L.
  1985 "The economic status of the oldest old." *Milbank Memorial Fund Quarterly/ Health and Society* 63 (Spring): 395–419.
  1988 "Making it last! Economic resources of the oldest old." Forthcoming in R. Suzman and D. Willis (eds.), *The oldest old.* New York: Oxford University Press.

Bankoff, E. A.
  1983 "Aged parents and their widowed daughters: A support relationship." *Journal of Gerontology* 38 (2): 226–230.

Bass, D. M., and L. S. Noelker
  1987 "The influence of family caregivers on elders' use of in-home services." *Journal of Health and Social Behavior* 28 (2): 184–196.

Béland, F.
  1984 "The family and adults 64 years of age and over: Co-residency and the availability of help." *Canadian Review of Sociology and Anthropology* 21 (3): 302–317.

Bengtson, V. L., and J. Treas
  1980 "The changing family context of mental health and aging." Pp. 400–428 in J. E. Birren and R. B. Sloane (eds.), *Handbook of mental health and aging.* Englewood Cliffs, NJ: Prentice-Hall.

Besdine, R. W.
  1985 "Rational and successful health care of tomorrow's elderly." Pp. 259–269 in C. M. Gaitz and T. Samorajski (eds.), *Aging 2000: our health care destiny.* Vol. 1, *Biomedical issues.* New York: Springer-Verlag New York.
  1987 "Normal human aging." Pp. 11–16 in *Proceedings of the 1987 public health conference on records and statistics.* Hyattsville, MD: U.S. Department of Health and Human Services.

Binstock, R. H.
  1983 "The elderly in America: Their economic resources, income status, and costs." Pp. 19–33 in W. P. Browne and L. K. Olson (eds.), *Aging and public policy.* Westport, CT: Greenwood Press.
  1985 "The oldest old: A fresh perspective or compassionate ageism revisited?" *Milbank Memorial Fund Quarterly/Health and Society* 63 (Spring): 420–451.
  1987 "Title III of the Older Americans Act: An analysis and proposal for the 1987 reauthorization." *The Gerontologist* 27 (3): 259–265.

Bishop, C.
  1986 "Living arrangement choices of elderly singles: Effects of income and disability." *Health Care Financing Review* 7 (3): 65–73.

Blau, Z. S.
  1973 *Old age in a changing society.* New York: New Viewpoints.

Blenkner, M.
  1965 "Social work and family relationships in later life with some thoughts on filial maturity." Pp. 46–59 in E. Shanas and G. F. Streib (eds.), *Social structure and the family.* Englewood Cliffs, NJ: Prentice-Hall.

Bond, J.
1976 "Dependency and the elderly: Problems of conceptualization and measurement." Pp. 11–23 in J. M. A. Munnichs and W. J. A. Van den Heuvel (eds.), *Dependency or interdependency in old age.* The Hague: Martinus Nijhof.

Borzilleri, T. C.
1978 "The need for a separate consumer price index for older persons." *The Gerontologist* 18 (3): 230–236.

Branch, L. G.
1985 "Health practices and incident disability among the elderly." *American Journal of Public Health* 75 (12): 1436–1441.

Branch, L. G., and D. J. Freedman
1985 "A case study of financial risk from Massachusetts." Pp. 50–59 in U.S. Congress, House Select Committee on Aging, *Twentieth Anniversary of Medicare and Medicaid.* Hearings, July 30. Washington, DC: U.S. Government Printing Office.

Brody, E. M.
1981 " 'Women in the middle' and family help to older people." *The Gerontologist* 21 (5): 471–480.
1985 "Parent care as normative stress." *The Gerontologist* 25 (1): 19–29.
1986 Interview by Lindsy Van Gelder. *Ms. Magazine* 14 (1): 47–48, 100.

Brody, E. M., P. T. Johnsen, and M. C. Fulcomer
1984 "What should adult children do for elderly parents?" *Journal of Gerontology* 39 (6): 736–746.

Brody, S.
1987 "Strategic planning: The catastrophic approach." *The Gerontologist* 27 (2): 131–138.

Brody, S., and N. Persily
1984 *Hospitals and the aged: The new old market.* Rockville, MD: Aspen Publishers, Inc.

Brody, S., and G. Ruff (eds.)
1986 *Aging and rehabilitation: Advances in the state of the art.* New York: Springer Publishing Company.

Cafferata, G. L., R. Stone, and J. Sangl
n.d. "The caregiving role: Dimensions of burden and benefits." Unpublished paper.

Callahan, D.
1987 "Rethinking health care for the aged." *The New York Times* (September 25).

Cantor, M. H.
1979 "Neighbors and friends: An overlooked resource in the informal support system." *Research on Aging* 1:434–463.
1983 "Strain among caregivers: A study of experience in the United States." *The Gerontologist* 23 (6): 597–604.

Caplow, T.
1977 Foreword in B. B. Manard, R. E. Woehle, and J. M. Heilman, *Better homes for the old.* Lexington, MA: Lexington Books.

Chenoweth, B., and B. Spencer
1986 "Dementia: The experience of family caregivers." *The Gerontologist* 26 (3): 267–272.

Chown, S. M.
1981 "Friendship in old age." Pp. 231–246 in S. Duck and R. Gilmour (eds.), *Personal relationships 2: Developing personal relationships.* New York: Academic Press.

Clark, C.
1983 "Sickness and social control." Pp. 346–365 in H. Robboy and C. Clark (eds.), *Social interaction.* 2d ed. New York: St. Martin's Press.
1987 "Sympathy biography and sympathy margin." *American Journal of Sociology* 92 (2): 290–321.

Clark, M.
1972 "Cultural values and dependency in later life." Pp. 263–274 in D. O. Cowgill and L. D. Holmes (eds.), *Aging and modernization.* New York: Appleton-Century-Crofts.

Cohen, M. A., E. J. Tell, and S. S. Wallack
1986 "Client-related risk factors of nursing home entry among elderly adults." *Journal of Gerontology* 41 (11): 785–792.

Cohler, B. J.
1983 "Autonomy and interdependence in the family of adulthood: A psychological perspective." *The Gerontologist* 23 (1): 33–39.

Cohler, B., and H. Grunebaum
1981 *Mothers, grandmothers, and daughters.* New York: John Wiley and Sons.

Collins, J., and J. McDonald
1984 "Health care for Medicare beneficiaries: The HMO option." *Nursing Economics* 2 (4): 259–265.

Congressional Quarterly Inc.
1988 "Major provisions of housing authorization bill." (January 2): 19.

Conner, K. A., E. Powers, and G. L. Bultena
1979 "Social interaction and life satisfaction: An empirical assessment of late life patterns." *Journal of Gerontology* 34 (1): 116–121.

Connidis, I.
1983 "Living arrangement choices of older residents: Assessing quantitative results with qualitative data." *Canadian Journal of Sociology* 8 (4): 359–375.

Conrad, P., and J. Schneider
1980 *Deviance and medicalization: From badness to sickness.* St. Louis: The C. V. Mosby Company.

Consumer Reports
1988 "Who can afford a nursing home?" *Consumer Reports* 53 (5): 300–311.

Cowley, M.
1980 *The view from 80.* New York: The Viking Press.

Crystal, S.
1982 *America's old age crisis.* New York: Basic Books.

Cumming, E., and W. E. Henry
1961 *Growing old: The process of disengagement.* New York: Basic Books.

Davis, K., and D. Rowland
1986 *Medicare policy: New directions for health and long-term care.* Baltimore, MD: Johns Hopkins University Press.

Deimling, G. T., and D. M. Bass
1986 "Symptoms of mental impairment among elderly and adults and their effects on family caregivers." *Journal of Gerontology* 41 (6): 778–784.

Diamond, L. M., and D. E. Berman
1981 "The social/health maintenance organization." Pp. 185–217 in J. Callahan,

Jr., and S. S. Wallack (eds.), *Reforming the long-term care system.* Lexington, MA: Lexington Books.

Dickens, W. J., and D. Perlman
1981 "Friendship over the life-cycle." Pp. 91–122 in S. Duck and R. Gilmour (eds.), *Personal relationships 2: Developing personal relationships.* New York: Academic Press.

Doty, P., K. Liu, and J. Wiener
1985 "An overview of long-term care." *Health Care Financing Review* 6 (3): 69–78.

Dowd, J.
1980 *Stratification among the aged.* Monterey, CA: Brooks/Cole Publishing Company.
1984 "Beneficence and the aged." *Journal of Gerontology* 39 (1): 102–108.

Duncan, G. J., M. S. Hill, and W. Rodgers
1986 "The changing economic status of the young and old." Paper presented at the annual meeting of the American Academy for the Advancement of Science, Philadelphia, May 25–30.

Elwell, F.
1981 "Old-age institutions: A study in social stress." Ph.D. diss., State University of New York.
1984 "The effects of ownership on institutional services." *The Gerontologist* 24 (2): 77–83.

Essex, M. J., and M. J. Lohr
1986 "Chronic life strains and depression among older women." Paper presented at the annual meeting of the American Sociological Association, New York, August 30–September 3.

Estes, C. L.
1983 "Fiscal austerity and aging." Pp. 17–39 in C. L. Estes, R. J. Newcomer, and associates (eds.), *Fiscal Austerity and Aging.* Beverly Hills, CA: Sage Publications.

Estes, C. L., and C. Harrington
1985 "Future directions in long-term care." Pp. 251–271 in C. Harrington, R. J. Newcomer, C. L. Estes, and associates (eds.), *Long-term care of the elderly.* Beverly Hills, CA: Sage Publications.

Estes, C., J. H. Swan, and L. E. Gerard
1981 "Dominant and competing paradigms in gerontology: Towards a political economy of aging." *Aging and Society* 1 (2): 151–164.

Evashwick, C. J.
1987 "Definition of the continuum of care." Pp. 23–43 in C. J. Evashwick and L. J. Weiss (eds.), *Managing the Continuum of Care.* Rockville, MD: Aspen Publishers, Inc.

Exton-Smith, A. N.
1977 "Functional consequences of aging: Clinical manifestations." Pp. 41–53 in A. N. Exton-Smith and J. G. Evans (eds.), *Care of the elderly: Meeting the challenge of dependency.* London: Academic Press.

Fahey, Monsignor C. J.
1984 "National perspective on issues of long-term care." Pp. 5–13 in R. Bennett, S. Frisch, B. J. Gurland, and D. Wilder (eds.), *Coordinated service delivery systems for the elderly.* New York: The Haworth Press.

Fann, W. E., and B. W. Richman
1985 "Considerations for treating the elderly with psychotropic medications." Pp.

317–325 in C. M. Gaitz and T. Samorajski (eds.), *Aging 2000: Our health care destiny*. New York: Springer-Verlag New York.

Faye, E. E.
1984 "Maintaining visual functions in the elderly." *Bulletin of the New York Academy of Medicine* 60 (10): 987–993.

Feller, B. A.
1983 "Americans needing help to function at home." *Advance Data from Vital and Health Statistics* 92 (September 14): 1–11. Hyattsville, MD: U.S. Department of Health and Human Services.
1986 "Americans needing home care, United States." National Center for Health Statistics, *Vital and Health Statistics* Series 10, No. 153. DHHS Pub. No. (PHS) 86–1581. Public Health Service. Washington, DC: U.S Government Printing Office.

Field, D., and M. Minkler
1987 "Stability in social support between young-old and old-old or very-old age." Paper presented at the 40th meeting of the Gerontological Society of America, Washington, DC, November 18–22.

Fisher, C. R.
1980 "Differences by age groups in health care spending." *Health Care Financing Review* 1 (4): 65–90.

Fitting, M., and P. Rabins
1985 "Men and women: Do they give care differently?" *Generations* 10 (Fall): 23–26.

Freudenheim, M.
1988 "Nursing homes face pressures that imperil care for elderly." *The New York Times* (May 26).

Gay, G. E., and J. J. Kronenfeld
1987 "Changing hospitalization patterns for the oldest old." Pp. 379–384 in *Proceedings of the 1987 public health conference on records and statistics*. Hyattsville, MD: U.S. Department of Health and Human Services.

George, L. K., D. G. Glazer, I. Winfield-Laird, P. J. Leaf, and R. L. Fischbach
1988 "Psychiatric disorders and mental health service use in later life: Evidence from the epidemiologic catchment area program." Forthcoming in J. Brody and G. L. Maddox (eds.), *Epidemiology and aging*. New York: Springer.

Gibson, M. J.
1985 "Caregiving in the Third World." Paper presented at the 38th meeting of the Gerontological Society of America, New Orleans, November 22–26.

Gibson, M. J., R. O. Andres, B. Isaacs, T. Radebaugh, and J. Worm-Petersen
1987 "The prevention of falls in later life." *Danish Medical Bulletin* 34, Gerontology Special Supplement Series Number Four (April): 3–24

Gillman, A. E., A. Simmel, and E. P. Simon
1986 "Visual handicap in the aged: Self-reported visual disability and the quality of life of residents of public housing for the elderly." *Journal of Visual Impairment and Blindness* 80 (2): 588–590.

Goffman, I.
1961 *Asylums*. Garden City, NY: Doubleday and Company.

Goleman, D.
1985 "Clues to suicide: A brain chemical is implicated." *The New York Times* (October 8): C1, C8.

Greenberg, J., et al.
1985 "S/HMO: The social health maintenance organization and long-term care." *Generations* 9 (Summer): 51–55.

Gubrium, J. F.
  1975 *Living and dying at Murray Manor.* New York: St. Martin's Press.
Guhleman, P.
  1987 "Health status variability among the oldest old." Pp. 388–392 in *Proceedings of the 1987 public health conference on records and statistics.* Hyattsville, MD. U.S. Department of Health and Human Services.
Gurland, B., J. Copeland, J. Kuriansky, M. Kelleher, L. Sharpe, and L. L. Dean
  1983 *The mind and mood of aging.* New York: The Haworth Press.
Gutkin, C. E., J. N. Morris, S. Sherwood, and H. S. Ruchlin
  1987 "The relationship of housing and case-managed home care to the substitution of formal for informal care." Paper presented at the 40th meeting of the Gerontological Society of America, Washington, DC, November 22.
Haber, D.
  1986 "In-home and community-based long-term care services: A review of recent AOA projects involving self-determination." *Journal of Applied Gerontology* 5 (7): 37–50.
Hanley, R.
  1988 "Utilization and financing of long-term care for the elderly: The next three decades." Paper presented at the 34th annual meeting of the American Society on Aging, San Diego, March 20–22.
Harahan, M., and L. V. Hamm
  1987 "National long-term care channeling demonstration program." Pp. 89–91 in *Proceedings of the 1987 public health conference on records and statistics.* Hyattsville, MD: U.S. Department of Health and Human Services.
Harrington, C.
  1985a "Crisis in long-term care: Part 1, the problems." *Nursing Economics* 3 (1): 15–20.
  1985b "Crisis in long-term care: Part 2, policy options." *Nursing Economics* 3 (2): 109–115.
Harrington, C., and R. Newcomer
  1985 "Social/health maintenance organizations: New policy options for the aged, blind, and disabled." *Journal of Public Health Policy* 6 (2): 204–222.
Harris and Associates
  1986 *Problems facing elderly Americans living alone.* New York: Louis Harris and Associates.
Harris, T., M. G. Kovar, J. Feldman, and R. Suzman
  1987 "Robust old: Health status and health utilization." Pp. 385–387 in *Proceedings of the 1987 public health conference on records and statistics.* Hyattsville, MD: U.S. Department of Health and Human Services.
Harvard Medicare Project
  1986 *Medicare: Coming of age.* Cambridge, MA: Center for Health Policy and Management, John F. Kennedy School of Government.
Hays, J. A.
  1984 "Aging and family resources: Availability and proximity of kin." *The Gerontologist* 24 (2): 149–153.
Health Care Financing Administration
  1987 "National health expenditures, 1986–2000." *Health Care Financing Review* 8 (4): 1–36.
Heaney, R. P.
  1983 "Prevention of age-related osteoporosis in women." Pp. 123–144 in Louis V. Avioli (ed.), *The osteoporotic syndrome.* Orlando, FL: Grune and Stratton.

Heinemann, G. D.
    1985 "Interdependence in informal support systems: The case of elderly urban widows." Pp. 165–186 in W. A. Peterson and J. Quadagno (eds.), *Social bonds in later life*. Beverly Hills, CA: Sage Publications.

Hendricks, J., and C. D. Hendricks
    1986 *Aging in mass society*. Boston: Little, Brown and Company.

Hill, R.
    1970 *Family development in three generations*. Cambridge, MA: Schenkman Publishing Company.

Hollonbeck, D., and J. C. Ohls
    1984 "Participation among the elderly in the Food Stamp Program." *The Gerontologist* 24 (6): 616–621.

Horowitz, A., and L. Cassels
    1985 "Vision education and outreach: Identifying and serving the visually impaired elderly." New York: The New York Association for the Blind.

Hospital Research and Educational Trust
    1986 *Emerging trends in aging and long-term care services*. Chicago, IL: Hospital Research and Educational Trust.

Hudson, R. B.
    1978 "The 'graying' of the federal budget and its consequences for old-age policy." *The Gerontologist* 18 (5): 428–440.

Hussar, D. A.
    1985 "Drug interactions in geriatric drug use." Pp. 135–143 in S. R. Moore and T. W. Teal (eds.). *Geriatric drug use—Clinical and social perspectives*. New York: Pergamon Press.

Illich, I.
    1976 *Medical nemesis: The expropriation of health*. New York: Pantheon Books.

Iversen, L., C. Polich, and J. Dahl
    1985 *The 1985 Medicare and HMOs data book*. Excelsior, MN: InterStudy Center for Aging and Long-Term Care.

Iversen, L., C. Polich, J. Dahl, and L. Secord
    1986 *Improving health and long-term care for the elderly*. Excelsior, MN: InterStudy Center for Aging and Long-Term Care.

Johnson, C. L.
    1983 "Dyadic family relations and social support." *The Gerontologist* 23 (4): 377–383.

Johnson, C. L., and L. A. Grant
    1985 *The nursing home in American society*. Baltimore, MD: Johns Hopkins University Press.

Johnson, J. H., and I. G. Sarason
    1978 "Life stress, depression and anxiety: Internal-external control as a moderate variable." *Journal of Psychosomatic Research* 22:205–208.

Johnston, M., and K. A. Roberto
    1987 "The impact of osteoporosis on the quality of informal relationships." Paper presented at the 40th meeting of the Gerontological Society of America, Washington, DC, November 18–22.

Jonas, K., and E. Wellin
    1980 "Dependency and reciprocity: Home health aid in an elderly population." Pp. 217–238 in C. Fry (ed.), *Aging in culture and society*. New York: Praeger.

Kahana, E., B. Kahana, and R. Young
  1987 "Strategies of coping and postinstitutional outcomes." *Research on Aging* 9
        (12): 182–199.

Kahn, E. S.
  1985 "Service credits: The new currency." Mimeographed paper. Miami, FL:
        Florida International University, Southeast Florida Center on Aging.

Kahn, R. L.
  1979 "Aging and social support." Pp. 77–91 in M. W. Riley (ed.), *Aging from
        birth to death*. Boulder, CO: Westview Press.

Kalish, R. A.
  1979 "The new ageism and the failure of models: A polemic." *The Gerontologist*
        19 (4): 398–402.

Kane, R. A., and R. L. Kane
  1981 *Assessing the elderly*. Lexington, MA: D. C. Heath and Company.

Kane, R., et al.
  1980 *Geriatrics in the United States: Manpower projections and training con-
        siderations*. Santa Monica, CA: Rand Corporation.

Kannel, W. B., T. R. Dauber, and D. L. McGee
  1980 "Perspectives on systolic hypertension: The Framingham study." *Circulation*
        61:1179–1182.

Katz, S., A. B. Ford, R. W. Moskowitz, B. A. Jackson, and M. W. Jaffe
  1963 "The index of ADL: A standardized measure of biological and psychosocial
        function." *Journal of the American Medical Association* 185: 914–919.

Kaye, L. W., and A. Monk
  1987 "Social network reciprocity in enriched housing for the aged." Paper pre-
        sented at the 40th meeting of the Gerontological Society of America,
        Washington, DC, November 18–22.

Keith, P. M., K. H. Hill, W. S. Goudy, and E. A. Powers
  1984 "Confidants and well-being: A note on male friendships in old age." *The
        Gerontologist* 24 (3): 318–320.

Kelsey, J., A. A. White III, H. Pastides, and G. E. Bisbee
  1979 "The impact of musculoskeletal disorders in the population of the United
        States." *Journal of Bone and Joint Surgery* 61-A (10): 959–964.

Kerson, T. S., with L. A. Kerson
  1985 *Understanding chronic illness*. New York: The Free Press.

Kingson, E. R., B. A. Hirshorn, and J. M. Cornman
  1986 *Ties that bind*. Washington, DC: Seven Locks Press.

Kleban, M. H., C. B. Schoonover, and C. Hoffman
  1988 "EQS models for effects of caregiving on adult daughters." Philadelphia,
        PA: Philadelphia Geriatric Center.

Kodner, D., and E. Feldman
  1982 "The service coordination/delivery dichotomy: A critical issue to address in
        reforming the long-term care system." *Home Health Care Service Quarterly* 3
        (1): 59–68.

Kosberg, J. I.
  1988 "Preventing elder abuse: Identification of high risk factors prior to place-
        ment decisions." *The Gerontologist* 28 (1): 43–57.

Kovar, M. G.
  1987 "The longitudinal study on aging: Some estimates of change among older
        Americans." Pp. 397–398 in *Proceedings of the 1987 public health conference*

on records and statistics. Hyattsville, MD: U.S. Department of Health and Human Services.

Kuypers, J. A., and V. L. Bengtson
1973 "Social breakdown and competence: A model of normal aging." *Human Development* 26 (3): 181–201.

Lammers, W. W., and D. Klingman
1984 *State policies and the aging.* Lexington, MA: Lexington Books.

Larson, R.
1978 "Thirty years of research on the subjective well-being of older Americans." *Journal of Gerontology* 33 (1): 109–125.

Lasch, C.
1977 *Heaven in a heartless world.* New York: Basic Books.

Lawton, M. P., and E. M. Brody
1969 "Assessment of older people: Self-maintaining and instrumental activities of daily living." *The Gerontologist* 9 (3): 179–186.

Leutz, W., et al.
1985 *Changing health care for an aging society: Planning for the social health maintenance organization.* Lexington, MA: Lexington/Heath.

Liang, J.
1982 "Sex differences in life satisfaction among the elderly." *Journal of Gerontology* 37 (1): 100–108.

Lieberman, M. A., and S. S. Tobin
1983 *The experience of old age: Stress, coping and survival.* New York: Basic Books.

Linsk, N. L., S. M. Keigher, and S. E. Osterbusch
1986 "States' policies regarding paid family caregiving." Unpublished paper. Chicago, IL: University of Illinois.

Lipman, A., and C. F. Longino
1986 "Living arrangements among the residentially dependent old population in the U.S." Paper presented at the 39th meeting of the Gerontological Society of America, Chicago, November 19–23.

Litwak, E.
1985 *Helping the elderly.* New York: The Guilford Press.

Liu, K., and K. G. Manton
1983 "The characteristics and utilization pattern of an admission cohort of nursing home patients." *The Gerontologist* 23 (1): 92–98.

Lohr, M. J., and M. J. Essex
1986 "The effects of health, coping, and self-esteem on life satisfaction." Paper presented at the 39th meeting of the Gerontology Society of America, Chicago, November 19–23.

Longino, C. F.
1988 "The oldest Americans: Their demographic, socioeconomic, relational and environmental characteristics." *The Sociological Quarterly* (forthcoming).

Lowenthal, M. F., M. Thurnher, and D. Chiriboga
1975 *Four stages of life.* San Francisco: Jossey-Bass.

Lozier, J., and R. Althouse
1975 "Retirement to the porch in rural Appalachia." *International Journal of Aging and Human Development* 6 (1): 7–15.

Lubben, J. E.
1987 "Models for delivering long-term care." *Home Health Care Services Quarterly* 8 (2): 5–22.

Macken, C. L.
  1985 "A profile of functionally impaired elderly persons living in the community." Unpublished manuscript.
  1986 "A profile of functionally impaired elderly persons living in the community." *Health Care Financing Review* 7 (4): 33–49.
Manard, B. B., R. E. Woehle, and J. M. Heilman
  1977 *Better homes for the old.* Lexington, MA: Lexington Books.
Manton, K. G.
  1986 "Past and future life expectancy increases at later ages: Their implications for the linkage of chronic morbidity, disability and mortality." *Journal of Gerontology* 41 (5): 672–681.
  1988 "Planning long-term care for heterogeneous older populations." Forthcoming in G. Maddox and P. Lawton (eds.), *Annual review of gerontology and geriatrics.* New York: Springer.
Manton, K. G., D. G. Blazer, and M. A. Woodbury
  1987 "Suicide in middle age and later life." *Journal of Gerontology* 42 (2): 219–227.
Manton, K. G., and J. Soldo
  1985 "Dynamics of health changes in the oldest old: New perspectives and evidence." *Milbank Memorial Fund Quarterly/Health and Society* 63 (Spring): 206–285.
Marshall, T. H.
  1963 *Citizenship and social class.* Garden City, NY: Doubleday and Company.
Matthews, S. H.
  1988 "The burdens of parent care: A critical assessment of findings." *Journal of Aging Studies* (forthcoming).
McCrae, R. R.
  1982 "Age differences in the use of coping mechanisms." *Journal of Gerontology* 37 (4): 454–460.
McKinlay, J.
  1987 "Medicalization of aging: Social construction of the male climacteric." Keynote address at the first International Conference on the Future of Adult Life, The Netherlands, April 1–5.
McMillan, A., J. Lubitz, and D. Russell
  1987 "Medicare enrollment in health maintenance organizations." *Health Care Financing Review* 8 (3): 87–93.
Meiners, M.
  1983 "The case for long-term care insurance." *Health Affairs* 2 (2): 55–79.
  1988 "State initiatives: Developing the marketplace for long-term care insurance." Paper presented at the American Health Care Association's conference, Private Long-Term Care Insurance, Washington, DC, March 1–2.
Melton, L. J. III, and B. L. Riggs
  1983 "Epidemiology of age-related fractures." Pp. 45–72 in L. V. Avioli (ed.), *The osteoporotic syndrome.* Orlando, FL: Grune and Stratton.
Minaker, K. L., and J. W. Rowe
  1985 "Health and disease among the oldest old: A clinical perspective." *Milbank Memorial Fund Quarterly/Health and Society* 63 (Spring): 324–349.

Moore, S. R., and J. K. Jones
1985 "Adverse drug reaction surveillance in the geriatric population: A preliminary view." Pp. 70–77 in S. R. Moore and T. W. Teal (eds.), *Geriatric drug use—Clinical and social perspectives.* New York: Pergamon Press.
Mouser, N. F., E. A. Powers, P. M. Keith, and W. J. Goudy
1985 "Marital status and life satisfaction: A study of older men." Pp. 71–90 in W. A. Peterson and J. Quadagno (eds.), *Social bonds in later life.* Beverly Hills, CA: Sage Publications.
Munnichs, J. M. A., and W. J. A. Van den Heuvel (eds.)
1976 *Dependency or interdependency in old age.* The Hague: Martinus Nijhof.
Muse, D., and D. Sawyer
1982 *The Medicare and Medicaid data book, 1981.* Baltimore, MD: U.S. Health Care Financing Administration.
Myers, D. A., R. V. Burkhauser, and K. C. Holden
1988 "The transition from wife to widow: The importance of survivor benefits to the well-being of widows." *Journal of risk and insurance* (forthcoming).
Naiditch, Z.
1984 Statement of Zena Naiditch, executive director, Developmental Disabilities Protections and Advocacy Board, Chicago, IL, in U.S. Senate, Special Committee on Aging, *Social Security disability reviews: The human costs.* Hearing February 16. Washington, DC: U.S. Government Printing Office.
National Center for Health Statistics
1979 *National nursing home survey: 1977. Summary for the United States.* Hyattsville, MD: U.S. Department of Health and Human Services.
1986 "Aging in the eighties, impaired senses for sound and light in persons age 65 years and over." *Advance Data from Vital and Health Statistics* 125 (September 19). Hyattsville, MD: U.S. Department of Health and Human Services.
1987a "Discharges from nursing homes: Preliminary data from the 1985 National Nursing Home Survey." *Advance Data from Vital and Health Statistics* 42 (September 30). Hyattsville, MD: U.S. Department of Health and Human Services.
1987b "Use of nursing homes by the elderly: Preliminary data from the 1985 National Nursing Home Survey." *Advance Data from Vital and Health Statistics* 135 (May 14). Hyattsville, MD: U.S. Department of Health and Human Services.
National Institute on Aging
1984 *Report on education and training in geriatrics and gerontology.* Bethesda, MD: National Institute on Aging.
Neugarten, B. L.
1982 "Policy for the 1980s: Age or need entitlement?" Pp. 19–32 in B. L. Neugarten (ed.), *Age or need?* Beverly Hills, CA: Sage Publications.
New York State Department of Social Services
1985 "Respite Demonstration Project." New York: New York Department of Social Services.
Newcomer, R. J., and C. Harrington
1983 "State Medicaid expenditures: Trends and program policy changes." Pp. 157–186 in C. L. Estes, R. J. Newcomer, and associates (eds.), *Fiscal austerity and aging.* Beverly Hills, CA: Sage Publications.
Newman, S. J.
1986 "Demographic influences on the future housing demand of the elderly." Pp.

21–32 in R. J. Newcomer, M. P. Lawton, and T. O. Byerts (eds.), *Housing an aging society*. New York: Van Nostrand Reinhold Company.

Newman, S. J., et al.
1976 "Housing adjustments of older people: A report from the second phase." Ann Arbor, MI: University of Michigan, Institute for Social Research.

Ory, M. G.
1985 "The burden of care: A familial perspective." *Generations* 10 (Fall): 14–18.

O'Shaughnessy, C., and K. Price
1987 "Financing and delivery of long-term care services for the elderly." Pp. 191–224 in C. J. Evashwick and L. J. Weiss (eds.), *Managing the continuum of care*. Rockville, MD: Aspen Publishers, Inc.

Osteen, F. L., and D. L. Best
1985 "Components of subjective age identification among older adults." Paper presented at the 38th meeting of the Gerontological Society of America, New Orleans, November 22–26.

Palmore, E.
1976 "Total chance of institutionalization among the aged." *The Gerontologist* 16 (6): 504–507.
1985 "Predictors of the longevity difference." Pp. 19–29 in Palmore et al. (eds.), *Normal aging III*. Durham, NC: Duke University Press.

Paringer, L.
1985 "Forgotten costs of informal long-term care." *Generations* 9 (Summer): 55–58.

Parsons, T.
1951 *The social system*. Glencoe, IL: The Free Press.

Pear, R.
1987 "Crisis predicted in care of the elderly." *The New York Times* (September 13).

Pearlin, L. I., and C. Schooler
1978 "The structure of coping." *Journal of Health and Social Behavior* 19 (1): 2–21.

Pesznecker, B., B. Horn, J. Werner, and V. Kenyon
1987 "Home health services in a climate of cost containment." *Home Health Care Services Quarterly* 8 (1): 5–21.

Phillipson, C.
1982 *Capitalism and the construction of old age*. London: Macmillan.

Pollack, L. M., and R. J. Newcomer
1986 "Neighborhoods and the aged." Pp. 119–126 in R. J. Newcomer, M. P. Lawton, and T. O. Byerts (eds.), *Housing an aging society*. New York: Van Nostrand Reinhold Company.

Powell, L., A. Roth, and K. Gelburg
1987 "Measurement of coping styles among the elderly." Pp. 136–139 in *Proceedings of the 1987 public health conference on records and statistics*. Hyattsville, MD: U.S. Department of Health and Human Services.

Preston, D. B., and P. K. Mansfield
1984 "An exploration of stressful life events, illness, and coping among the rural elderly." *The Gerontologist* 24 (5): 490–494.

Pynoos, J., B. Hade-Caplan, and D. Fleisher
1984 "Intergenerational neighborhood networks: A basis for aiding the frail elderly." *The Gerontologist* 24 (3): 233–237.

Quadagno, J., D. A. Squier, and G. Walker
1987 "Long term care community services and family caregiving." Pp. 116–128

in T. Brubaker (ed.), *Aging, health and family*. Beverly Hills, CA: Sage Publications

Rabin, D. L., and P. Stockton
1987 *Long-term care for the elderly: A factbook*. New York: Oxford University Press.

Ragan, P. K., and J. B. Wales
1980 "Age stratification and the life course." Pp. 377–399 in J. E. Birren and R. B. Sloane (eds.), *Handbook of mental health and aging*. Englewood Cliffs, NJ: Prentice-Hall.

Rathbone-McCuan, E., and R. T. Coward
1985 "Male helpers: Unrecognized informal supports." Paper presented at the 38th meeting of the Gerontological Society of America, New Orleans, November 22–26.

Reif, L.
1984 "Making dollars and sense of home health policy." *Nursing Economics* 2 (6): 382–390.

Rice, D.
1985 "The health care needs of the elderly." Pp. 41–66 in C. Harrington et al. (eds.), *Long term care for the elderly: Public policy issues*. Beverly Hills, CA: Sage Publications.

Rich, B. M., and M. Baum
1984 *The aging*. Pittsburgh, PA: University of Pittsburgh Press.

Riley, G., J. Lubitz, R. Pirhoda, and E. Rabey
1987 "The use and costs of Medicare services by cause of death." *Inquiry* 24 (Fall): 233–244.

Riley, M. W., and A. Foner (eds.)
1968 *Aging and society*. Vol. 1, *An Inventory of Research Findings*. New York: Russell Sage Foundation.

Rimer, S.
1987 "Buses link elderly to city life." *The New York Times* (September 29).

Rives, N. W., Jr., and W. J. Serow
1984 *Introduction to applied demography*. Beverly Hills, CA: Sage Publications.

Rivlin, A., and J. Wiener, with R. Hanley and D. Spence
1988 *Caring for the disabled elderly: Who will pay?* Washington, DC: The Brookings Institution.

Roberto, K. A.
1987 "Adjusting to chronic disease: The osteoporotic woman." Paper presented at the 40th meeting of the Gerontological Society of America, Washington, DC November 18–22.

Roberto, K. A., and J. P. Scott
1984–1985 "Friendship patterns among older women." *International Journal of Aging and Human Development* 19 (1): 1–10.
1986 "Friendship of older men and women: Exchange patterns and satisfaction." *Psychology and Aging* 1 (2): 103–109.

Rosenfeld, J. P.
1979 "Bequests from resident to resident: Inheritance in a retirement community." *The Gerontologist* 19 (6): 594–600.

Rosenwaike, I.
1985a "A demographic portrait of the oldest old." *Milbank Memorial Fund Quarterly/Health and Society* 63 (Spring): 187–205.
1985b *The extreme aged in America*. Westport, CT: Greenwood Press.

Rossdale, M.
   1965   "Health in a sick society." *New Left Review* 34 (November–December): 82–90.
Rowe, J. W.
   1983   "Systolic hypertension in the elderly." *New England Journal of Medicine* 309:1246–1247.
   1985a   "Health care of the elderly." *New England Journal of Medicine* 312 (12): 827–835.
   1985b   "Interaction of aging and disease." Pp. 247–257 in C. M. Gaitz and T. Samorajski (eds.), *Aging 2000: Our health care destiny*. Vol. 1, *Biomedical issues*. New York: Springer-Verlag New York.
Rowe, J. W., and R. L. Kahn
   1987   "Human aging: Usual and successful." *Science* 237 (July 10): 143–149.
Rubinstein, R. L.
   1986   *Singular paths: Old men living alone*. New York: Columbia University Press.
Sahlins, M. D.
   1965   "On the sociology of primitive exchange." Pp. 139–227 in M. Banton (ed.), *The relevance of models for social anthropology*. London: Travistock.
Sanborn, B., and P. Erlich
   1985   "Informal caregiving: Proximate and dispersed." Paper presented at the 38th meeting of the Gerontological Society of America, New Orleans, November 22–26.
Sankar, A., R. Newcomer, and J. Wood
   1986   "Prospective payment: Systemic effects on the provision of community care for the elderly." *Home Health Care Services Quarterly* 7 (2): 93–117.
Schneider, E. L.
   1983   "Aging, natural death and the compression of morbidity: Another view." *New England Journal of Medicine* 309 (10): 854–856.
   1985   "Implications for aging and diseases of aging." Paper presented at the 38th meeting of the Gerontological Society of America, New Orleans, November 22–26.
Schulz, J. H.
   1984   "SSI: Origins, experience, and unresolved issues." Pp. 1–39 in U.S. Senate, Special Committee on Aging, *The Supplemental Security Income Program: A 10-year overview*. Washington, DC: U.S. Government Printing Office.
   1985   *The economics of aging*. Belmont, CA: Wadsworth Publishing Company.
Schwartz, S., S. Danziger, and E. Smolensky
   1984   "The choice of living arrangement by the elderly." Pp. 229–253 in H. J. Aaron and G. Burtless (eds.), *Retirement and economic behavior*. Washington, DC: The Brookings Institution.
Shanas, E.
   1979   "Social myth as hypothesis: The case of the family relations of old people." *The Gerontologist* 19 (1): 3–9.
Shanas, E., and G. F. Streib (eds.)
   1965   *Social structure and the family: Generational relations*. Englewood Cliffs, NJ: Prentice-Hall.
Sheehy, T. W.
   1982   "An overview on geriatric medicine." *Resident and Staff Physician* (6): 29–40.

Simons, R. L., and G. E. West
   1984–1985   "Life changes, coping resources, and health among the elderly." *International Journal of Aging and Human Development* 20 (3): 173–189.
Smeeding, T., B. B. Torrey, and M. Rein
   1986   "The economic status of the young and the old in six countries." Paper presented at the annual meeting of the American Association for the Advancement of Science, Philadelphia, May 25–30.
Smyer, M. A.
   1980   "The differential use of services by impaired elderly." *Journal of Gerontology* 35 (2): 249–255.
Snow, R., and L. Crapo
   1982   "Emotional bondedness, subjective well-being, and health in elderly medical patients." *Journal of Gerontology* 37 (5): 609–615.
Soldo, B. J., and J. Myllyluoma
   1983   "Caregivers who live with dependent elderly." *The Gerontologist* 23 (6): 605–611.
Soldo, G. J., M. Sharma, and R. T. Campbell
   1984   "Determinants of the community living arrangements of older unmarried women." *Journal of Gerontology* 39 (4): 492–498.
Spector, W. D., and S. Katz
   1985   "The hierarchical relationship between activities of daily living and instrumental activities of daily living." Paper presented at the 38th meeting of the Gerontological Society of America, New Orleans, November 22–26.
Spence, D.
   1988   "The costs of public long-term care insurance." Paper presented at the 34th annual meeting of the American Society on Aging, San Diego, CA, March 20–22.
Stoller, E. P., and L. L. Earl
   1983   "Help with activities of everyday life: Sources of support for the noninstitutionalized elderly." *The Gerontologist* 23 (1): 64–70.
Stone, R., G. L. Cafferata, and J. Sangl
   1986   "Caregivers of the frail elderly: A national profile." Unpublished paper. Baltimore, MD: Health Care Financing Administration, Office of Research.
   1987   "Caregivers of the frail elderly: A national profile." *The Gerontologist* 24 (5): 616–626.
Straus, R.
   1985   "Risk factors in geriatric drug use: Biobehavioral issues." Pp. 160–167 in S. R. Moore and T. W. Teal (eds.), *Geriatric drug use—Clinical and social perspectives.* New York: Pergamon Press.
Streib, G. F.
   1983   "The frail elderly: Research dilemmas and research opportunities." *The Gerontologist* 23 (1): 40–44.
Struyk, R. J.
   1986   "Future housing assistance policy for the elderly." Pp. 53–61 in R. J. Newcomer, M. P. Lawton, and T. O. Byerts (eds.), *Housing an aging society.* New York: Van Nostrand Reinhold Company.
Struyk, R. J., and B. J. Soldo
   1980   *Improving the elderly's housing.* Cambridge, MA: Ballinger Publishing Company.
Suzman, R., and M. W. Riley
   1985   "Introducing the 'oldest old'." *Milbank Memorial Fund Quarterly/Health and Society* 63 (Spring): 177–186.

Taeuber, C.
1987 "New census data on the oldest old." Paper presented at the 40th meeting of the Gerontological Society of America, Washington, DC, November 18–22.

The Commonwealth Fund Commission
1987a *Medicare's poor: Filling the gaps in medical coverage for low-income elderly Americans.* The Commonwealth Fund, 624 N. Broadway, Baltimore, MD.
1987b *Old, alone and poor.* The Commonwealth Fund, 624 N. Broadway, Baltimore, MD.

The New York Times
1987 "House votes insurance against catastrophic ills." (July 26): E4.

Thomas, S. G.
1985a "The significance of housing as a resource." Pp. 391–414 in R. J. Vogel and H. C. Palmer (eds.), *Long-term care.* Rockville, MD: Aspen Publishers, Inc.
1985b "Transportation and dependency." Pp. 463–482 in R. J. Vogel and H. C. Palmer (eds.), *Long-term care.* Rockville, MD: Aspen Publishers, Inc.

Thompson, L., and A. Walker
1984 "Mothers and daughters." *Journal of Marriage and the Family* 46 (2): 313–322.

Titmuss, R. M.
1962 *Income distribution and social change.* London: G. Allen and Unwin.
1971 *The gift relationship.* New York: Pantheon.

Tobin, J. J.
1987 "The American idealization of old age in Japan." *The Gerontologist* 27 (1): 53–58.

Tobis, J., S. Reinsch, A. Rubel, J. Ashurst, R. Friis, and B. Fallavollita
1986 "A profile of the robust very old." Paper presented at the 39th meeting of the Gerontological Society of America, Chicago, November 19–23.

Tolchin, M.
1988 "For many, help is near on health costs." *The New York Times* (May 31).

Torrens, P.
1987 "The continuum of care: The patient and the family's view." Pp. 295–309 in C. J. Evashwick and L. J. Weiss (eds.), *Managing the continuum of care.* Rockville, MD: Aspen Publishers, Inc.

Torrey, B. B.
1985 "Sharing increasing costs on declining income: The visible dilemma of the invisible aged." *Milbank Memorial Fund Quarterly/Health and Society* 63 (Spring): 377–394.

Torrey, B. B., and C. M. Taeuber
1986 "The importance of asset income among the elderly." *Review of Income and Wealth* 32 (4): 443–449

Townsend, P.
1981 "The structured dependency of the elderly." *Aging and Society* 1 (3): 5–28.

Turner, L.
1986 "Public policies and individual housing choices." Pp. 42–52 in R. J. Newcomer, M. P. Lawton, and T. O. Byerts (eds.) *Housing an aging society.* New York: Van Nostrand Reinhold Company.

Turner, R. J., and S. Noh
1988 "Physical disability and depression: A longitudinal analysis." *Journal of Health and Social Behavior* 29 (3); 23–37.

U. S. Bureau of the Census

1975 *Historical statistics of the United States: Colonial times to 1970.* Part 1. Washington, DC: U.S. Government Printing Office.

1983 *Residential finance. U.S. census of housing,* Series HC80-5 Washington, DC: U.S. Government Printing Office.

1984a *Annual housing survey: 1983 current housing reports.* Series H-150-83. Washington, DC: U.S. Government Printing Office.

1984b "Detailed population characteristics. Part 1, U.S. Summary." Chapter D in *Census of the population: 1980.* Vol. 1, *Characteristics of the Population.* Washington, DC: U.S. Government Printing Office.

1984c *Persons in institutions and other group quarters.* Vol. 2, *Subject Reports.* Series PC-80-2-4D. Washington, DC: U.S. Government Printing Office.

1984d Spencer, G, "Projections of the population of the United States, by age, sex, and race: 1983 to 2080." *Current Population Reports.* Series P-25, No. 952. Washington, DC: U.S. Government Printing Office.

1985 "Characteristics of the population below the poverty level: 1983." *Current Population Reports.* Series P-60, No. 147. Washington, DC: U.S. Government Printing Office.

1987 "Characteristics of the population below the poverty level: 1985." *Current Population Reports.* Series P-60, No. 158. Washington, DC: U.S. Government Printing Office.

U.S. Congress, House Select Committee on Aging

1978 *Poverty among America's aged.* Washington, DC: U.S. Government Printing Office.

1985 *Twentieth anniversary of Medicare and Medicaid: Americans still at risk.* Hearings, July 30. Washington, DC: U.S. Goverment Printing Office.

U.S. General Accounting Office

1987 *Long-term care insurance: Coverage varies widely in a developing market.* Publication no. GAO/HRD-87-80. Washington, DC: U.S. Government Printing Office.

U.S. Senate, Special Committee on Aging

1983 *Life care communities: Promises and problems.* Senate hearings, 98–276, May 25. Washington, DC. U.S. Government Printing Office.

1984a *Medicare and the health costs of older Americans: The extent and effects of cost sharing.* Washington, DC: U.S. Government Printing Office.

1984b *Section 202 housing for the elderly and handicapped: A national survey.* Washington, DC: U.S. Government Printing Office.

1985a *Compilation of the Older Americans Act of 1965.* Washington, DC: U.S. Government Printing Office.

1985b *The pension gamble: Who wins? Who loses?* Hearings, June 14. Washington, DC: U.S. Government Printing Office.

1985c *Unnecessary surgery: Double jeopardy for older Americans.* Hearings, March 14. Washington, DC: U.S. Government Printing Office.

1987a *Developments in aging: 1986.* Vol. 3. Washington, DC: U.S. Government Printing Office.

1987b *Older Americans Act amendments of 1987: A summary of provisions.* Washington, DC: U.S. Government Printing Office.

U.S. Social Security Administration

1984 Wade, Alice H. "Social Security area population projections, 1984." Actuarial Study No. 92. Washington, DC: U.S. Government Printing Office.

Valentine, C. A.
  1971 "Deficit, difference, and bicultural models of Afro-American behavior."
        Harvard Educational Review 41(5): 137–157.
Vicente, L., J. A. Wiley, and R. A. Carrington
  1979 "The risk of institutionalization before death." *The Gerontologist* 19 (4):
        361–367.
Vladeck, B. C.
  1980 *Unloving care.* New York: Basic Books.
  1987 "The continuum of care: Principles and metaphors." Pp. 3–10 in C. J.
        Evashwick and L. J. Weiss (eds.), *Managing the continuum of care.* Rock-
        ville, MD: Aspen Publishers, Inc.
Vladeck, B., and G. Alfano
  1987 *Medicare and extended care: Issues, problems and prospects.* Owings Mills,
        MD: National Health Publishing.
Vogel, R. J., and H. C. Palmer
  1985 Introduction and Summary in R. J. Vogel and H. C. Palmer (eds.), *Long-
        term care.* Rockville, MD: Aspen Publishers, Inc.
Waldron, I.
  1976 "Why do women live longer than men? Part I." *Journal of Human Stress* 2
        (1): 2–13.
Walker, A. J., H. Shin, L. Jones, and C. C. Pratt
  1987 "Mothers' and daughters' reasons for daughters' caregiving." Paper presented
        at the 40th meeting of the Gerontological Society of America, Washing-
        ton, DC, November 18–22.
Ward, R. A., S. R. Sherman, and M. LaGory
  1984 "Informal networks and knowledge of services for older persons." *Journal of
        Gerontology* 39 (2): 216–223.
Warlick, J. L.
  1982 "Participation of the aged in SSI." *Journal of Human Resources* 17 (2): 236–
        260.
  1983 "Aged women in poverty: A problem without a solution." Pp. 35–66 in
        W. P. Browne and L. K. Olson (eds.), *Aging and public policy.* Westport,
        CT: Greenwood Press.
Watkins, S. C., J. A. Menken, and J. Bongaarts
  1987 "Demographic foundations of family change." *American Sociological Review*
        52 (3): 346–358.
Watson, W. H.
  1983 "Selected demographic and social aspects of older blacks." Pp. 42–49 in R.
        L. McNeely and J. Colen (eds.), *Aging in minority groups.* Beverly Hills,
        CA: Sage Publications.
Wentowski, G. J.
  1981 "Reciprocity and the coping strategies of older people: Cultural dimensions
        of network building." *The Gerontologist* 21 (6): 600–609.
Wiener, J.
  1988 "Private long-term care insurance: Product experience." Paper presented at
        the American Health Care Association's conference, Private Long-Term
        Care Insurance, Washington, DC, March 1–2.
Wiener, J., D. Ehrenworth, and D. Spence
  1987 "Private long-term care insurance: Cost, coverage, and restrictions." *The
        Gerontologist* 27 (4): 487–502.
Wild, D., U. S. Nayak, and B. Isaacs
  1981 "How dangerous are falls in old people at home?" *British Medical Journal*
        282:266–268.

Wilkinson, D. Y.
   1988   "Mother-daughter bonds in the later years: Transformation of the 'help pattern'." Pp. 183–195 in S. K. Steinmetz (ed.), *Family and support systems across the life span*. New York: Plenum Press.
Winklevoss, H., and A. Powell
   1984   *Continuing care retirement communities: An empirical, financial, and legal analysis*. Homewood, IL: Richard D. Irwin.
Wood, J.
   1986   "The effects of cost containment on home health agencies." *Home Health Care Services Quarterly* 6 (4): 59–78.
Wood, J. B., and I. A. Parham
   1987   "Coping with perceived loss of control: Ethnic and cultural issues in Alzheimer's family caregiving." Paper presented at the 40th meeting of the Gerontological Society of America, Washington, DC, November 18–22.
Woods, A. M., G. Niederehe, and E. Fruge
   1985   "Dementia: A family systems perspective." *Generations* 10 (Fall): 19–23.
Zarit, S. H.
   1985   "New directions." *Generations* 10 (Fall): 6–8.
Zarit, S. H., K. E. Reever, and J. Bach-Peterson
   1980   "Relatives of the impaired elderly: Correlates of feelings of burden." *The Gerontologist* 20 (6): 649–655.
Zarit, S., P. Todd, and J. Zarit
   1986   "Subjective burden of husbands and wives as caregivers: A longitudinal study." *The Gerontologist* 26 (3): 260–266.
Zawadski, R.
   1984   *Community-based systems of long-term care*. New York: The Haworth Press.
   1985   "So you don't like the rules: A critical overview of waivered demonstration projects." *The Coordinator* 4 (1): 16–19.
   1988   "Consolidated care organization for dependent adults: Findings from On Lok's program of services." Speech given at the 34th annual meeting of the American Society on Aging, San Diego, CA, March 20–22.
Zopf, P. E.
   1986   *America's older population*. Houston: Cap and Gown Press.

Index

(n) indicates reference is in note.

AARP. *See* American Association of Retired Persons
Abuse, preventing, 119
Action, direct, as ineffective coping strategy, 80, 81
Acute conditions
  defined, 57
  prevention of, 119, 120
  treatment, with Medicare, 160
Administration on Aging, 158, 182
Aging, in absence of disease, 75–76
Aging network, 158
Agriculture, Department of, 130
Alcohol abuse, 67(n)
Alone, demographics of those living, 34, 39–40
Alzheimer's disease, 12, 55, 65, 74, 110, 114–115, 117, 165, 192
American Association of Retired Persons (AARP), 49, 194
Antidepressive drugs, problems with, 68
Arteriosclerosis, 61–62, 75
Assets of oldest old, 140–141. *See also* Economic resources

Atherosclerosis, 62
Availability of caregivers, 101–103
Avoidable dependence, 13–16

Bathing, problem of, 10, 56
Behavioral change, caregiver attention to, 119–120
Black oldest olds, demographics, 43–45
Blindness, 63–64
Bone and joint problems, 59–61
  osteoarthritis or degenerative joint disease, 59–60
  osteoporosis, 60–61
Bronchitis, 72
Brookings Institution, 190
Burden, caregiver, 113–119
Burnout, caregiver, 123

Cahn, Prof. Edgar, 96(n)
Cancer, 72
Cardiovascular diseases, 61–63

Multi-infarct dementia, 65
Multiple resource limitations, 19–20

National Center for Health Services Research (NCHSR), 103(n)
National Center for Health Statistics (NCHS), 2(n), 28, 54
National Health Interview Survey, 28, 37, 39(n), 52(n)
National Institutes of Health, 63(n)
National Institute of Mental Health, 2, 66
National Institute on Aging (NIA), 27, 59, 75
National Long Term Care Survey, 60, 103(n)
National Society to Prevent Blindness, 64
NCHS. *See* National Center for Health Statistics
NCHSR. *See* National Center for Health Services Research
Neighbors
as caregivers, 110
importance of, in interdependence, 8
Network, social support, importance of, 83, 84–94
shrinkage of, with age, 85
New ageism, 24
NIA. *See* National Institute on Aging
"911 cycle," 152
Normative stress, 49, 102
Nursing homes
numbers of oldest old in, 3, 33–34
paying for, 189–194. *See also* Economic resources. Finances. Medicaid. Medicare
as synonymous with dependence, 4, 5, 6
those with cognitive impairment in, 65
those with functional disabilities in, 53–56

OAA. *See* Older Americans Act of 1965
Old Age Assistance, 138
Older Americans Act of 1965 (OAA), 156–158, 170
Title III, 25, 155
Oldest old
defined, 27
growth of numbers in group, 2–3, 32–35
Old old, defined, 27
On Lok Senior Health Services, 186–187, 188–189
"Optimistic attitude" coping strategy, 80
Orshansky, Mollie, 130
Osteoarthritis, 59–60, 63, 74
Osteoporosis, 60–61, 70, 74

PADLs. *See* Personal activities of daily living
Paratransit programs, 111, 148, 155, 169
Parkinson's disease, 150, 160
Pensions, 133–135, 145–146
Pepper, Claude, 18
Personal activities of daily living (PADLs), 5(n), 17, 37(n), 52
Personal coping resources, 77–84
interpersonal skills, 82–84
Personal-psychological resources, limitations, and assistance needed, 16–18, 174–175
Pervasive depression, 67, 68
Physiological resources, limitations, and assistance needed, 16–17, 174–175
Pneumonia, 75
Poverty, of oldest old, 127–133
women, 20, 40–42, 135–137, 139, 145–146
Poverty line, government, 129–132
Prevention, of disease and disability, 74
Primary caregiver, defined, 99
Project LINC, 111
Psychological-personal resources, limitations, and assistance needed, 16–18, 174–175

Spouse (*continued*)
  demographics of oldest old living
    with, 34, 35, 38–39
  loss of, 85
SSI. *See* Supplemental Security Income
Staying at Home Project, 112
"Sticking to oneself," as ineffective cop-
  ing strategy, 81
Stroke, 61–62, 65, 73
"Structured dependency," 163
Substitution effect, 148–149
Suicide, 67–68
Supercopers, 78
Supplemental Security Income (SSI),
  14, 23, 138–139
Sweden, and equality of income, 127–
  128, 132, 133
Systolic hypertension, 63

Tasks, caregiver, 111–113
Tax Equity and Fiscal Responsibility
  Act of 1982 (TEFRA), 182–183,
  185
TEFRA. *See* Tax Equity and Fiscal
  Responsibility Act of 1982
Third Age Center, 164
Toilet, using, problem of, 54, 56
Traditional caregivers, 103–104
Transportation, Department of, 168, 169
Transportation, problem of, 95, 111,
  148, 155, 168–169

Treatment-oriented model for service delivery, 177–179

Urban versus rural, demographics of oldest old, 48
Urinary incontinence, 71, 72

The View from 80, 1
Vision problems, 63–64, 72, 73, 74
Volunteer Payee programs, 112

Weight, excessive body, and disability,
  73
Widower, oldest old, as atypical case, 49
Windsor, Duchess of, 18, 125–126, 127
Women
  and fractures, 70
  and marriage lottery, 135–137
  and osteoporosis, 61
  and pensions, 133–135, 145–146
  and poverty, 20, 40–42, 135–137,
    139, 145–146
  as special demographic case, 40–42
  and SSI, 139

Yale Project on Stress and Coping in
  the Elderly, 79
Young old, defined, 27